E   McClellan, Irina
184   Igorevna, 1938-
.R9
M43   Of love and Russia
1989

$19.45

Of Love
and
Russia

Of Love and Russia

THE ELEVEN-YEAR FIGHT FOR MY HUSBAND AND FREEDOM

Irina McClellan

Translated by Woodford McClellan

W · W · NORTON & COMPANY · *NEW YORK* · *LONDON*

Author's Note

I have changed six names in this book: "Olga," "Maria," "Zoya," "Ludmila," "Father Nikolai," *and* "Grisha" *are pseudonyms.*

The text of this book *is composed in Avanta, with display type set in Skjald. Composition and manufacturing by the Haddon Craftsmen, Inc. Book design by Marjorie J. Flock.*

First Edition

Library of Congress Cataloging-in-Publication Data
McClellan, Irina Igorevna, 1938–
  Of love and Russia / by Irina McClellan. — 1st ed.
    p. cm.
    1. McClellan, Irina Igorevna, 1938–   . 2. Russian Americans—
Biography.   3. Soviet Union—Emigration and immigration.   4. United
States—Emigration and immigration.   I. Title.
E184.R9M43 1989
325'.247'0924—dc19
[B]   88–8542

ISBN 0-393-02680-9

W. W. Norton & Company, Inc., 500 Fifth Avenue, New York, N. Y. 10110
W. W. Norton & Company Ltd., 37 Great Russell Street, London WC1B 3NU

1 2 3 4 5 6 7 8 9 0

To the memory of my grandmother,
Aleksandra

Contents

Book 3

Acknowledgments

TO WRITE THIS, my first book, I had not only to learn the principles of narrative writing but also to relive the past, adjust to freedom in a new country and culture, and rediscover my husband. Thus I am more than ordinarily grateful to all the people who have helped me.

My heartfelt thanks go to my editor, Edwin Barber, vice-president of W. W. Norton and Company. Demanding but extremely patient with a novice writer and sympathetic to my determination to tell the story in my own words, Ed Barber became my teacher.

Eliza Klose, of *Surviving Together: A Journal on Soviet-American Relations,* read the penultimate draft meticulously and made many suggestions for improvement. Her professional expertise proved invaluable; I am deeply in her debt. Staige Blackford, editor of the *Virginia Quarterly Review,* studied an early version carefully and provided splendid editorial advice and warm encouragement.

My special friend Judith de Kovacsy helped me immensely through difficult times in general and the writing of this book in particular. My friends David Satter, Marie-Hélène Satter-Gugenheim, Sam Berner, and Lynn Crane read the penultimate draft and sharpened the focus of the final version, while Tom Romer read some early chapters, offered useful insights, and helped me in many other ways. I am grateful to Karen Whitehill for her excellent adaptation of my translation of the poem that constitutes the epigraph to Book One, and to my friend Martin Davis for providing enormous technical assistance with word processing and for digging out historical information.

Father Victor Potapov of St. John the Baptist Russian Orthodox Church in Washington read Book Three and helped me fine-tune the story of the great transformation in my life. I am profoundly grateful to him. Warmest thanks go also to Charles McClellan, who read the manuscript and made useful suggestions.

Finally, a special acknowledgment goes to my husband, Woodford—Vadim—McClellan, who translated the book, including the epigraphs to Books Two and Three and the passage from *The Brothers Karamazov*. Most importantly, his encouragement and his own hard work made it possible for me to complete the project. It was not easy to overcome the difficulties of such a lengthy separation, but through the reliving of it in this book we were able to restore our relationship.

I.M.

Alexandria, Virginia
July 16, 1988

Of Love
and
Russia

Foreword

THE TELEPHONE call came in late morning on Monday, December 30, 1985.

"Citizeness McClellan? This is Karakulko of OVIR. Happy New Year!"

"Thank you," I replied tersely.

"Your exit visa is ready. You can pick it up Thursday."

I had waited eleven and a half years for that telephone call. Before the words sank into my consciousness, Karakulko continued:

"But your daughter cannot go with you to the United States."

I gasped, unable to speak for a moment, then:

"You mean you'll reunite one part of my family and separate the other!"

I slammed down the receiver.

There was no New Year's celebration in my home. Instead, I composed a letter to General Secretary Gorbachev:

Respected Mikhail Sergeevich:

Thank you very much for granting me permission to join my husband in the United States after eleven and a half years of separation. This manifestation of your campaign to improve Soviet-American relations appears threatened by opponents in the Soviet government. How else can I understand OVIR's decision to deny my twenty-six-year-old daughter permission to leave with me? She has paid for my ordeal with her health: she has had two major operations for ulcers, the second of which cost her half her stomach.

You said in your New Year's address to the American people that it is essential to begin now to mend Soviet-American relations. Can that be done when an agency of the Soviet government has made such a barbaric decision?

I hope very much that you will intervene in our case and help bring all my family together.

Sincerely,
Irina McClellan

Book 1

If it all won't come true,
will it fade, be forgotten—
the glow of those moments,
the glow of our souls
                    gone astray?

— *Veronika Tushnova*

Above: No. 7, Chernyshevsky Street, Moscow. My window is on the third floor at the extreme right. Below: Chernyshevsky Street from my window. *Loren Graham photos*

1

A Turn of Fate

THAT SUMMER of 1972 we lived on Chernyshevsky Street a few blocks east of Red Square, close enough to hear the Kremlin chimes. I had spent most of my life in this part of old Moscow, even on the same street, which begins at the Elijah Gates and leads away to the east to the Holy Protector Gates. The central city had always been my home. I felt utterly at ease on those streets and crooked lanes, the pastel-colored stucco houses with ornate window frames and double-glazed windows, shops at ground level and crowded communal apartments above.

In the 1930s the Moscow City Council razed the northeast corner of the intersection of Chernyshevsky Street and Potapov Lane to erect a massive seven-story apartment building totally out of keeping with the architectural harmony of the neighborhood. There my thirteen-year-old daughter Lena and I occupied two rooms in a three-room kommunalka, or communal apartment. We shared the hall, tiny kitchen, toilet, and bath with another family—husband, wife, and small daughter—who lived in the third room. Neither family relished the living arrangements, the norm for perhaps half Moscow's eight million inhabitants, but Lena and I felt fortunate to live in the very center, a five-minute walk from three metro stations.

I liked my work in the protocol section of the Institute of World Economy and International Relations—IMEMO is the Russian acronym—even though my salary was low. A kind of "think tank," IMEMO advises the government and the Central Committee of the Communist Party on foreign policy. I worked as an interpreter and translator for English-speaking visitors and

handled my boss's correspondence with English-speaking countries.

My second husband, Yuri, who taught the Thai language at a
secret Moscow military academy, had moved out in the spring.
We had no children in common and had been married only a few
months; I did not anticipate complications with the divorce. But a
gnawing concern that I was unsuited for married life made the
summer of 1972 a difficult one. Approaching thirty-four, I had my
slender, chestnut-haired daughter to see through adolescence and
my own future to think of. Burdened by my marital failures and
uncertain of my ability to shoulder so many responsibilities alone,
I took long, solitary walks and tried to sort out my life. After a
while I reached some decisions. I would devote myself to helping
Lena through the teenage years and begin work on a master's
thesis in the hope of being promoted at IMEMO. And I made a
resolution: never again would I become deeply involved with a
man.

At the end of July, needing a rest, I eagerly accepted an invitation from my friend Zaira to spend part of the August vacation together at her parents' home in Ordzhonikidze, capital
of the North Ossetian Autonomous Republic 1,500 kilometers
south of Moscow in the foothills of the Caucasus Mountains. My
daughter was away at a Pioneer camp, so I did not have to worry
about her.

Zaira's parents greeted us with overwhelming southern hospitality, giving us their own bedroom with two large beds and pam-
pering us night and day. They stuffed us with garden-fresh
vegetables, lamb shashlik, succulent baked potatoes drenched in
butter, melons, pears, plums, apples, Georgian and Azerbaijani
wine, Borzhomi mineral water. The abundance of the southern
republics always astonishes people from the north, where fresh
vegetables and fruit are expensive and in such short supply that
parents save most of what they find for their children. Every day
Zaira's mother prepared pine-oil baths for us; worn out by life in
Moscow, we luxuriated in the warm, fragrant water. Afterward,
soaking up the sun on the balcony, we would revel in the musky

odor of the nearby vineyards and in late afternoon stroll to the city center, enjoying the aromas the huge outdoor market brought to us on a semi-tropical breeze. Northern tensions melted away.

After a week of complete rest and idle luxury, Zaira and I looked forward to the arrival of my college classmate, Olga. She worked as a guide for Intourist and was escorting a group of foreigners around the country. The group was scheduled to visit Ordzhonikidze for a day and a half on the way to Georgia and Armenia. We went to the hotel to meet her. Suddenly she appeared, tall and brassy, at the top of the stairs, talking animatedly with a foreign man, no doubt one of her tourists. When she caught sight of us she raced down the steps with squeals of delight to embrace Zaira and me; our student years were not far behind and we were still close. We chatted for a few moments and then Olga beckoned her tourist, who stood nearby, to join us.

"This is the American leader of my tour group," she said, touching his shoulder lightly, "Woody . . . but Russians call him Vadim."

His full name was Woodford McClellan; I liked the dignified English-Scottish sound of it. In the early 1960s he had been an exchange student at Moscow University where Soviet students had christened him—Russian having no "W" sound—Vadim. Dressed in lightweight khaki trousers, short-sleeved blue button-down shirt, and loafers, he had thick brown hair, a full mustache, and large, piercingly blue eyes that sparkled behind horn-rimmed glasses and bristling eyebrows. His snubbish Baltic or even Slavic nose and sensual mouth, on a far from handsome face, projected a passionate magnetism. Here was a man whose story lay in his eyes—at once apprehensive, intelligent, and mischievous—eyes that proclaimed him to be not entirely at peace with himself or the world. For some reason I felt a sudden impulse to embrace him, calm him down, reassure him.

Zaira immediately played the coquette: she chattered away, pirouetted on long, shapely legs, languidly ran her fingers through her luxurious jet black hair. When Olga introduced me, I concealed my impulse and said with more formality than the occasion demanded, "A pleasure to meet you. My name is Irina."

Zaira and I had spoken in English; he answered in Russian and instantly bewitched me with his accent. In a lilting voice that clearly delighted in forming Russian sounds, he tended to harden vowels the way people from the middle Volga region do, saying "oh" instead of "ah," and to soften consonants.

"Why don't we go to my room for a drink?" he suggested. "I've got some vodka."

We women looked at each other and burst into laughter: no Soviet man would dream of offering vodka to a woman he had just met. Not that Soviet women do not drink, but most prefer wine to vodka. Amused by the American's artless grace, we followed him up the stairs.

In his small second-floor room, Woody—as I will name him in this book, although I was never to call him anything but Vadim— poured some Stolichnaya vodka, a treat available almost exclusively to foreigners in the hard-currency shops. It was not ice-cold as Russians prefer, and there were no *zakuski*, or appetizers, to go with it, but impromptu parties have their own flavor.

Zaira chirped away in her marginal English and flashed those dark Ossetian eyes. Olga and Woody talked animatedly too, switching back and forth between English and Russian. He turned often to me, seeking to draw me into the conversation, but—by nature more reserved than Olga and Zaira—I sipped my vodka silently.

"Are you a professional tour guide?" Zaira asked.

"No, no. Just a professor." Woody grinned.

"Then how . . . ?"

"A Montreal travel agency offered me a free trip around the Soviet Union in exchange for giving a few lectures at each stop. No point turning down such an offer."

"But you never had a trip like *this* one!" Olga joked. It was clear that she and Woody had developed a good working relationship. She attended to the practical needs of the tourists, he to their interest in history.

"I'd been to Kizhi and the lakes north of Leningrad," Woody said, "but never to the Pskov region . . . it's magnificent."

He quoted a few well-known lines from our great poet Aleksandr Pushkin, whose estate was near Pskov. When he spoke Russian, I observed a subtle personality change. Even though more animated than in English, he seemed also more relaxed, as though Russian freed him to be more natural, at ease.

"You say you teach Russian history?" I asked, joining the conversation at last.

"Yes. I taught at the Military Academy while I was in the Army, and for the past few years at the University of Virginia."

He said "Military Academy" in a matter-of-fact voice, but the words raised my defenses another couple of notches. My husband taught in such an institution and was forbidden to breathe a word about his work to anyone. Why was this American so candid?

"Where is your university?" I asked.

"In a little place called Charlottesville . . . a hundred miles or so south of Washington."

"Ugh!" Olga said with an exaggerated grimace. "How can you stand to live in a small town?"

"I go to Washington and New York quite a bit," Woody replied with a smile.

"How did you get interested in Russian history?" I asked.

"Who *wouldn't* be! To me it's the most fascinating subject imaginable."

"But why not *American* history?" Zaira wanted to know. "Isn't it . . . "

"Hah!" Woody interrupted. "One of my professors used to say that they built a railroad across the country and agreed to hold elections every four years—and that was that. No Mongol invasion, no Ivan the Terrible, no Peter the Great, no . . . "

He hesitated, possibly deciding not to mention any modern historical figures, then continued, "Our country has been so fortunate . . . maybe success and peace are always dull."

He went on to say that he had had excellent teachers at Stanford and Berkeley, including Russian émigrés.

"Did you learn Russian from émigrés?" Zaira asked.

"If he did, they must have been from Vologda," I interjected drily, referring to the town on the Volga famous as the home of those broad vowels.

"My professors were from the post-revolutionary emigration," Woody replied. "And by the way—all three of you speak English with a kind of BBC accent. Where does that come from?"

"We graduated from the Institute of Foreign Languages," I answered. "Some of our teachers were British. Unfortunately, we haven't been able to go abroad to practice."

Woody shot me a look of understanding. As a specialist in Soviet history, he would know how severely restricted our lives were.

"How is your tour connected with your work?" Zaira asked.

"It gives me a chance to see the country. This is the third tour I've led. I usually spend a few weeks in the libraries after the tours, but this time I've got to get back for the fall semester."

The history of Old Russia was one thing, but, recalling required classes in high school and college, I could not see what he found exciting about Soviet history—Lenin, Stalin, and the infallible Communist Party. But the time had come to change the subject. History can get uncomfortably close to politics, a subject no prudent Soviet citizen discusses with a foreigner in a hotel room. To my relief Olga turned to the latest Moscow gossip.

Only half-listening to her stories, I tried to understand the turmoil that had welled up within me. Entering into a genuinely personal relationship with a foreigner was the last thing I could imagine for myself—yet I was drawn to this man with a suddenness that bewildered me. How to explain it? I'm not sure anyone can explain falling in love, the sudden, unexpected attraction.

After an hour or so we thanked Woody for his hospitality and left.

The next day Olga and Woody invited Zaira and me to dine with the tour group. Zaira was busy with her family, so I went alone through the evening heat to the courtyard restaurant of the hotel, where we ate in the shade of a massive beech tree. The sidewalk was visible through a large archway; on the street, all Ossetia seemed to be on promenade. The tourists—an assortment of people from the United States, Canada, France, and Holland—ten in all, introduced themselves: the Dutch Ambassador to Italy and his wife, a Kansas woman and her daughter, a New York stockbroker, a research chemist from New Jersey, two retired Frenchwomen from Paris, and a couple of others. All received me cordially, obviously happy to meet a private Soviet citizen.

Over dinner, we discussed jobs and families; I spoke chiefly about my daughter. Woody sat at the opposite end of the table. He smiled at me frequently, but we were too far apart to converse.

That dinner remains in my memory as the first we shared. The waiters produced *zakuski:* plates of smoked tongue garnished with horseradish, green onions, olives, and pickles; cold salmon and sturgeon; pickled herring with sliced onion; Armenian salami and smoked sausage; and large clear-glass dishes of black Caspian caviar set in ice-filled pewter containers, caviar we spread with a little butter on crisp white bread. For the main course I ordered *tsyplyata tabaka,* a Georgian specialty—pressed, butterflied spring chicken sauteed in oil and covered in a thick garlic sauce, served with fresh herb grasses, especially *kinza,* or coriander, green onions, sliced cucumbers, tomatoes. Standing sentinel around the table were bottles of Georgian wine, Azerbaijani cognac, Stolichnaya vodka. Such feasts are for foreigners with hard currency and Soviets of high rank. Most Soviet people have to stand in queues just to put bread, cabbage, and potatoes on the family table.

Toward the end of the meal Woody rose, raised his glass of *Kinzmarauli,* Stalin's favorite red wine, bowed in my direction, and proposed a toast: "To our lovely Russian guest!" Flattered but embarrassed, I thought everyone must notice the intimacy of his tone. I smiled, trying to conceal my emotions. Before I could thank the group with a toast of my own, Woody rose again:

"Shall we invite Irina to travel with us to Tbilisi and Yerevan?"

"Yes!" two or three of the tourists cried out in unison. "There's room in the bus."

Olga quickly sized up the situation.

"Irka, davai!" she exclaimed. Come on . . . let's do it!

Never having been to Georgia or Armenia, I wanted very much to go . . . and to see more of this American professor. But I did not want to offend Zaira by leaving so abruptly; and it would be a violation of Intourist rules to travel with foreigners. Grasping my dilemma, Olga winked as if to say, Let me handle it.

We went to Zaira's parents. Olga took the initiative as usual and argued that I should take advantage of the opportunity; she would simply pass me off as her sister and no one would be the wiser.

"Are you sure it will be all right?" Zaira's father asked. "The KGB watches foreigners so closely . . . is it a good idea for Irina to travel with them?"

Her mother also expressed concern, but by this time my mind was made up.

The next morning I thanked my hosts for their hospitality, kissed them goodbye, and walked the dozen or so long blocks to the center, carrying my one small suitcase. A little before nine o'clock I found Olga near a big Hungarian bus, one of several parked in front of the hotel. At her signal I hopped aboard and settled as inconspicuously as possible into a back seat. The driver worked for Intourist and would know the rules, but so long as the foreign tourists raised no objections (they almost never did), guides could get away with taking a relative or a friend on bus trips—one of the perquisites of a low-paying job.

A few minutes later Olga and the tourists boarded. Woody got on last; I watched him peer around the people milling in the aisle until he caught my eye and grinned. He took the guide's swivel chair in the stairwell next to the driver, clipped a microphone to his shirt, and said a few words about the day's itinerary. Olga sat near him in the front seat.

The wheat fields were behind us now and the road led ever upward into the mountains, through great stands of oak and pine and Caucasian beech, occasionally leveling out in a meadow or descending into valleys where peasant men and women worked the fields with horses. The hotel had provided box lunches, and early in the afternoon the driver stopped in a meadow near a holly and boxwood copse. I was last off. Woody was there to offer me his arm—and make me overly conscious of his touch.

The trip took us along the Georgian Military Highway through the Caucasus to Tbilisi, capital of Georgia, where we spent a couple of days. I slept on a cot in Olga's hotel room, tagged along on excursions around the city and into the country-side, ate with the tourists, tried to answer questions about life in the Soviet Union . . . and could not get Woody out of my mind. Intrigued by a new point of view, I listened to his talks on Russian and Georgian history on the bus or outside churches and mu-seums and castles. In those informal settings he could obviously be more relaxed than in the classroom, but I was struck by the absence of stock phrases about classes and masses, his concern with the human condition. Woody spoke cultivated English de-void, so far as I could tell, of any regional accent, and spiced his talks with wry, often self-deprecating humor.

From Tbilisi we drove the 175 kilometers over the mountains to the Armenian capital, Yerevan. The first evening there, Friday, August 18, 1972, Woody invited me to have dinner away from the group at another restaurant.

Emotions mixed, I felt myself blush. I wanted to accept, but at the same time I feared that being alone with a foreigner would be claiming a privacy that the government expressly forbade. And yet I agreed.

When I told Olga, she approved, warning, "Be careful . . . watch out for the KGB." The secret police is especially vigilant in Yerevan because Armenians have so many foreign contacts; hotels are kept under close watch. As I would soon learn, the extra per-son in Olga's group had not escaped notice.

In the early evening, Woody and I strolled to the Hotel Ani, the oldest and best in Yerevan. Over dinner he talked at length of

his successes and disappointments, his two unsuccessful marriages. He had begun to doubt he was suited for family life; at
thirty-eight, four years older than I, he was evidently experiencing
a personal crisis. His lack of reserve—common among Russians
but rare among Americans I had met—puzzled me; we had
known each other only five days. Why was he unburdening himself? Or was that the key, the fact that he barely knew me and
would soon say goodbye? Unable to answer those questions, I was
struck by the similarity of our lives. We were both reasonably
successful at our careers but failures at marriage.

The restaurant, like many in the Soviet Union, had live music.
The orchestra struck up a tango, a dance never out of fashion at
hotel restaurants in our country, and Woody invited me to the
floor. He touched me very lightly, but my skin shuddered a little
voluptuously. When the music stopped, he kissed me gently on
the forehead and whispered, "I'm happy."

The restaurant closed around eleven-thirty. We went into the
street and for a long time walked slowly through the center of
Yerevan, stopped under trees to kiss, finally ending up in a park
where an elegant, soaring piece of stone hollowed at the center for
an eternal flame perpetuates the memory of the dead of World
War II. We were alone, and the park belonged to us . . .

We were still holding hands when we walked back into the
hotel after midnight. A couple of clerks at the registration desk
shot insolent looks our way, and three or four men in dark business
suits who sat far apart from each other in the spacious lobby
looked on silently. Woody released my hand. Suddenly uneasy, we
said goodnight and went to our separate rooms.

2

Stones Fly

THE SHARP, ominous ring of the telephone awakened us early; a peremptory summons to Olga to come to Room 1 immediately. The number was significant. In many Soviet hotels, Room 1 is reserved for the KGB. Her habitual self-assurance badly shaken, Olga dressed quickly and dashed downstairs. Twenty minutes later, pale, mouth trembling, she reported that a middle-aged man had confronted her with questions about me—and Woody.

"Why is this woman with your group?" he had demanded. "You know that's not allowed. And why did that *American* go out with her alone?"

Olga had pleaded innocence.

"We haven't done anything wrong . . . she's my cousin . . . used to work for Intourist herself. She's never been to Armenia . . . I let her come along. That's all."

We were not cousins, but I had worked briefly in the Moscow home office.

"You've broken the rules. I'll inform your superiors!" the man barked.

In an effort to placate him, Olga swore I was flying home the next day. Hand poised over the telephone, he stared at her for several seconds. Olga's innocent look—she was an accomplished actress—and tone evidently won him over. He relaxed.

"All right. But keep her away from the foreigners until she leaves!"

We tried to guess the identity of the informer. The local Yerevan guide, noticing Woody's absence at dinner? The hotel clerks? Those men who watched Woody and me enter the lobby

together late last night? We would never know. But there was no
time to speculate. Olga had to leave for breakfast and then an
excursion to Echmiadzin, the Vatican of the Armenian Apostolic
Church.

On top of the world at midnight, eight hours later I found
myself practically under house arrest. The last few days had left
me confused. The trip had begun so innocently . . . and so *what* if
the American and I liked each other. Whose business was that but
ours? Olga returned at sunset and we decided to defy the orders
from Room 1.

"Get dressed," she commanded. "We're going to dinner. The
tourists want to say goodbye."

"How did you explain my absence?"

"A white lie—you had a headache."

At dinner, one by one the tourists brought me little souvenirs
of our few days together: perfume, a pocket tape recorder, a couple of books, records. I found the unexpected gesture touching.
The three of us—Olga, Woody, and I—tried to maintain the
cheerful atmosphere so as not to spoil the group's easy camarade-
rie.

When I had said goodbye to everybody, Woody suggested a
walk. We left the hotel separately and met in a dimly lit nearby
park. There we sat on a bench and talked, pausing when the
occasional passer-by approached.

"I'll try to see you in Moscow," Woody said. "We'll be there
for three days at the end of the tour."

I nodded agreement. "You can't come to my apartment—it's
a kommunalka."

"I don't want to lose this . . . what we've found," he said
haltingly. "It sounds silly, but I would just like to be with you in a
small quiet room with a bottle of wine, some music . . . "

"That's what I want, too."

We separated a block from the hotel and I went on alone.
Woody walked around a few minutes before following.

Sunday, August 20: I left without seeing him and caught an
early flight to Moscow.

My month-long vacation would soon be over. I was happy but nervous. One afternoon my friend Galya and I took a bus to a lake near Kuskovo, a Moscow suburb where, stretched out lazily in the sun on a sandy beach, I told her the whole story. Galya listened, now and then nodding understandingly. When I finished, she said sensibly, "You can't have all the answers at once. Just be patient."

Russians are supposed to be patient by nature. I am Russian to the core, but that did not help. I could hardly wait for Woody to come to Moscow.

"You look so happy and relaxed," Galya continued. "It would be ridiculous not to see him again."

Meanwhile, in Central Asia, Woody traveled through Samarkand and Bukhara, Khiva and Tashkent, gave his mini-lectures to the tour group and nearly drove Olga crazy—she later reported—talking about me.

At last the tourists reached Moscow, on Sunday, August 27. Despite her misgivings, Olga arranged for Woody and me to see each other; her sister, Svetlana, had an apartment not far from Moscow University. Svetlana was away at the family dacha, or country cottage, with her children, but her husband, Kostya, agreed to have a party.

Unable to wait, I took some sandwiches, salad, wine, and went to the apartment early. I tried to help Kostya set the table but my agitation made me useless; he chattered good-naturedly in an attempt to calm me down. Curious to meet an American—so much is forbidden Soviet people!—Kostya would be a good host.

I listened for the knock at the door so anxiously that I jumped when it finally came, around eight o'clock. I jerked the door open—and there stood Woody and Olga. No mistake . . . I was ominously close to falling in love with this man. I barely had time to formulate the thought. He pulled me to him and we embraced. Olga brushed past us with some ribald comment and closed the door behind her.

After a few minutes we went inside, then a little later Galya, her husband Konstantin, and Woody's friend Valeri Tishkov arrived. A shortish man in his late twenties with thick blond hair, big ears, and a gap-toothed, curiously artificial smile, Tishkov immediately made me uneasy; he held my hand a fraction of a second too long and stared too intently into my eyes when Woody introduced us. Later, when Tishkov was talking with the others, Woody took me into the kitchen and warned me to be careful around him. Taken by surprise, I asked why Tishkov had been invited.

"Valeri always shows up when I'm in the Soviet Union," Woody replied. "It's obviously his job to keep an eye on me. Best to make it easy for him."

"How did you meet him?" I asked.

In the summer of 1967 Intourist had assigned Tishkov, then a graduate student at Moscow University, to accompany a group of American specialists in Soviet history that Woody was taking around the USSR. His English was good, but aside from that Tishkov was an absurd choice: his specialty was nineteenth-century Canadian history.

The party amused Woody and me only for a couple of hours. We began to resent each new topic of conversation. Like Chagall creatures who hover over merrymakers in a peasant hut, we longed to be outside the party, wanted each other. Tishkov watched us throughout the evening. Superficially affable, he never relaxed, hung on every word, noticed the slightest gesture. He was the last to leave.

Then Kostya went to his room . . . and Woody and I were alone. The tension of the last two weeks slowly evaporated into the soft, still Moscow night.

Dark windows and the light from a small lamp in the corner of the room outlined the limits of our tiny world. Now there were only the two of us, so close there was almost no distance between us, and then the final barrier that separates two people disappeared completely, and that which our minds and souls had expressed during the day our bodies now shared . . . He tamed my passion so gently, expertly, my whole body sang, rejoicing in how well, how thoroughly, he knew it. Then followed the relaxation that momentarily calms but never replaces desire . . .

Morning came, and a feeling of complete, perfect harmony.

Kostya went out to the store for bread and yogurt. A few moments later the phone rang. It was my husband, Yuri. Calling from a pay phone across the street, he ordered me downstairs. Astounded, I refused.

"What do you want?" I asked. "Why did you follow me here?"

Shaking uncontrollably, unable to utter a word to Woody, who stood perplexed at my side, I replaced the receiver. The phone rang again.

"So you've brought your lover back from Georgia," Yuri sneered. "Come down immediately!"

I hung up; he rang back. I took the phone off the cradle, but as soon as I replaced it, it rang again. I could not leave it off the hook lest Svetlana or someone else should need to call Kostya. The apartment became a madhouse.

Woody and I hugged hurriedly, then he and Kostya left. I could not see the street from the fifth-floor apartment, which was on the courtyard side. Kostya was gone fifteen minutes. The phone rang for the first few moments, then went silent.

When he returned from escorting Woody to the metro, Kostya reassured me: "There's no one anywhere near the phone booth and no one approached us. Vadim will have Olga call you."

I relaxed a little and had some breakfast. Svetlana and the children arrived in a flurry of greetings. As I was describing what had happened, the doorbell rang. Svetlana and I looked at each other as Kostya reached for the knob.

My mother—who lived halfway across Moscow—stood there with Yuri. Normally an outgoing, friendly woman in her late fifties, she now wore a contorted, angry expression and was gesturing wildly; my tall, urbane husband remained silently behind her. She stormed in like a police matron. Furious at my "sluttish behavior" and ostensibly sympathetic to my husband, she raged on about saving the marriage.

I let her rant for a while, then said: "Mama, *enough*. I may have many men"—I stared coldly at Yuri—"but you've got only one daughter. If I left him, perhaps he deserved it. Go away now. We'll talk later, privately."

I had no idea how Yuri had found me nor how much he knew. We were all frightened, especially Svetlana and Kostya, who could be reported to the police for allowing a foreigner to spend the night in their apartment. I castigated myself for bringing them such trouble. And yet it all seemed so innocent: two people met and fell in love. What was wrong with that?

Distraught and embarrassed, I thanked my hosts, apologized for the trouble, and took my leave. But where to go? I did not want to be alone, but who could help me? I wandered through Moscow for several hours before I finally ended up at my own apartment.

Yuri sat at the table, in front of him a meat platter covered with dozens of cigarette butts. I had forgotten he still had a key. God knows how long he had been there, a man possessed: mouth set in implacable rage, eyes glazed, hair and clothes disheveled, traces of whitish foam around his lips. An enormous screwdriver lay next to the platter. Before I could react he jumped up, locked the outer door, yanked the telephone cord out of the wall, and began shouting insults, threats, humiliating questions.

"I'll *kill* your goddamned Georgian," he hissed, brandishing the screwdriver.

"He's an American," I replied quietly.

Yuri stared at me speechless for a few moments, then changed his tune.

"What are you saying? Have you lost your mind? You'll lose your *job!*"

It was hard to determine what would happen to my job, but Yuri might well lose his if it became known his wife was involved with a foreigner.

An attack of madness seemed to seize him. He leapt at me, tore off my clothes, and threw them down the garbage chute.

"I'm going to cleanse you," he babbled over and over. He dragged me into the bathroom and dumped me into the tub, turning on the water full force. In a frenzy he began to scrub away my "shame," mumbling unintelligibly all the while. I hated and despised him, but I was powerless. We were alone in the apartment. The neighbors were at their dacha, and the telephone was cut.

Rage spent, he allowed me dress, then made coffee for us both. Sitting in an armchair, I silently sipped from my cup, lit a cigarette, thought of Woody, who was leaving Moscow. Would I be able to see him again?

The next day Yuri was rational again.

"I'll save you," he promised. "Taking up with a foreigner— what an idea! You're so naive . . . it was just a fling."

Treating me like an addled child, he talked quietly, soothingly, trying to persuade me to give our marriage another chance. Finally, on Friday, he let me out to pick up Lena at the camp. She would have to start school the following week. Once on the street I immediately called Olga.

Woody had left Moscow . . . but there was a letter for me. I hurried to her apartment.

My dearest Irochka,

This all weighs heavily on me—what will become of you? Where will it end? Can you find the strength to endure? Do you know how terribly my inability to help you torments me?

. . . You changed my life, brought happiness I didn't know existed, and now your misery brings nothing but sorrow. . . . I can only ask you to believe in our moment of happiness as I do and to look beyond your present agony to a lifetime of happiness.

I love you, Irochka, and my heart reaches out to you. Always remember that you gave me a precious human gift—always remember that I am with you.

Vadim

3
Waiting for Vadim

A SINGLE LETTER and memories were all that remained. Yet even if I never saw him again, falling in love with Woody had destroyed my fear of being alone, a fear that had driven me into an unhappy marriage. Perhaps my subconscious had chosen an unattainable object, a man who offered no prospects for my future but did release me from my past.

Mama disapproved of my plans to divorce Yuri: "Losing a second husband, and no angel yourself!" She never actually said that to me, but she thought it loudly enough, and we rarely saw each other. For a time Olga avoided me; I had brought her too many problems. Only to Galya could I unburden myself, but once I had told her the story there remained no outlet for my emotions. Woody had disappeared like a desert mirage. My letters went unanswered. Only later did I learn he never received a single one.

It took several weeks to sort out the situation with Yuri. For a while he acted decently, but his anger festered and one day he started a row that ended in violence: he hit me and split my lip. That was it.

"If you're here when I come home from work," I screamed, "I'll go to your accursed Party cell! They'll be happy to learn your wife has an American lover!"

Like any careerist, Yuri, a member of the Communist Party, feared for his job and his standing. I went off to work looking like a battered wife; but that evening Yuri and his things were gone.

I was at my desk at IMEMO one November afternoon when the telephone rang. A man mumbled something I could not catch—no doubt his name—and then said, "I have a letter from Woody."

He must have heard me gasp, sensed me sit up with a start. Hope that had dwindled all that dreary autumn sprang instantly to life.

"He'd like to see you again," the voice was saying, " . . . might come to Moscow."

It was Valeri Tishkov. As he rambled on, elation gave way to apprehension: why was he speaking so openly about my friendship with a foreigner? Every IMEMO telephone is monitored, as anyone with half a brain knew. Tishkov worked at one of the Institute's sister organizations, the Institute of the United States and Canada. He was surely familiar with the system.

"Maybe we could meet someplace," I interrupted, anxious to stop the flow of words.

At eight o'clock that evening I waited in front of the Lenin Library, a massive, mausoleum-like structure across from the Kremlin's Kutafya Tower. Only parking lights are permitted in Moscow city traffic, and the use of horns is forbidden except in emergencies. Cars, buses, and trolleys glide silently from one set of barely visible traffic signals—a coin-sized dot of color centered in a black disc—to the next. Never boisterous, Moscow's streets assume a kind of mechanical life in late fall and winter. People hurry along wrapped in dark clothes and personal cares, rarely making eye contact. I did not immediately recognize Tishkov when he approached.

"Why don't we sit in my car?" he suggested. "You don't have to stand here in the cold."

Tishkov was my only link to Woody. He began to read out Woody's letter.

If you see Irina, please give her my warmest regards and tell her I think of her often. My wife and I have separated and I'm living alone in two rooms above my lawyer's offices. I miss my son terribly, there's no

hot water and no kitchen, but I'm free, or at least on the way to being
free. Divorce is a sad business but this one had been coming for years.

Tishkov prattled on but my mind was continents away. The
man I loved was in pain; it was all too easy to understand him.
Again, as at our first meeting, a sudden strong desire to comfort
him, let him absorb my strength, swept over me. The letter went
on:

A colleague of mine is leading a tour of the Soviet Union over the
Christmas holidays—the group will be in Leningrad three days, Moscow
four. It's fairly inexpensive and I'm considering tagging along. I could
use a couple of days in the Moscow libraries to check sources for my
book. Do you think Irina would like to see me again? Please let me know
soon because I'll have to make reservations and get a visa.

Tishkov looked at me quizzically, waiting for a reaction.
"I want to see him," I said quietly.
"All right," he responded. "I'll send a cable and say we're
waiting . . . sign it 'Valeri and Irina.' "
Why was everything so simple for this Tishkov? No fear of
associating with foreigners, or with a Soviet citizen—a virtual
stranger—who dared to do so? Something was fishy, but in November 1972 the path to Woody led through him.

If all went well, Woody would arrive in less than a month. I
began to scheme. Taking him home was out of the question: even
though my husband had moved out, the neighbors would certainly inform the police if a foreigner appeared in the kommunalka, and beyond that I had said nothing about Woody to my
daughter. Staying with him in a hotel was also impossible. I do not
know whether it was against the law or merely against the rules; in
any event you could not do it. On every floor of every Soviet hotel
that caters to foreigners sits a concierge whose main job is to
report everything to the KGB.
My loyal friend Galya offered to ask her mother for advice. A
retired bookkeeper, Anastasiya Nikolayevna Khovanskaya lived
with her granddaughter in a three-room apartment on Architect

Vlasov Street on the west side of Moscow, near the Novye Cheryomushki metro station; her husband, an investigating magistrate, was frequently away on business. I scarcely dared hope, but within a few days Galya told me everything was arranged: her mother had no objection to my staying in her apartment with my American friend.

It was a stroke of incredible luck. A total stranger was willing to give me a roof over my head—aware I would bring my lover, a foreigner. A few days later I went with Galya to meet her mother.

Anastasiya Nikolayevna turned out to be a short, plump woman of about sixty in a simple housedress. Her short gray-blond hair was carelessly combed; a gold front tooth flashed when she smiled. She greeted me warmly and offered us tea in the small main room, furnished with an oilcloth-covered table, four straight chairs, sofa, large cupboard, and a television set on a wooden stand. A tiny kitchen was visible through an open door; the doors to the other two rooms were closed.

At first glance Anastasiya Nikolayevna's face appeared coarse, and her rapid-fire, guttural speech gave the impression of a farm woman transplanted to the city. Only a few minutes at her table, however, revealed something noble beneath the rough exterior.

" . . . doesn't matter what nationality somebody is," she was saying, "as long as he's honest. You say he's American?"

"Ye—yes," I stammered nervously.

"And what's wrong with that? They just came over here a few months ago to sign a treaty, and now you can't drink a bottle of wine with one of 'em? *Of course* you'll stay here with him." A gentle smile lit her face.

"Anastasiya Nikolayevna," I said, "I'm so grateful. It's just for a few . . . "

"Don't worry about it," she interrupted, dismissing my protests with an airy wave. "I'm for love. Nothing else matters. If you love him, that's all that counts."

We talked for a long time, or rather, Galya and I listened to a captivating monologue. If Galya had heard the stories before, she gave no sign; I was spellbound. Anastasiya Nikolayevna spoke

devotedly about her husband, Sergei Yakovlevich, who was away
on a case in Mahach-Kala, the capital of Dagestan on the Caspian
Sea.

"Better man never lived," she said. "He'll hunt all over Moscow for some fish for Filka"—their Persian cat. "And he treats me
like the czarina."

It was time to go. Anastasiya Nikolayevna showed me her
spare room, a tiny rectangle just big enough for a sofa, night table,
and small wardrobe. A radio sat on the night table. I remembered
Woody saying he wanted only a little room, some wine, maybe
some music . . . and me. I'll bring the wine, I thought with a secret
smile.

For the next few weeks I walked on air. I had found not only a
place where we could be alone but also a new friend.

Tishkov called to say that Woody had made all the necessary
arrangements.

He was to arrive on December 28. A week before, there came
another telephone call: Lev Sukhanov, head of the KGB section
at the Academy of Sciences—IMEMO's parent organization—
wanted to see me. I shuddered. My boss had to clear visiting
foreign delegations and foreign travel for IMEMO employees
with that office; I normally handled the paperwork. But in December 1972, about to go on vacation for two weeks, I was caught
up with my work. The summons must surely concern Woody's
visit.

I had met Sukhanov twelve years earlier at the Afro-Asian
Solidarity Committee, where I had been a secretary; he worked as
a referent, or all-purpose "specialist." Ostensibly the Committee
was a public organization composed of four hundred or so public
figures—authors, scientists, teachers, workers, peasants—whose
responsibility was to support Soviet ideology and foreign policy in
the Third World. They signed speeches and appeals, went on
goodwill trips abroad, and in general acted as Kremlin spokespeo-
ple. The dozen or so referents assisted them in all this. Only some
years later did I learn that the Committee is a KGB agency entrusted by the Party Central Committee with the care and feed-

ing of potential recruits to the Soviet cause and the advancement of Soviet interests in Asia and Africa. At least half the referents are always KGB employees, and Lev Sukhanov was one of these.

In 1971 I had encountered Sukhanov a second time. Now a big boss, he was no longer familiarly Lyova, but the very proper Lev Sergeevich. I had just started working at IMEMO; he asked me to come to his office at the Academy of Sciences. We exchanged a few pleasantries about the old days, then he said, "I understand you've been assigned to work with Professor Polk."

Head of the Near East Institute at the University of Chicago, William Polk would be the guest of IMEMO.

"Yes, he and his wife will be here in a few weeks. I'm to take them to Leningrad and Central Asia."

Sukhanov looked at me probingly for several seconds.

"He's an important man. We want to learn more about him. You're attractive and smart—you could help us."

It was a proposal to work for the KGB, to undertake the surveillance of some unsuspecting person, become an informer. I found the very thought repugnant and wanted no part of it. Trying to make light of his request, I said, "You've got the wrong person. I'm just a guide and interpreter—you know, 'On your right you see this, on your left you see that.'"

He started to object but I would not let him. Looking him straight in the eye, I said quietly, "It's no use, Lev Sergeevich. Find somebody else."

Making an excuse about an urgent meeting, I left. From then on I was wary. When Sukhanov summoned me to his office in December 1972, I was prepared for the worst.

This time he did not bother with small talk, limiting himself to a curt "Hello." Nodding toward a chair in front of his large desk, behind which hung portraits of Lenin and Feliks Dzerzhinsky, founder of the secret police, he gave me a cold look and waited, expressionless, while I removed my coat and sat down.

He spoke, exposing rotted, nicotine-stained teeth.

"All right," he said, fixing me with a stare, a cigarette drooping insolently from his puffy lips, "what's between you and this American?"

"I beg your pardon."

I met his gaze, trying to keep my expression neutral.

"Don't give me that. Why have you taken up with the ugly bastard?"

"Lev Sergeevich," I replied, addressing him formally, "I'm not sure I understand your language. And why are you taking such an interest in my private life? When I need your advice I'll ask for it."

He snorted contemptuously.

"Listen, Irochka," he said with a sneer, using the familiar pronoun *tu* instead of *vous* as the relationship demanded, "you will stop writing to this man and break off all contact with him. Do I make myself clear?"

"What gives you the right to pick my friends?"

A straight answer would have been, "My position as a KGB officer." Even straighter was the one he actually gave.

"If you don't do as I say, we'll send you off to Siberia—along with your daughter and your mother." His voice grew shrill. "None of you will ever see Moscow again . . . you've taken up with a spy!"

Siberia—who in our poor country has not heard about Stalin's Terror? Innocent people disappeared, families suffered, lives were shattered. Out of control now, Sukhanov continued to shout. Drops of saliva flew from his mouth. Eyes squinting, cheeks puffed out, he looked like a caricature movie villain. I struggled to follow his threats but could not slow my thoughts long enough to understand what was happening. Suddenly the stupidity of it all dawned on me: I was simply in love with a man.

"All right," I said firmly, "now let me tell *you* something. We're not in Stalin's time any more, and they don't send people to Siberia just like that. Second, if this American is a spy, then *you*, Lev Sergeevich, will go to Siberia because your KGB let him get away. All I did was fall in love."

My fear momentarily dissipated. My bold declaration of love

for the "spy" discomfited Sukhanov, my determined tone restrained him. He changed his tack.

"What's this—thinking of marrying him?"

When I did not react, his anger broke out anew.

"Aren't a hundred million Soviet men enough for you?"

Instantly I stood up to leave.

"Anything else?" I demanded icily.

"Yes. I'll give you three days to think it over. If you decide to break this liaison, call or come to see me."

On the street, my boldness deserted me. I felt alone and helpless. I was afraid to get on a bus lest the doors close and block escape. Gray skies, gray asphalt, gray buildings, everything around me suddenly turned a metallic, impersonal gray. I dragged myself along Lenin Prospect, powerless, my last ties to the known world hanging in shreds. Instinctively I looked behind: someone was following me, keeping me under surveillance. No, no one . . . only fear dogged my heels.

I do not know how much time passed before I found myself at home.

On December 28 I hurried to Architect Vlasov Street around noon with food, a couple of bottles of wine, and a magnum of Soviet champagne, ready to celebrate our reunion. I was much too early. To pass the hours, I talked to Anastasiya Nikolayevna and her eight-year-old granddaughter Marina, in whose presence we had agreed not to speak the word "American." Then I excused myself and walked to the metro.

The plane was due in at one o'clock. Passport control, customs, the trip to the hotel, and registration would consume at least two hours. Valeri Tishkov was to meet Woody at the Hotel Berlin and pass on a simple message: Take the metro to the Novye Cheryomushki station.

I paced the platform for an hour, went outside, took fright lest Woody get off a train and not find me, rushed back inside, paced back and forth. The sparkling clean trains painted in blue and light green pulled in, disgorged passengers, and continued on their way punctually every four minutes. Contradictory feelings assaulted me: I wanted so badly to see this man, proclaim my love, tell him all that had happened to me. But then I thought: My God! what if I've just *imagined* all these emotions? What if I've mistaken a fleeting, danger-spiced, lusty romance for love?

At last, a little after four, a train pulled in, the doors opened, and there he was, my funny American, stepping onto the platform in a silly green English cap and a Western-style overcoat not warm enough for Russia and breaking into a broad grin when he caught my eye. We locked into an embrace with foreheads touching, hands cupping each other's face, barely breathing. We stood that way for a long moment, then I whispered, "Welcome back. Let's go."

We said little as we made our way through the dark snow-covered streets and courtyards. I told him briefly about *Matushka,* or Mother—Anastasiya Nikolayevna—but my words probably did not register. No less excited and nervous than I, he had been flying for many hours.

Anastasiya Nikolayevna let us in, smiled at Woody, whom I introduced as Vadim, helped us with our coats and boots, and showed us to our room.

"Make yourselves comfortable," she said as she closed the door. "Rest. Be at home. We'll have a bite after a while."

Alone, we collapsed silently on the sofa, held hands, and looked at each other. It was a silence that answered all questions. It had not been merely a vacation fling.

Then Woody took off his jacket and leaned back, closing his eyes.

"It's good to be here," he said gently. "With you."

A few hours later Anastasiya Nikolayevna called us to the table, where she had set out the things I had brought, some vodka, and appetizers. She filled shotglasses from a bottle she kept on her window ledge and proposed a simple toast of welcome. We touched glasses, drank, and reached for black bread and salted herring. Marina, daughter of Anastasiya Nikolayevna's son Konstantin, stared silently at this "uncle" with the strange accent.

Unable to contain her curiosity, she asked cautiously,
"*Vy . . . otkuda?*" Where are you from?
Woody grinned at her and replied, "*Iz demokraticheskoi strany!*" From a democratic country.
In Soviet jargon, which Marina already knew from school, "democratic countries" are those allied with the Soviet Union. Woody's answer satisfied her; one hurdle surmounted.
Anastasiya Nikolayevna and Woody liked each other instantly. At my prompting he told her a story he had heard in Leningrad last August:
Crudely lettered announcements had appeared in the entryways of several apartment buildings: "The Public Health Office requests residents who will be away for the weekend to leave jars outside their doors for free roach spray." Dozens of people complied. When they returned they found their apartments ransacked by thieves . . . the authors of the anti-roach campaign.
Anastasiya Nikolayevna laughed uproariously, then recounted the latest Moscow scam, swearing it was true. Maybe so; it was a time of widespread, blatant corruption:
Two men come to a factory manager's apartment around noon on a workday. The wife answers the doorbell.
"We work for your husband," they tell her excitedly. "He's been arrested! Sent us to tell you to gather up everything you can . . . we'll take you to the dacha. He'll try to get things fixed."
In a panic, the wife gathers up jewelry, fur coat, a large sum of cash, and follows the men to their car.
"Wait!" says one of the men. "Wasn't that a Sony television? Better take it, too—the KGB will ask how you got it."
Leaving the valise with her valuables in the car, she dashes back upstairs with one of the men to get the television set. When they return, the car is gone. The second man puts the set on the sidewalk and says he's going for the police.
The wife never sees them again.
Doubling up with laughter, Woody spurred Anastasiya Nikolayevna to one tale after another of life in the Soviet Union; she was surprised at his knowledge of the country. Asking the right questions and laughing in the right places, he gave impetus to her

natural storytelling abilities. I listened and said little, rejoicing in
the company of two people I loved. Although I had known one of
them four months, the other only a month, they had become part
of my happiness.

Having forgiven me for the anxious moments I had caused
her, Olga came along one evening with Galya to Architect Vlasov
Street. She strode into the room and boomed out in that low,
almost masculine voice, *"Nu, rebyata, vo dela!"* Hey, you guys,
just *look* what's going on!

Troubles forgotten, everyone glad to be together, a lively party
ensued. Olga proposed the most popular toast of the evening—to
love.

The four days Woody was in Moscow are fixed in my memory
as a time of almost dreamlike perfection, when all was right with
the world. Nothing special happened. A man came from across
the ocean to love me. We went for long walks in the snow; vast
open fields surrounded the new residential district and we strolled
across them talking quietly, reveling in each other's company and
the unusually clear, sunny days. We talked about our lives during
the four months we had been apart, touched only lightly on troubles, tried to put the most optimistic, positive face on everything.
It was not contrived. The strength we drew from each other as our
love grew reduced outside difficulties, made them seem manageable, their solution certain.

We spoke of the future, making no concrete plans but promising to be together as often as possible. At work on a project that
required him to do research in Moscow and Leningrad, Woody
intended to apply for a slot on the official American-Soviet exchange of professors.

There were days, nights, only four of them . . . but full of wild
ecstatic sharing of all we possessed. Never had I felt so comfortable with a man, so complete, so whole. Our parting was sad, but
not desperate: I knew he would come back, and soon.

4

KGB in Action

WHEN I RETURNED to work at IMEMO after those few days with Woody, Milochka, the secretary of the section where I worked, looked at me quizzically, her striking Modigliani head inclined to the side.

"What in the world have you been up to?" she exclaimed. "You look positively radiant!"

Pretending to dismiss the compliment, I said offhandedly, "Nothing special. A good rest . . . saw some friends."

Unable to keep a straight face, I erupted in giggles and whispered something about a big secret to be revealed when we went for coffee.

Personal secrets in the Soviet Union sometimes become state business. Milochka had nothing to do with it, but a couple of days later I was summoned to the boss's presence.

Yuri Aleksandrovich Kostko, chief of the protocol section where Milochka and I worked, had a small, tastefully furnished office. Because the number of foreign visitors to the Institute had increased in the early 1970s, he had recently redecorated to impress them: thick Bukhara rug, modern sofa and two armchairs from Finland, and a large, expensive mahogany desk.

Kostko's IMEMO title was "scientific secretary"; in Sovietese that always means KGB. Although on paper they outranked him, the director and two deputy directors kept their doors open to Kostko.

Thin, middle-aged, of medium height, Kostko had a nondescript face with a small, squarish, "German" mustache. Out of nervous habit he fumbled in his trouser pocket with his left hand in the unconscious way one might pull at an earlobe or run one's fingers through one's hair. A Byelorussian, he did not speak or write Russian very well. When he had to compose an official letter, he gave me the general idea and I wrote it for him. Though his knowledge of English was slight, Kostko would try to converse with English-speaking visitors. The results were often comic: he would ask people to stand down on a chair or promise to come see them yesterday.

Kostko read proscribed books. In the summer of 1972, the year I met Woody, everyone was discussing the strident media campaign against Aleksandr Solzhenitsyn. One day I came to work with an issue of *The Literary Gazette* in which both "our great Soviet writers" and many "simple workers" condemned Solzhenitsyn's "betrayal of the motherland." It was not clear how the writers, much less the workers, could judge works never published in our country. Many forbidden books circulated in *samizdat,* or the underground press, of course, and the intelligentsia devoured them voraciously, but no one dared acknowledge that fact of Soviet life publicly. When Kostko came to work that day I produced the newspaper and asked innocently, "Yuri Aleksandrovich, what do you think of this article about Solzhenitsyn?"

He fidgeted, poked around in his pocket, sat down, got up again, then finally stammered, *"Vsyo . . . vsyo . . . vsyo pravilno, kak napisano!"* It's . . . it's . . . just as it is, the way it's written!

"But how can we know?" I persisted. "His works aren't published. Have you read *Cancer Ward, The First Circle?"*

Sensing danger from an unexpected corner, he peered at me quizzically. He had expressed his opinion on officially forbidden literature more than once in my presence, as much to prove his manhood, I suspected, as to demonstrate his sophistication. Finally he replied, "Yes, I've read them."

"And? What do you think?"

"I don't have time to discuss this now," Kostko said abruptly, turning to go into his own office. "Read the article. You'll understand."

Kostko liked to listen to Western popular music on cassettes bought on his frequent trips abroad, journeys that also inspired his own homemade movies. Once after he had been in France, he invited Milochka and me to stay after work. When everyone else had left, he produced champagne, a hamper of fresh fruit, imported chocolates, and a projector. We admired the usual tourist shots of Notre Dame, the Eiffel Tower, the Arc de Triomphe, and so forth, but then the itinerary led to Place Pigalle, where prostitutes beckoned shamelessly to passers-by, including filmmaker Kostko. Naturally he had not accepted the invitations; so much is forbidden Soviet people! He pretended to have found the decadent West disgusting and was anxious to share his contempt with us.

Milochka had worked at IMEMO several years and knew all the gossip. Kostko had once had an affair with the wife of a high-ranking KGB man that had almost cost him his job. Somehow he wriggled out of trouble—more than once I watched him flatter the powerful—and was given a chance to redeem himself by keeping IMEMO on the correct political path.

Kostko determined the composition of IMEMO delegations on trips abroad; needless to say, the most interesting ones demanded his presence. He called himself a "doctor of military science" even though he had never earned an advanced degree. Had he decided to produce a dissertation, however, it would have been no problem: any of several young scholars would gladly have ghost-written one in exchange for a trip to London or Paris.

IMEMO employees without a doctoral degree—I among them—received low salaries, around one hundred twenty-five rubles a month at a time when the average was about one hundred fifty. Those with higher degrees had bigger salaries and enjoyed several perquisites, notably foreign travel. Westerners find it difficult to understand why Soviets regard travel as such an extraordinary privilege. In the West, anyone who wants to go somewhere and has the money simply goes, no questions asked. In the Soviet Union, the state has never recognized a citizen's right to travel beyond the country's frontiers. A journey abroad is one of the most precious gifts the authorities have to offer, and they reserve

it for people of proven reliability. Sometimes the state bestows it
unwisely and a traveler defects; that leads to still more severe
restrictions.

People permitted to go abroad on official business invariably
leave someone at home as a hostage. The ones who remain at
home are not called that officially, of course, but that is what they
are. Until the era of Gorbachev and *glasnost,* or openness, promi-
nent defectors and people expelled from the country were almost
never permitted to return to visit their loved ones.

With all the problems and dangers associated with foreign
travel, why do Soviet people, or at least millions of the educated,
want it so badly? For the same reason they read more books than
any other nation: they are intensely curious about the world, especially the forbidden West.

Permission to go abroad on IMEMO business depended not
only on one's job performance but also on one's relations with
Comrade Kostko. It was understood that anyone allowed to travel
could be asked—that is, required—to collect information for the
KGB. Those whom Kostko chose to perform this service came to
his office before departure for instructions.

Some people at IMEMO believed that everyone in the protocol section worked for the KGB; that was not the case. As our low
salaries and lack of special privilege clearly indicated, Milochka
and I had no connection with the secret police. We worked for
Kostko the IMEMO official, not Kostko the KGB man.

Although I did not like him personally, Kostko was not a bad
boss; generally he let me do my work without interference. Not
the most stimulating job in the world, but a lot better than the
secretarial work I had done earlier. As a referent I translated articles and sections of books on economics and politics, wrote letters
in English and Russian, occasionally acted as guide-interpreter for
visitors to the institute.

My summons to Kostko's office came on January 8, 1973. I
found him pacing back and forth and assumed he was collecting
his thoughts for a letter.

Finally he stammered, "I . . . ah . . . hope you haven't forgotten your talk with Sukhanov."

"No, I haven't forgotten," I answered.

"Well?"

Kostko met my gaze only briefly, then turned his head to stare out the window.

"You can't continue to work in the protocol section," he grunted. "I'll have to transfer you to the typing pool."

When I did not reply, he continued, "And I'll need to tell the board of directors why."

I cared nothing for the board of directors but found the idea of them discussing my love affair ludicrous and insulting. Woody had come to the Soviet Union legally, we had met and fallen in love, he had returned to Moscow to see me, we spent a few days together—and for that I would be fired and publicly humiliated? It made no sense. It was inconceivable that our love affair could have the slightest impact on the mighty Soviet state. Or so I thought then.

Trying to collect my thoughts, I realized that Kostko and Sukhanov had backed me into a corner from which there was no escape. Even if I gave up Woody, my reputation and career prospects were ruined.

"Say what you like to the board of directors," I replied as coolly as possible. "I'm resigning." I hesitated for a long moment, then added, "For personal reasons."

The expression on Kostko's face was one of immense relief.

So, after only two years on the job, I would leave; or rather, the KGB had made it impossible for me to stay. As I tended to the business of resignation, I remembered my first visit. I had wanted the job badly and was terribly nervous at the interview, but to my delight they hired me. Milochka later confided that my competitors had all been from the elite, offspring of high-ranking officials of the Ministry of the Foreign Affairs, the Central Committee of the Communist Party, and so on. Those officials try to place their children in prestigious agencies such as IMEMO and the Institute of the USA and Canada, which are regarded as stepping stones to good careers.

Then why, I asked Milochka, had Kostko selected me? I was not from the elite. Her theory was that hiring yet another spoiled brat could lead to complications. Concerned for his own security, Kostko did not want office gossip passed along to someone in a position of power. Beyond that, work had to be done. He could not have someone sitting idle, protected by parental rank.

Senior employees at IMEMO had to be in their offices only two days a week for meetings and receptions; the rest of the week they worked—at least in theory—in libraries and archives on assignments. The two days when everyone was present resembled working weekends: people came dressed in their best clothes, visited and gossiped endlessly, took lengthy coffee and lunch breaks, acted as though at a social gathering. Foreign visitors were received.

The only people at their desks the other three days were the secretaries, librarians, and researchers using the IMEMO library or "special repository" of restricted works. The building seemed almost empty; those of us who had to be there took advantage of the slower pace. We got our work done quickly, took several breaks and a long lunch, even did our shopping in the neighborhood. It was like having two jobs. At one you were on display and did a lot of unproductive wheelspinning two days a week. At the other, you had three days to do the real work and take care of personal business. As I hoped to get permission to write a master's thesis, I planned to use the quiet days to get it done.

Gradually disenchantment set in. Like any other organization, IMEMO looks different from the inside. As I became accustomed to the people and the routine, the luster wore off and I began to see the reality behind the facade. The economists were the first to open my eyes. These highly if narrowly educated people inundated the Central Committee of the Party with elaborate socialist schemes for the Third World, but they lacked the courage to analyze the catastrophic mess in our own country, where people spend sixty-five billion hours a year waiting in lines to buy food. They produced nothing but politically orthodox, economically meaningless theses, dissertations, and papers studded with quotes from Marx and Lenin and Brezhnev. Had they actually *believed* what they wrote, they might not have been so obnoxious, but after a short time on the job I realized that these people merely told the leaders what they wanted to hear, namely, the same shopworn, discredited nonsense that had passed for economic and social thought in our country since 1924, the year of Lenin's death.

The members of the junior Soviet elite at IMEMO paraded their hypocrisy daily but displayed it most strikingly when they returned from abroad. Whether they had memorized a script or simply imbibed the lines with their mothers' milk, they spoke them perfectly. Afraid to express approval of anything they had seen abroad, they condemned the West and loudly praised our Soviet homeland as the best, freest, most wonderful country in the world. But these same patriots came back dressed in clothes unavailable in any Soviet store, bragged about the Japanese stereo equipment and Danish furniture that now graced their apartments, showed photos and slides of marvelous, expensive itineraries. If they considered you trustworthy, they would offer to sell you a few leftover items at astronomical prices.

The day after my encounter with Kostko, I found a new job: a school in my district needed someone to teach English. The former instructor had left in November and the principal was desperate. I had never intended to enter the teaching profession, but at least there would be bread on the table. Kostko was surprised to find my letter of resignation on his desk.

"What's the hurry?" he asked. "I'm not chasing you out."

"I've found a new job," I replied in a tone that discouraged further conversation.

That turned out to be my final, bizarre day at IMEMO. I was required to obtain the signatures of the director and the two deputy directors on my letter of resignation. Puzzled, all three tried to persuade me to change my mind. Had someone offended me? Did

I need time off? I gave my crisp explanation—personal reasons—
to everyone, declined to be more specific, and stood silently while
they signed.

Kostko waited nervously in the corridor, groping in his pocket,
while I was with the bosses. What if I suddenly decided to explain
my "personal reasons"? He could be accused of having hired
someone who proved to be a security risk. He followed me everywhere, ready to jump in immediately if I said the wrong thing.

Around noon I returned to my desk to find a book that had
come in the morning mail, one on Balkan history Woody had
published a few years earlier. He had inscribed it "To my darling
Irochka." Fortunately, Kostko was momentarily out of the office.
I quickly stuffed the book into my bag. They had opened the
package in the mail room—had anyone seen the inscription? At
least Kostko would not.

I had just managed to calm down when the telephone rang:
the secretary in the "special repository" section announced that a
book had arrived for me. I could look at it there, but it would be
IMEMO property.

Another book? Was someone playing a game? I stole a glance
at the one in my bag.

In the restricted collection room the secretary handed me
some sort of bibliography on Yugoslav foreign relations, which
was to have been the subject of my master's thesis.

"You can read it here if you like," she said, "but it stays in the
room."

I sat down at a desk, opened the book, and there it was again:
"To my darling Irochka." I closed it quickly. Now what? Sooner
rather than later everyone would know my "secret." I went out for
a cigarette and tried to think.

From my own office I got the single-edge razor blade we used
to sharpen pencils. Back in the "special repository," the secretary
was busy. I pretended to turn the pages, then, satisfied she was not
looking, put the book on my lap beneath the desk, sliced out the
flyleaf, and put it in my sweater. I returned the volume, thanked
the secretary, and left the room trembling with relief.

Back in my office I sat at my desk dreading a summons to Kostko's office. It did not come. I had gotten away with it. IMEMO had the book, but I had the page that proved it was mine.

There was one last surprise. The payroll clerk, holding my last pay envelope back as though reluctant to let go of it, tapped it on the counter and said, "Irina, look at this: an order raising your salary by twenty-five rubles a month, signed today. You're walking away from it!"

Her eyes searching my face, she awaited my reaction. By now inured to surprises, I was tired of explaining, or rather, not explaining.

"Sometimes you just do what you have to do," I said flatly.

If my eyes were still not completely open, at least I was beginning to see some light. My innocence about my country was behind me: I was now a security risk, a person suspected of being suspect, as they put it in the French Revolution. I had lost my job and with it all prospects for a decent future in the Soviet Union.

The KGB had struck. Not for years would I wean myself from a search for logic in its actions. Of course, there was none.

5

My Mother

WITH ONLY ONE free day between my departure from IMEMO and my new job at the school, I tried to put the apartment in order—cleaned, dusted, washed, straightened, put things away, and thought about the abrupt change in my life. Tomorrow I would face four classes, each of about twenty students who had not had an English teacher for three months and had spent their language periods in unsupervised study halls.

My experience in the classroom was limited to a month of practice teaching during my studies at the Institute of Foreign Languages. I remembered little from a couple of education courses and did not even have any textbooks at home.

In the middle of the afternoon Anastasiya Nikolayevna telephoned—a letter from Woody had arrived. Thank God! I thought. Today of all days I need to hear from him. I dropped everything and hurried across the city.

Happy New Year to my beloved *Dekabristka!* ["December woman"—a reference to the wives of the "Decembrist" rebels against the czar in 1825.] You waited for me so many months last fall without any news, and then we met in that glorious week in December. I still find it difficult to believe that it all happened as it did. . . .

You are literally never out of my thoughts . . . did you begin divorce proceedings? Any more unpleasantness with your husband? Keeping your promise to smoke no more than five cigarettes a day? . . .

I hope to come at the end of March, while the low-season air fares are still in effect . . . I'll keep you posted.

. . . I am committed to you heart and soul. You brought me a love so new and overpowering I still can't fully comprehend it . . . it's nothing short of a miracle. . . .

He had also written to Anastasiya Nikolayevna. We read and reread the letters and discussed them over cups of tea.

The hectic first week of teaching wore me out. With four Monday-Wednesday-Friday classes and five on Tuesday and Thursday, I taught pupils from the fifth through the senior grades. The majority came from working-class families, and many were disadvantaged some way due to divorce, alcoholism, poverty—or all three. Physically and morally worn out in the attempt to cope with their own problems, the parents paid little attention to their children's education and tended to regard foreign language as unnecessary and even frivolous.

The beginners among my students had forgotten whatever they had learned, the ones in the middle considered ignorance fashionable, and the seniors were at first surly and uncooperative. It would take several months to establish rapport and instill a certain respect for the English language.

At the end of the first week I came home tired, listlessly cooked some dinner, chatted with Lena for a while, and was about to go to bed around nine thirty when the telephone rang. My mother rasped an order: "Come over here immediately!"

"Mama, it's late and I'm sleepy. Couldn't it . . . "

"I said *immediately!*" She hung up abruptly.

She and my stepfather lived several metro stops away. I left the perplexed Lena—who knew nothing about Woody—with a flimsy excuse for my disappearance, bundled myself against the January cold, and wearily trekked to Mama's apartment.

All their lives together, my parents had lived in one room. In this, their latest and most modern quarters, one corner served as a dining room, another as a living room, and the rest as their bedroom. The place was barely lit: only one of six bulbs in the brass ceiling-light fixture was turned on. Such economizing was a generational habit. Electricity is cheap in the Soviet Union, about four kopecks (six cents) a kilowatt, but my parents were accustomed to saving, cutting corners, making do without, because they had grown up in the aftermath of the Revolution and Civil War,

when the country was devastated. Living through the still greater
horror of World War II only reinforced their frugality.

My stepfather sat as usual in an armchair near the television
set, reading *Pravda*. An intelligent, devout Communist, he spent
hours every day with the Party newspaper, though it normally has
only six pages. He was mildly shocked to see me so late in the
evening. I mumbled a greeting and we talked for a few moments,
then Mama concocted some lie and hustled me back out the door.
Private conversations were impossible in the tiny apartment.

It was about 25 below zero Celsius that moonless night; lights
in the courtyard reflected off dirty snow which had not been
removed in weeks. My mother's mood matched the atmosphere;
she turned on me in fury: "You've ruined me! Ruined my career!"

At first I could not make sense of what she was saying. Finally
it emerged that after thirty-six years with a spotless record, she
had been dismissed from her job. She had worked all those years
for the KGB, the secret police. Despite her conscientious service
and devotion, they had forced her into retirement because of her
daughter's unworthy conduct.

My shock at the IMEMO reaction to my affair with an American had proved how much I had to learn about my own country.
As I listened to Mama rant, I thought, Dear God! Is Stalinism still
alive? Must parents still pay for their children's sins, and vice
versa? Perhaps they don't shoot people on a mass scale any more,
but the guiding principles seem the same.

Mama's dress peeked out from under a coat misbuttoned in
her rage. She wore a scarf over her head, and beneath it her eyes
were angry slits. Her plump rosy cheeks were made even more
round and red by cold and spleen. She stood there a blustering
virago, punishing me with an unwavering glower. I felt sorry for
her—sorry she could not recognize the absurdity of being called
to account for the "mistakes" of a thirty-four-year-old daughter. I
had not lived in her home for over fifteen years.

"You've sold yourself for pantyhose! Sold out to the imperialists!"

I did not even try to suppress a smile. The emotional, romantic, incautious Woody hardly fit the imperialist mold.

"Be quiet," I hissed. "You know the walls have ears."

"Quiet!" she yelled. "You want quiet? You should have thought about *quiet* earlier! Tell me what's been going on!"

The circumstances did not dispose me to enlighten her, and anyway the KGB had obviously done all the explaining necessary. Whatever I said, she would believe her masters' version. That was the way she had brought me up, to render unquestioning obedience to authority. The bosses always knew what was best and were not required to explain anything.

Not only had I violated my mother's principles: I had also caused her to lose a good job, one she loved. She could of course have retired four years earlier at fifty-five; Lena and I had urged her to. We pleaded with her to rest, travel, relax with her friends and with us, read, enjoy life more. She always resisted. They needed her, she said, and clearly she needed them.

Now they had booted her out, of course with thanks, even honors. They gave her a certificate of meritorious service and so many presents that an official car barely held them all, as Mama later told us proudly.

She kept demanding that I reveal everything, but it was cold and late.

"When you've calmed down," I said, "we'll meet again and talk. I've got to be in class tomorrow at eight thirty."

We parted on the worst of terms. The KGB had taken my mother from me as well as my job. We would not see each other again until her birthday in April.

Exhausted though I was, instead of taking the metro I dragged myself through the cold streets in the general direction of home, thinking about Mama.

She was born in 1914 into a simple working-class family, the Babyshkins, nominally Russian but in reality chiefly Tatar, a blend of Turkic, Mongol, and other ethnic stock whose oriental blood flows in the veins of millions of Russians. The Babyshkins lived in the town of Balashikha, thirty kilometers east of Moscow, in a forest zone of oak, beech, fir, and birch. Economic life centered around a couple of textile mills. Aside from those massive red-brick nineteenth-century buildings there is not much else in the town even today, except apartment houses and a few shops. Eight barrack-like, pre-revolutionary workers' dormitories are still used as dwellings. Each of the four-story buildings is painted a different color; in the old days people would say they lived in the "white sleeper," the "red sleeper," or whatever.

Ivan Babyshkin, my maternal grandfather, worked in one of the mills until World War I, in which he served and died. His death left Grannie Sanya, a diminutive of Aleksandra, to care for two young daughters, my mother, Elizaveta, and my aunt, Anna. As soon as the girls were old enough they took their places at the looms but somehow managed to finish high school while holding down jobs. Elizaveta and Anna welcomed the new regime enthusiastically and adopted communism as their religion despite its outlawing of the Russian Orthodox faith in which Grannie had raised them. They joined the Komsomol—the Communist Youth League—at fourteen and entered the ranks of the Communist Party as soon as permitted. Obeying Party discipline, they forbade Grannie to keep icons and demanded that she abandon the Church.

Family photographs reveal my mother as a pretty, brown-haired, brown-eyed, young woman with the high cheekbones and wide skull of her Tatar ancestors. She had a voluptuous figure: large bust, thin waist, rounded hips, shapely legs. At family reunions I heard stories about the young men who chased after her, and Grannie Sanya often told me, "Eat lots of sauerkraut so your titties will grow like your mother's."

The blond Anna was attractive rather than pretty. Though she never went to college, she was always considered the intellectual in the family. Aunt Anna and her husband, Mikhail, lived all their lives in Balashikha, but the ambitious Elizaveta wanted to escape the little town; the bright lights and excitement of Moscow drew her like a magnet. Relatives helped her find work as a laboratory assistant at the Bauman Higher Technical School, and it was there that she met Igor Shvetsov, who had come to visit his father, a chemistry professor. They fell in love, had a whirlwind courtship, and married.

This was in 1936–37, a time when the secret police recruited new cadres to replace the ones Stalin and his henchmen were eliminating at a catastrophic rate. The recruiters appeared at the Bauman School and persuaded several young Communists, among them my mother, to come to work at the Lubyanka— KGB headquarters. Forty years later I asked Mama why she had taken such a job.

My mother in 1936, about the time she entered the KGB.

In essence they coerced her; when the recruiters encountered resistance, they responded with threats. Once they had selected you—you never knew on what basis—there was little choice but to accept. They offered my mother, a twenty-three-year-old woman without a higher education, the chance to serve both the motherland and the moral-philosophical ideals in which she fervently believed. The salary was above average and the job carried various perquisites: preferential treatment for housing, a month's vacation and free stays at the best health resorts, a free round-trip rail ticket every year anywhere in the country, and access to special comparatively well-stocked food and clothing stores. Masters of the country, the secret police could offer its employees a slightly higher standard of living in that desperately poor time when Stalin enslaved our people to build an industrialized state and prepare it for the possibility of war with Germany or Japan or both.

Such offers were almost irresistible. With KGB benefits, my mother could help her family, perhaps even protect it if the great dragnet of the Terror came too close.

And so my mother began a career and a second education, both based on cruelty, deceit, and power. An alternate personality came into existence: brought up a Christian, she now donned the cloak of a tough, atheistic policewoman. The two personalities oscillated within her, depending on circumstances. Once inside the system, she could see, or at least guess, that in those years arrest and punishment did not depend on real guilt or innocence. Both innocent, apolitical people and manifestly loyal Party members disappeared and perished. But my mother did not allow herself the luxury of thinking about that, much less speaking. Like so many others, she did as she was told, convinced that the leaders were acting in the best interests of the motherland.

I grew up in my mother's home knowing nothing of her work beyond the bare fact of its existence. To me, the KGB was like the Red Army or any other important state agency. Ignorant of both life and politics, for years I preserved a childlike faith in our institutions and leaders. Until 1956, the Soviet people were never told anything about the horrible crimes of the secret police, which we—simple believers—indeed regarded as the "sword and shield of the Revolution," the KGB's own description. As the world now knows, untold numbers of victims of the Terror went to their graves *defending* the secret police, and those who did not champion it were too terrified, too broken in body and spirit, to speak out.

My mother almost never mentioned her work. When she did say something, it was only a terse, mysterious comment about how important it was. The adults in the family called her *"Minister-sha"*—Madame Minister—more in respect than jest. To this day I do not know what Mama did for the KGB. Lacking a college degree, she probably did not hold high rank. In an unguarded moment at her sixtieth birthday party in 1974, relaxed and a little tipsy after a couple of glasses of wine, she revealed more than she intended:

"Ah, if I could do it all over again I'd never enter either the Party or the KGB!"

Appalled by her own confession, she abruptly began to sing *"Shumel kamysh"*—"The Reeds Are Moaning," a melancholy folk song.

My father appears in family photographs as handsome, intensely masculine; there is an intelligent quality about his long face. He had a strong, aquiline nose, nervous, sensuous mouth, elegantly cut dark hair. Something about those photographs makes me think he wore his good looks unself-consciously, the way people of forceful character always do. Highly educated and well mannered in the way of the pre—revolutionary landowning gentry from which he came, he was—as Mama declared on those rare occasions when his name was mentioned—the most charming man my mother ever met. For his part, my father was attracted by the vivacious good looks and simple purity of a country girl. He worked as an editor at the Znanie, or Knowledge, publishing house.

The Shvetsovs belonged to a far higher social class than the Babyshkins, but after the Revolution such distinctions favored the poor. The Moscow townhouse the Shvetsov family had occupied for generations had been converted into communal apartments; in the 1930s my grandfather, the professor, and his family had only a few rooms there.

I believe that Elizaveta has loved Igor all her life, the way women do their first love. But their happiness lasted only a few years, during which time I was born, and ended when Mama could not forgive her husband's betrayal.

She worked long hours at her new job: on duty at 9:00 A.M., a three-hour break for dinner at 6:00 P.M., then back to the Lubyanka until midnight. My parents had a room in a kommunalka

My parents with their first and only child, spring 1939.

five minutes' walk from KGB headquarters; at the time I was usually with Grannie Sanya in Balashikha.

One evening my mother got off early and came home around eleven to find the door to the room locked from the inside. At her knock there was a commotion and she heard two voices, one of them female. My father, who worked normal daytime hours, had brought a woman to the room. Genghis Khan's proud Mongol blood boiled up in my mother.

They were divorced in 1940. The following year Igor Shvetsov went off to fight in World War II.

I cannot remember seeing my father before 1946 or 1947, right after the war, when he came to our apartment on crutches in terrible pain. He stayed only a short time. A leg wound had become gangrenous, necessitating amputation below the knee. Although I did not know him, the agony of that healthy, happy, good-looking man in the photos made me sick with sorrow.

My father, Igor Shvetsov, during World War II.

Our second, final meeting took place in 1954, when I was sixteen. My father lived then on Gorky Street, Moscow's Park Avenue, in a fashionable apartment building divided into communal apartments; he had one small room. Someone had called my mother—obviously at his request—to say that he was desperately ill and wanted to see me. My first reaction was negative, but my mother insisted I respect his wishes.

One of the neighbors showed me into my father's room and at once I understood the extent of his illness: he could not get out of bed. Thin, pale arms stretched out on the dingy blanket, by now he had lost his other leg. I approached and greeted him rather stiffly, trying to conceal my shock at his appearance. Only fifty-two, he had aged terribly. Toothless, cheeks sunken, he lay there in abandoned misery, gray hair damp with perspiration seemingly glued to his skull.

The room itself seemed part of the tragedy. The several pieces of antique furniture were covered in thick layers of dust. Bookshelves, cobwebs in every corner and crammed with books, covered one entire wall from floor to ceiling. To one side of the bed was an armchair, on the other an intricately carved cherrywood buffet on top of which rested an overturned packet of tea, scattered dried leaves like tiny islands in a sea of dust, and a partially eaten smoked fish. If that fish had been on a table in some café, people would have been pulling at the dried, salty flesh between gulps of beer, enjoying one of the great simple pleasures still to be had in our country. But here, in this dark, musty, room over which death hovered like a shroud, it appeared like something out of a morbid, surrealistic still life. The dying man and the apprehensive schoolgirl had nothing in common save a name and a past which she never knew and he had remembered too late. He was a stranger, grasping at me as the drowning man reaches for a straw.

No sooner had I entered the room than he asked me to kiss him. I experienced a rush of revulsion. To a priggish adolescent, he presented a disgusting, repulsive sight—but it would have been unthinkable to refuse. Leaning over the bed, I pressed my lips to his cheek and felt sick, knowing in that moment I would never see him again. Because there was nothing else to talk about, I tried to amuse him with stories about my school.

After half an hour, I said goodbye and fled. I spent the rest of the afternoon wandering the streets of central Moscow in a daze, pondering my parents' fate. If only they had been able to overcome that family crisis and stay together, how different our lives might have been.

Not long after my parents' divorce, one of Mama's neighbors introduced her to a friend, a man twelve years older. Also divorced, he lived alone with his daughter. Mama had not recovered from her trauma, but the solicitous attentions of this new acquaintance brightened her life. Gradually she melted.

Izmail Dokhov really entered my life only after the war, and when he did I disliked him. Like most children of divorced parents, I was jealous of a stranger's intimacy with my mother, and beyond that his looks repelled me. Tall and rather thin, a proud, dignified man, he had a large eagle-like nose and a stern, commanding chin. Not a Russian, he spoke our language with an accent that annoyed me: he was a Cherkess, a Muslim from the Caucasus Mountains. Grannie Sanya mistrusted him. She never said anything, but I think she feared his strange non-Christian blood. Aware of her disapproval and knowing that our family revolved around her, Izmail Dokhov tried his best to win Grannie over.

In June 1941, Germany attacked Russia. Our whole nation mobilized. Personal quarrels were put aside, and my mother sent two men to the front. Hoping the war would wipe out his sins and that she would take him back, my father came to beg forgiveness and ask her blessing. Izmail Dokhov also came to say goodbye. Given my mother's inflexible moral code, he had more reason to hope she would be waiting when he returned.

This new man in my mother's life rose to the rank of lieutenant colonel and commanded a battalion. Captured in 1943 and imprisoned in a POW camp, three times he tried unsuccessfully to escape. The Wehrmacht usually shot prisoners after one attempt; apparently only the fact that Izmail Dokhov was not a Slav saved him. The Germans had plans to use the minority peoples to rule various parts of Russia after Hitler's victory.

Finally liberated by the Red Army, Izmail Dokhov came home not to a hero's welcome but to prison. That was the fate of almost all Soviet POWs, whom Stalin in his madness considered traitors. Red Army soldiers had standing orders to die rather than surrender. Izmail Dokhov was released after only eighteen months, long before the post-Stalin amnesty. Again, so far as anyone knew, it was his nationality that saved him: the minority peoples emerged from the Gulag a few years before the Slavs. My mother was waiting.

They let him out of prison but did not give him his freedom. The stigma of having been taken prisoner remained; Izmail Dokhov could not return to his old job as director of the Museum of the Northern Caucasus. He had no other profession except that of dedicated Communist, and now even that did not help: they expelled him from the Party. He had to do something, and soon— he found work repairing shoes and earned a few rubles, not enough to live on.

My mother came through magnificently, and her behavior after the war made it all the more difficult for me to understand when, years later, she denounced me for fighting for my own love. Living practically in the shadow of the Lubyanka, she of all people knew how families and friends of "traitors to the motherland" were treated. Nevertheless she secretly continued her relationship with her lover, gave him food and money, saw him on the sly. Had the KGB found out, at the very least she would have been dismissed in disgrace.

When I learned this story, I respected my mother's courageous defiance. Long before my own struggle with the KGB began, she herself took great risks for the man she loved—who incidentally was as much a "foreigner" in the forties as my American in the seventies.

Finally Dokhov found a job in a factory, and following the 20th Party Congress he was "rehabilitated." His Party card, taken away eleven years earlier, was restored. Our family celebrated the event as though the Communist Party had not committed a crime at all.

As a metalworker, Izmail Dokhov stood at a lathe all day and inhaled enormous quantities of metal dust. When his lungs began to fail after a decade, the factory granted him early retirement and disability compensation. His devotion to Communist ideals, heroic if belatedly recognized service during the war, excellent record as a worker, his suffering and humiliation and disability—all this in the end brought him an additional twelve rubles (fifteen dollars) a month to his pension and free public transportation.

Although my mother did not actually marry him until some years later, Izmail Dokhov was her husband in all but name from the time he was released from prison until his death in 1978.

During the war the KGB evacuated my mother and me to Kirov, a medium-sized town on the Vyatka River 700 kilometers east of Moscow. Thinking as always of the family, Mama brought twenty-six-year-old Zoya, her favorite niece, along and shared her rations among the three of us. We lived in a wooden two-story house near the edge of a leafy old park. Almost every evening Mama would bring me a honey roll, something almost as rare in those terrible years as bird's milk, or at least caviar on white bread with butter. At a time when millions of Soviet people could barely survive, she was able to bring me special food because the KGB took care of its employees and rewarded them for their "important work." My mother even managed to send food parcels to Grannie Sanya and Aunt Anna.

In 1985 Mama told me she had been chief censor in Kirov during the war. At first I was surprised: why should a God-forsaken backwater like that need censors? They were not publishing much there during the war. Of course, that was not the point; my mother censored letters to and from the front. Whenever the soldiers mentioned the location of their units or complained about harsh conditions and danger, my mother and her crew took out their black pencils. They did the same when people at home wrote of shortages and low morale. I understood the need to keep

My mother and Izmail Dokhov, my stepfather, vacationing on the
Black Sea, 1953.

information of potential military significance secret, but it seemed cruel to me to deny people the right to share their fears and worries.

My mother had gone to work for the KGB as a young woman who believed deeply in its ideals and those of the Communist Party. This shaped her personality and made her a strict disciplinarian. I had to study hard and, "like the great Lenin," get all 5's and 4's, A's and B's, and keep my things in perfect order. Hers was a Stalinist discipline: in those days people were sent to prison for being a few minutes late to work. Closely following my every step, Mama often telephoned to issue orders when I came home after school.

Competing with her stern, austere personality was the warm, generous one she showed to the family. My mother would collect the provisions she obtained through her job, pack them in two suitcases, and on her free day take the elektrichka, the suburban electric train, to Balashikha. She tied the bags with rope to keep them from bursting open and swung them up on her shoulders like a yoke. We would be waiting at the station when she tumbled out of the carriage "like a pack camel," as she put it. Mama always arrived exhausted but satisfied that she had fulfilled a sacred obligation. We used to call her our our "honeybee-provider." Without her, life would have been much harder for Grannie, Aunt Anna, and Uncle Misha, who during the war and for many years after would have had to exist on the puny rations that were the norm in our country.

At home in Moscow, my mother would stay up half the night to bake snow white napoleons, kneading the dough, spreading the cream, sprinkling the sugar on those many-layered treats. Enjoying her privacy, she made them when everyone else in the building was asleep and placed them on the wide marble windowsill of our room. In the morning I awakened to an aroma so delicious it made my head spin. I was a thin, pale child, and Mama racked her brains for ways to put weight on me. She thought the napoleons would tempt me, but the rich confections made me gag. I just liked the smell, and the pleasure Mama took in baking them. She was forever fussing over me: "My *bylinochka,*" little blade of grass, "you're so thin. Let me fix something for you!"

Her concern led her to overdo things. She would put a big pat of butter into the cup of cocoa she brought me in the morning. The stuff nauseated me, but she begged, "Drink, drink—it'll make you stronger!"

Mama usually washed at night. There was no other time to do it, and anyway at night there was no waiting for the improvised washtub in the communal kitchen. Running hot water did not exist; it had to be heated on the stove, and of course no one even dreamed of washing machines. Mama used an old-fashioned washboard on which she scrubbed so vigorously she often finished with bloody fingers. She was proud that our clothes were always bright and clean and our linens snowy white, delighting in the respect this brought from the neighbors in the kommunalka.

Every summer Mama sent me to a Young Pioneer camp for the children of KGB personnel. In the years right after the war it was a great privilege to go to any camp; the KGB ones were the best of all. My first, a huge one not far from Moscow, had thirty-two sections of about thirty children each. Nearly seven in the summer of 1945, I had never been away from home. My mother kept my childish letters—dictated to counselors—full of tears and homesickness, and came to see me on her free days. Parents were rarely permitted to visit, lest they introduce infections. Hiding in the bushes whenever a counselor approached, they would hang on the fence asking each child who passed to fetch little Ivan or Olga. When their darling finally appeared, Mama or Papa would shove sweets through the fence and stroke heads and faces with their fingers.

I was always happy when Mama came. I cried at first, then gorged on the treats she brought. The counselors never gave us candy, and a wave of diarrhea invariably raced through the camp after these illicit visiting days.

I participated in sports, won prizes in the high jump and gymnastics, and was designated to perform free-style exercises at a camp show. At that time I dreamed of going to the circus school and learning to walk the high wire. We went on the usual camp hikes, learned songs about Stalin and Lenin and the Party, our indisputable authorities.

The first few years at camp I came home with a headful of lice, yet another consequence of the war; all Russia was infested. Every September before I went back to school Mama scrubbed my head vigorously with kerosene, terrified lest I be disgraced at school.

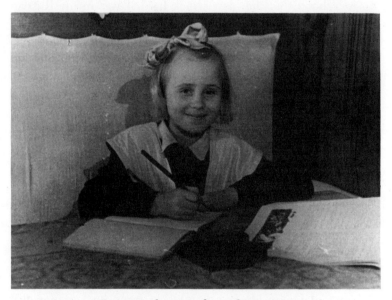

Doing my homework, 1948, age ten.

On March 5, 1953, Stalin died. The entire country mourned. Radio Moscow played funereal music twenty-four hours a day, interrupted only when Yuri Levitan, the chief announcer, periodically read tributes to the fallen leader. Levitan repeatedly broadcast an appeal from the Presidium—as the Politburo was then called—to the Soviet people to remain calm, to unite in this difficult hour and be worthy of Stalin.

My mother, a true Stalinist, was grief-stricken. She had lost

her source of inspiration and strength. To her and indeed to most
Soviet citizens, Stalin was the father of the nation. How could the
country survive without him?

Unfathomable sorrow engulfed our home. Mama paced aim-
lessly, occasionally pausing to exclaim, "Lord, Irochka, what's to
become of us now?" For days her eyes were never dry and at night
I could hear her sobbing. She continued to go to work and indeed
stayed at the Lubyanka even later than usual, telephoning several
times a day to check on me. She forbade me to go into the streets.

At school, too, the blow struck hard. I was in my Russian
literature class when the news came over the intercom; the
teacher, a strong, healthy woman in her mid-thirties, fell to the
floor in a faint. The next day the principal announced that the
semester's cohort of pupils eligible to join the Komsomol would be
admitted early to honor Stalin's memory. I worried that my name
might be left off the list.

They hung a huge portrait draped in black in the vestibule,
and bouquet after bouquet of flowers piled up on the floor beneath it. Black and red memorial streamers on tripods flanked the
portrait, in front of which Komsomol members stood at attention
in twenty-minute shifts around the clock. It was the same in all
schools in the country and in factories and offices.

My name was on the Komsomol list. Would I forget the oath?
No—and I took my turn in the honor guard. Mama was inordi-
nately proud of my participation in the nation's tribute.

The embalmed, awe-inspiring body lay in state in the Hall of
Columns of Union House a few blocks from our kommunalka,
and for three days the Soviet people were permitted to pay their
last respects. Gigantic crowds pushed toward the city center,
driven to bid farewell to the Father, Leader, Teacher. I too
wanted to take my leave of Stalin, and disregarding my mother's
orders, I hurled myself into the immense throng. I knew the central city like the back of my hand. Trotting through familiar back
streets and alleys now decked out in black and red banners and
portraits of Stalin studded with black ribbons, I crawled under the
trucks that blockaded the Lubyanka and Kuznetsky Most, or

Blacksmiths' Bridge, reached Neglinnaya unnoticed, and found myself behind the Bolshoi Theater, only a couple of hundred meters from Union House.

Here several rows of police, Army troops on horses, and trucks parked bumper-to-bumper formed a barrier behind which an ocean of bobbing heads and shoulders waved as if in slow motion, threatening to crush Union House like a matchbox if the barrier failed to hold. The trucks rocked as people surged against them, the outer line of guards buckled and bent. Horses pranced nervously as their riders viciously prodded the mob with long black hardwood batons, trying to keep order. Pressing forward, people slipped between horses and men only to encounter the second ring of guards; these soldiers swung rifle butts and kicked savagely at those who broke through. In another few seconds that chaotic tide of humanity would swallow me like a crippled minnow. Despairing of seeing our Stalin, I turned back and made my way home.

The next day Moscow was swept by rumors about the number of people trampled to death in the spectacular confusion, the likes of which the city had not seen even in 1917. The authorities never revealed the size of the death toll, which was apparently in the hundreds and maybe close to one thousand. Once again people had died with Stalin's name on their lips, just as in the war.

My political coming of age dates from 1956, when First Secretary Nikita Khrushchev denounced Stalin in the "secret speech" that became one of the most widely discussed addresses of the century—even though it has never been published in our country. Mama had little to say about the matter and dismissed my questions as too puerile to warrant answers. I could not understand how a man whose name we had been taught to pronounce reverently, as believers do the word "God," had suddenly become a monster. I asked Uncle Misha whether it was really true that Stalin had sent innocent people to prison. Why, if he were such an evil man, had our soldiers gone into battle screaming "For Stalin and the motherland"?

"You see," my uncle replied, "we faced death every moment. In those circumstances one does not reason. They gave us vodka, told us what to yell, ordered us to attack."

"And everybody obeyed?"

"Of course! We were soldiers . . . and there were secret police troops behind us. If anybody turned back, they shot him."

"Did the soldiers really love Stalin?"

"I suppose so . . . we certainly believed in him. The Fascists removed all doubts when they invaded. Stalin had been saying for years that our enemies were out to destroy us. Now we saw he was right."

Only later would I realize what a watershed the 20th Party Congress had been for the country and for me personally, and only later would I understand that Mama never accepted the toppling of her idol. She could not act differently; how could she admit to the horrors perpetrated by the KGB?

The 20th Party Congress constituted a turning point not only in my attitude toward my country but also in my relations with Mama, who was no longer unchallengeable; her authority, like that of Stalin and the secret police and Party that had faithfully executed his monstrous orders, was hopelessly compromised. She was part of the system that had doomed millions of innocent people. Since 1956 we have moved in different directions. My refusal at age twenty-eight to join the Communist Party disappointed her terribly, but as I matured I tried to establish a normal relationship. The example of my grandmother was always before me: Grannie Sanya never renounced her children even though the moral path they chose ran counter to her devout Christian beliefs. I used to remind Mama that no matter what happened she had only one child, I only one mother. No government or ideology should come between us.

The night I learned of my mother's dismissal from the KGB, my theory about our blood ties did not help. Years would pass before it did.

6

A New "Career"

AND SO through the vagaries of the Soviet system, I became a schoolteacher. Low salaries and corresponding lack of prestige make teaching an unattractive profession in the USSR. Beyond that, I had come to resent the school system because of the way it treated my daughter. The teachers constantly criticized Lena's poor grades and unsatisfactory conduct, blaming me, but never acknowledging their own failures in the classroom.

Obligatory teacher-parent conferences that sometimes resemble criminal trials take place in the evening after the workday; the children wait at home to learn their sentences. Calling out each pupil's name, stern-faced homeroom teachers publicly praise those who have done well, excoriate the dullards and troublemakers—and their parents. In the fall of 1971, when Lena was twelve and in the fifth grade, I sat at her desk during one of these conferences, trembling when the teacher looked over her small, round, metal-framed spectacles to fix a withering, contemptuous gaze on me.

"Well, as for Lena, what can I say? *Another* miserable performance! Grades bad, behavior even worse. Cut classes Monday and took two other girls with her. Hit the boy who sits in front of her with a ruler. *Unbearable* child!"

This was the worst of the many such encounters I had endured. My patience was exhausted. I jumped to my feet and spoke sharply in front of the classroom full of parents.

"Why do you delight in humiliating me? Wouldn't it make more sense to talk privately if you really want to help?"

She gaped in surprise. Parents, especially those whose children have academic problems, rarely argue with teachers. My outburst produced results: from that evening on, the teachers always invited me by telephone to come in for a personal meeting.

But the nagging pain of Lena's mediocre performance never went away; life would have been so much easier if she had lifted that burden. Woody wrote that he had the same problem: "When Charlie began misbehaving at school last year I knew he was reacting to the tension between his parents. Even if I had never met you I would have had to get a divorce; the miserable situation at home was hurting the child deeply."

My misbegotten marriage to Yuri obviously had not helped Lena cope with school, and now my mysterious behavior might worsen the situation further. I had told her nothing about Woody, in part because I had no idea where our affair would go. But although I felt guilty at concealing an increasingly important part of my life from Lena, the roots of her problems went deeper.

In kindergarten and primary school, Lena had been everyone's favorite, the rosy-cheeked, eternally smiling child of an attractive and ambitious young couple. The teachers admired her father and me, struggling as we were to get our college degrees by attending evening classes. Occasionally they helped us out by keeping Lena with the group of children who boarded at the kindergarten all week, going home to their parents only on weekends. My husband's factory provided this service for people who worked swing and night shifts; when he and I crammed for semester exams we sometimes took advantage of it.

Lena made no special effort to find love; it came naturally from everyone around her. But her babyhood ended. Each year the competition in school grew more intense, the large classes often had forty pupils, with teachers too busy to take a personal interest in each child. Now Lena had to fight to prove herself. She tried, but it was not easy. Slowly, she gave up.

Feeling her failures keenly, she sought to compensate with fantasy. One became part of family folklore. On Lenin's birthday in 1971, Lena participated in the annual Red Square ceremony in which children are admitted into the Pioneers. On that day, a few

Lena, on the left with a bow in her hair, at nursery school summer camp outside Moscow, 1963.

of Moscow's academically outstanding pupils, along with some children of the elite, customarily present flowers to the Party leaders assembled on the tribune of the Lenin Mausoleum. When she came home that afternoon Lena breathlessly announced that she had given a bouquet to Leonid Brezhnev, General Secretary of the Communist Party, who hugged her in return. It had not happened; she just wanted to please me.

The experience of Lena's school years did not make it any easier for me to accept a job with a monthly salary of ninety-five rubles—fifty-five less than the early 1970s' average. Our unpretentious food cost about a hundred rubles a month; rent, utilities, and transportation came to another thirty. We survived only because in addition to my salary I received sixty rubles a month in child support from Lena's father.

The more I learned about Soviet schools from the inside, the greater my disillusion and disappointment. The Soviet educational system aims less at imparting knowledge and developing creative intellectual skills than at ideological indoctrination. All history revolves around the sanitized, idealized saga of the Com-

munist Party; economics begins and ends with an ossified version
of Marxism that even Marx could not recognize; literature stresses
the class struggle; science instruction must conform to the "laws"
of dialectical materialism. Only mathematics remains pure.

Teaching English, I was obliged to use stories about Lenin
and lesser Communist heroes, but fortunately I could also assign
the works of Charles Dickens, Jack London, O. Henry, Theodore
Dreiser, Mark Twain, and a few other British and American writers. Foreign-language study enjoys little respect in the average
Soviet school. Special schools, where several subjects are taught in
foreign languages, involve only a tiny percentage of schoolchildren. When I began teaching, the school principal tried to use my
class hours and pupils for various housekeeping and extracurricu-
lar activities. Marching down the hall to my classroom, sturdy,
heavy-footed stride heralding her approach, Anna Markovna
opened the door unceremoniously and said in a commanding
voice, "All right, Irina Igorevna—Ivanov, Petrov, and Sidorov are
to come with me!"

Bewildered by her parade-ground manner, I stammered, "But
. . . what's happened? What's going on?"

"We have to move chairs from the auditorium to the gym."

Irritated, I managed with difficulty to restrain myself.

"Anna Markovna, when the lesson is finished, I'll send the
boys to you."

Disoriented by my resistance to her orders, she closed the door
and left.

The episode created a minor sensation; everyone discussed it
for a few days. Most of my fellow teachers were apprehensive.
Why was a newcomer so sensitive? *They* did not argue with orders.

Many of the parents in Moscow's proletarian Bauman District had only a primary school education themselves and displayed
little interest in the studies of their offspring. Uncommunicative
in teacher-parent conferences, more often than not they ignored
my invitations to come in for private talks. When children experi-

enced difficulties in school, we teachers could never depend on the parents for help.

One of my problem students, a personable boy named Mikhail, regarded his schoolwork with a contempt that hinted at some past trauma. On investigating I learned that some years earlier the system had tagged him a poor student; thereafter no one paid the boy much attention. Each teacher gave him a 3, or C, just to pass and be done with him, indifferent to the bleak future they were helping create.

Something about Mikhail told me he could do better. I singled him out, helping not only with English but also with other subjects; as tactfully as I knew how I counseled him. He began to respond. Sensing that at long last a teacher cared, Mikhail dug into his studies, for the first time in years actually did homework, and quickly improved his grades.

Yet every now and then he became terribly frustrated for no apparent reason; he would sulk at his desk and retreat into hostile silence. I decided to speak to his parents. For weeks there was no response, then late one afternoon the father appeared at the door of my classroom. A handsome, rough-looking working man in his thirties, dressed in dirty gray grease-stained workclothes, his stubby fingers grimy and nicotine-stained, he addressed me insolently as *tu* rather than *vous*.

"Well, you asked me to come. What's goin' on?" he asked in bored tones. "You're wastin' time with this damned English!"

"Let's use *'vous'* when we speak to each other, shall we, Ivan Petrovich?"

Being addressed formally and politely was evidently a new experience. He dropped his gaze in confusion and nodded assent.

"Then please sit down," I said.

A little sheepishly, he eased himself into one of the front-row desks. When I praised his son, Ivan Petrovich stared at me in confusion. Accustomed to negative reports when he bothered to listen at all, he seemed to think I had confused Mikhail with someone else. Listening intently to my encouraging words, gradually he relaxed. Then we turned to the family situation.

He admitted that he drank heavily and beat his son. As he spoke, I sensed that, worn out from hard work and the daily struggle to survive, Ivan Petrovich had no energy to think about anything else; alcohol and violence constituted his natural response to any obstacle. We talked for more than an hour and I tried to convince him to take an interest in his son's studies. He flashed a look of genuine gratitude at me as he left. I could almost hear him thinking, She's a strange one.

Mikhail continued to improve. When he shyly confessed one day that he could not decide whether to concentrate on English or mathematics, I knew I had gained his trust. He liked my class, but his favorite subject was mathematics; I sent him to the math teacher, my friend Ananii Moiseevich, who became his adviser. Eventually Mikhail entered one of the best engineering institutes.

Having no family of his own, Ananii—then about fifty—had devoted his life to teaching; the children adored him. We became friends, and through him I got to know Tamara, a young divorcée, also a math teacher, and Mark, a teacher of Soviet history and a thirtyish bachelor. The four of us tended to group together in faculty meetings and occasionally saw each other after school. Sharing an aversion to the drill-instructor behavior the system encourages, we rigorously avoided following the pedagogical example set by Anna Markovna. Barging into her Russian literature classroom, she invariably left the door open and boomed out for the whole school to hear, "All right, children, to your places! Good. Now, open your notebooks and *write!*"

She proceeded to dictate some text she had studied thirty years earlier. An official analysis had been established long ago; the children merely had to memorize it. No need to critique anything, no requirement to think, just copy. The possibility of a second opinion, an alternative explanation, was formally excluded. Needless to say, the children quickly lost all interest in Russian literature.

Sometimes the schoolchildren protested Party orders. More than a few incipient dissidents were loath to join the Komsomol, the Communist youth auxiliary which subordinates everyone and everything to one idea, the sham of total unanimity of people and state, the lie of Communist infallibility. In the spring of 1973, two boys stubbornly refused to join.

This was serious. Children join the Komsomol almost as automatically as they enroll in school. Unable to argue them into line, Anna Markovna summoned their parents and hurled threats: the Party organization at their workplaces would make things hot for people who did not raise their children properly. But the parents either could not or would not interfere, and the boys refused to give in.

"We're too young to enter the Komsomol," the two claimed innocently. "It's a serious step we need to think about carefully. We need more time to prepare ourselves to be worthy of the lofty calling of *Komsomoltsy.*"

Anna Markovna knew mockery of Communist cant when she heard it. She was infuriated. When she again threatened dire retribution, the boys asked, "Is joining the Komsomol voluntary or obligatory?"

Our principal was lost. How could she admit that the system forces children into the Komsomol regardless of their wishes?

I do not know how the story ended, but the boys almost certainly did not go on to higher education. Admission to the colleges and institutes is difficult under the best of circumstances, for "ideologically unreliable elements" virtually impossible.

Naturally I did not tell Woody about the Komsomol incident. Naive though I was, I knew better than to write anything remotely bearing on politics. But I did occasionally mention my frustration with teaching, and he tried to cheer me up: "Sometimes you have to wait a long time to see any results. I make notes on my own lectures and mark more than half of them as failures, but every now and then a student from a few years back will write and say something kind about my course—and I think, Well, maybe I can go on a bit longer. . . ."

To help pass the time in the summer of 1973 I decided to accompany a group of children from my school—including Lena, who had transferred—to work for a *kolhoz*, a collective farm. Schoolchildren fourteen and older are obliged work every summer; the state calls it "labor education," but in reality the Soviet Union's inefficient agriculture needs all the help it can get.

Teachers rarely go to the farms. Unaccustomed to physical labor, after nine months in the classroom they also tend to avoid children for as long as possible. But Lena had to go. A month in the fresh country air would do me good, and I was ready to do anything to make the wait for my lover easier. Two fellow teachers, one of whom taught German and the other physical education, also went along as counselors. The three of us had to supervise about thirty children.

The farm "sponsored" by our school was two hours by train from Moscow in a peaceful area of birch, fir, and oak woods. Clear, miraculously unpolluted creeks flowed lazily through grassy meadows full of ox-eyed daisies, wood anemones, horse sorrel mixed with red clover. Toadflax flashed burnt orange around the edge of every coppice, and inside the thickets a few raspberries still lingered on the briars.

In the village where the *kolhoz* peasants lived, almost all the modest, comfortable wooden cottages boasted flowerbeds of racemose, Anyuta's eyes, pansies, marigolds. Clay pots of bright red geraniums stood on windowsills painted white against the soft blues, greens, and apricots of the cottages themselves. In back gardens, carefully tended rows of cabbages, potatoes, carrots, and radishes promised full larders in July and August. Chickens cackled and pecked jerkily in the dirt street, penned-in piglets squealed behind a few of the cottages, and here and there tethered calves bawled for their mothers. Tucked away in a corner of each plot, dilapidated outhouses leaned at crazy angles at the end of well-beaten paths.

Assigned to weed 500-meter-long beet fields, the children hated the hard, dirty work in the hot sun; after half an hour everyone's back ached. I tried to set an example at the head of the line, though the heat soon made me strip down to my bathing suit. When I stood to wipe my face, I looked back and saw the children far behind, holding their hoes like Don Quixote's lance, pretending to do battle with the weeds. These were city kids who did not know the first thing about manual labor. For once I agreed with the authorities: the young ought to learn what hard work is.

We Muscovites marveled at the village vocabulary, which consisted chiefly of obscenities using the word "mother." The peasants addressed each other in curses, to which they merely added diminutives when speaking to children, and raised their animals to be fluent in the same language. Many afternoons we watched a young man trying to get the cows out of the creek where they had taken refuge from the heat:

"Burenka, davai," Burenka, let's go. "Come on, get up the bank . . . *Burenka, davai."*

Burenka would not budge. The cowherd urged her again in gentle terms, with the same lack of success. Then: *"Tvoyu mat!"* . . . Your mother!

It was her native language. Burenka obeyed.

The miserable village store seemed to stock little except vodka and fortified wine; nearly all the peasants drank heavily. I had never seen such general drunkenness before, never encountered up close the tragedy of these simple people. After work they spread cloths on the grass in front of their cottages and laid out bread, cucumbers, sausage if they had any, and vodka, vodka, vodka. Men, women, children gathered for the picnic. The gatherings began in quiet merriment, with lots of toasts and jokes, happy laughter and flirting. After an hour or so, however, some *muzhik,* some peasant man, would get drunk and start to pummel his woman. Few of the other villagers paid the slightest attention, scarcely looking up from their food and conversation. The peasant children went on playing.

We had brought a lot of canned food, flour, potatoes, and cabbage from Moscow, and needed to buy only bread, milk, eggs, and cheap cuts of meat on the rare occasions when they were available in the village. We teachers took turns cooking and quickly discovered it was easier to hoe beets than stand in the kitchen all day preparing food for so many people. I detest cooking under any circumstances and whenever one of my colleagues agreed to take my turn, I gladly escaped to the fields.

One day when kitchen duty could not be avoided, I asked Lena to help. We decided to spoil the group and cook bliny. Like workers on an assembly line, we divided up the mixing and pouring, put several big skillets on the stove, and set about frying, turning, piling up the thin pancakes. In the midst of the tedious work I made up my mind to tell Lena about Woody. It was simply too nerve-racking to go on concealing my love affair, especially since relations with Mama were so strained.

"Lena, there's something new in my life."

She looked at me quizzically.

"I've fallen in love."

Feminine curiosity shone in her eyes. She waited silently for me to continue.

"He's an American." I tossed the bombshell casually.

That she had not expected. Looking up at me with bulging eyes she exclaimed, "Aren't you something! Where did you meet him?"

I told her the whole story. The mountain of bliny grew rapidly but could not keep pace with her questions about Woody, his son, America, the future. Pride at being entrusted with her mother's secret colored her reaction positively, and I felt an enormous sense of relief. She paused for a few moments to reflect, then said, "*Now* I understand. Sometimes you sparkle, then you're sad for days on end, you run to this Anastasiya Nikolayevna . . . But what's going to happen?"

"I'm not sure. We want to be together."

Her face shining with the excited innocence of youth, she looked at me for a moment, broke into a huge smile, and said, "I'm for it!"

Lena was on my side.

7

Courtship Across the Oceans

TEACHING SCHOOL and being a mother to Lena consumed most of my emotional energy in the winter and spring of 1973. The rest I expended in the effort to divorce Yuri, who refused to cooperate. Exhausted by the end of the week, I often fled to Anastasiya Nikolayevna, with whom I could share memories of Woody. I spent many hours with her in Novye Cheryomushki, where Woody sent his letters and called me every two or three weeks. In the middle of February he announced that he was coming to Moscow for a week in March.

His calls and long, newsy letters full of love and plans and descriptions of life in Virginia kept my memories fresh and alive and sustained me through that long winter. He wrote of skiing and going to basketball games with his son, of a trip to a friend's pig farm in North Carolina, of trying to repair an ancient Studebaker, of his classes at the university. Like all lovers, we had a pathetically transparent romantic code. Had we realized that intelligence agencies on both sides were reading every line, we might have been more restrained.

Impatient with my difficulty in obtaining a divorce, Woody repeatedly urged me to move faster. At the end of January he wrote:

Of course it is . . . unfortunate that your husband doesn't cooperate . . . but you can and will get the divorce no matter what he does or doesn't do. And you have to try to understand him . . . he realizes what he has lost. . . . He wants to hang on at all costs, to try to persuade you to change your mind. I . . . can understand, at least to some extent, what he is going through, but I cannot agree with his tactics.

A week later, after we had talked on the telephone, he sent another letter:

How does your . . . divorce proceed? I gathered from what little you said . . . that it is going slowly. There is of course a grand total of *nothing* I can say or do here that would make any difference, except that I can tell you how much I love you and want you and will wait for you as long as it takes. I had always thought that divorce was easier in the USSR than here.

It *should* have been simple, not even necessary to go to court. The district ZAGS, or registry office, can grant the decree. After establishing that the couple has neither children nor property in common, a bored clerk merely asks a couple of questions:

"Have both of you thought this through? What is your reason for divorcing?"

The routine answer is, "We don't get along."

No one goes into details. The clerk is not a social worker, and the couple just want to be rid of each other. The decree is signed, a notation entered into each partner's internal passport—which every adult Soviet citizen must have—and the marriage is dissolved. The procedure hinges on mutual consent. When one partner contests the divorce, if children are involved, or when the parties cannot agree on the division of property, it is necessary to go to court.

Yuri favored the quick variant, but he was afraid to take the step so long as I was involved with an American. Guilt by association is a long-established principle of Soviet injustice—his career would almost certainly be compromised should his superiors learn of my affair. He hoped to wait it out until Woody disappeared from my life, then give me the divorce.

We had agreed to meet at the Bauman District ZAGS on February 23, but Yuri failed to appear. He remained, however, very much in my life, and refused to return his key to my apartment. Transformed into an aggressive, persistent stalker, he kept me under constant surveillance; I was never free of him. He now lived with his sister in another part of the city. Day and night he lurked in a corner of my courtyard, chain-smoking, standing watch.

In late March I discovered he was eavesdropping; every morning a mound of cigarette butts littered the hallway outside my door. He loitered there for hours, waiting for me to speak on the telephone. In a kommunalka, families share the telephone, which is usually in the corridor near the outside door. On March 8, International Women's Day, the man who was technically still my husband terrified me with a sick prank.

This widely celebrated holiday is the only day when Soviet women's femininity is officially recognized. Husbands and lovers bring home flowers and champagne, and at work the men chip in a ruble or so each to buy presents and throw a party. In 1973 I had no reason to celebrate. Continents and oceans separated me from Woody; I dreamed of his return to Moscow at the end of the month. The male teachers at my school gave their female colleagues a party the previous evening, and on the holiday itself I stayed at home alone with Lena. Unable to sleep, I was reading by the light of a small lamp, vaguely aware of an occasional trolleybus going by. Something amiss made me raise my eyes: Yuri's face loomed over me, distorted by the dim light and the alcohol he had obviously consumed—a face out of a horror film.

"Happy holiday," he cooed softly in a malicious, drunken voice.

Frozen with fear, I could not speak. Before I had recovered he disappeared, ghostlike, as quietly as he had entered.

There seemed no end to Yuri's vicious jokes. Woody's birthday was coming toward the end of March. One of my gifts was a handsome little book with color photos of the icons in Suzdal, an old Russian town, one of the centers of Russian Orthodoxy; I sent it through the regular international mail. Woody wrote that he had received the book and liked it. That ought to have been the end of the matter, but in mid-April Yuri called and asked what my lover thought of the special message inside the Suzdal book.

The next time we spoke on the telephone, I asked Woody to take a closer look at his present. He found two pages glued together and slit them apart. Yuri had added his greetings in English:

Fuck your own wife, not mine. And keep farther from Moscow. Woody, better stop in time unless you want your head broken and your career spoiled. Think of your kids. Happy birthday and best wishes. Be careful.

Having stood guard in the hall night after night for several months, finally he had heard me mention the book over the telephone. He had entered the apartment during the day, found it, and appended his poisonous note.

Woody had problems of a different kind. In the beginning it seemed, he and his wife would reach a reasonably amicable settlement, but financial disagreements clouded the picture. His letters reflected increasing dismay: "It appears I may lose everything, including my son. They'll leave me only my books and clothes. My wife's lawyer—a devout Catholic with an obscenely lucrative divorce practice—has made it clear he'll make me pay heavily for my freedom."

At such a distance we could not help each other, but his coming visit—which coincided with my spring break at school— would give us the chance to share our troubles. He breezed in on March 26 around 9:00 P.M. with whoops of delight and bear hugs and presents for everyone; his arrival brightened the apartment like an unexpected holiday. Anastasiya Nikolayevna cried "Welcome home!" and introduced him to her husband, Sergei Yakovlevich. Marina, the eight-year-old granddaughter, clung to him and jumped up and down with joy: "Uncle Vadim has come!" In the midst of all the happy confusion I put my arms around him and tried to calm my galloping heart . . . which only beat faster when Woody told us he had been selected to participate in the American-Soviet exchange of professors for the following academic year.

"Bog sam idyot vam na pomoshch!" Anastasiya Nikolayevna exclaimed. God Himself is helping you!

A couple of hours later Woody and I retired to "our" room, our little world.

Moscow in March is cold and damp, and that gave us yet another excuse not to leave the apartment except when we had to. We spent a great deal of time alone, storing up for the drought that lay ahead. Ravenous for each other after three months apart, in six days we would begin another long separation.

Late in the afternoon of his first full day in Moscow, we went to the Hotel Berlin in the center of the city, three minutes from KGB headquarters at the Lubyanka. Woody wanted to get some fresh clothes and rumple the bed for appearances' sake. I waited on the street. A dense, chilly fog shrouded the city. Weak street lights could not dispel the late afternoon gloom, and low-wattage lamps within were barely strong enough to outline old-fashioned sand-colored window shades in private dwellings and government offices. Woody said the setting reminded him of *The Third Man*, a movie I had not seen. After pacing the sidewalk opposite the hotel for a few moments, I strolled back and forth, looking into shop windows so as not to appear to be loitering near a hotel where foreigners stayed.

I could not have been gone more than ten minutes. When I came back, Woody was standing looking frantically in all directions. He stomped the sidewalk and uttered a curse. I quickened my pace.

"Vadim," I said softly as I came up to him, "what's the matter?"

He whirled around, stared in confusion for a second, then grabbed me into his arms. Even through our winter coats I could sense his wild heartbeat. After a few seconds he relaxed and murmured, "Darling . . . I thought I'd lost you again."

Our March 1973 week passed all too swiftly, full of love—but
how to describe that love? What made it so grand? Neither of us
sought to attract the other; attraction existed. We accepted each
other as we were the day we met, sensed a freedom to speak
honestly, without pretense or reservation. We again moved as one
being, as if our two bodies had no bones, no joints, no rough
edges, and thus merged and blended, became one . . .

Two days before Woody had to leave, we went to dinner in
the main restaurant of the Hotel Ukraina. Neither the cuisine nor
the atmosphere drew us there. With merely edible food, the huge,
cold, high-ceilinged room with its scattered potted palms was
about as gracious as an exhibition hall, or maybe an aircraft han-
gar. But the hotel was across the street from a Beriozka shop for
foreigners where Woody had bought some scarce goods for Lena
and me and for Anastasiya Nikolayevna's family, and he liked the
orchestra. To me it seemed just a routine hotel group that played
Western swing music of the thirties and forties, but Woody detected something different. When they began playing a song from
Rimsky-Korsakov's opera *Sadko,* he seemed to hold his breath and
relax his mouth in a mysterious smile.

I knew the haunting melody:

Western popular music of an earlier era knew this as "Song of India"; Benny Goodman's recording was very popular in the Soviet Union for decades. When the last notes faded away Woody grinned at me contentedly.

"*Molodtsy!*" Well done! he said quietly. "I liked that."

"Does the song mean something to you?"

"It does now."

"What?"

"Russian classical music, American swing orchestration, Soviet style . . . interesting blend." Looking deep into my eyes, he did not speak again for a long moment. Then he leaned across the small table, took my hands in his, and murmured softly, "Irko, marry me."

A thrill of ecstatic happiness shot through me—as through any woman when the man she loves asks her to spend all her days with him. I remained silent for a few moments, tried to preserve the feeling, gazed into his eyes.

We had not discussed marriage, except to comment on our failures. Early in our relationship we realized that we were part of that great band of romantic anarchists whose love is doomed as soon as society blesses it. Oddly, in our own countries we had followed nearly identical paths, plunging into early marriage out of deference to Victorian social conventions, then, when the first union soured, repeating the process for still less defensible reasons.

Now Woody had proposed a marriage that would be the third for both of us. He loved me, but there was another reason: unless we married, we could never be together outside the Soviet Union. Lev Sukhanov had made it clear that the state had its eyes on me;

the great privilege of foreign travel would never be mine.

These thoughts raced through my mind and then suddenly a cold wave drenched me: I did not *want* to get married again. The wave crested, broke, and was followed by a devastating second one: What if I were to lose this man? How often does one find what we had together?

"Vadim, I love you—but let's wait until you come back next winter. It's too early to decide anything."

"That means no?"

"It means I'll be waiting."

Woody left on Sunday, April 1. So far as we knew then, he would not return until late December.

Yuri seemed determined to interfere in my love affair. When he deceived me again in April and did not come to ZAGS to sign the divorce papers, I went after him. On a lusciously sunny May day I set out for his office. I gave his name to the guard and waited.

When he spotted me, Yuri turned pale. A crooked, nervous smile crossed his face. He instantly understood the seriousness of my visit. Composing himself, he came up and asked in a calm voice, "Why are you here? Is anything wrong?"

I looked at him grimly. Having rehearsed my speech a dozen times, I was prepared to argue for hours. But now the words would not come.

"Well, what's going on?" he demanded.

Finally I announced, "I'm going to your boss to tell him about our situation . . . and about myself. I have nothing to lose."

Yuri flinched, and his jaw went slack. *He* had something to lose—his job. After a moment of silence he said in resigned tones, "All right. I'll meet you at ZAGS next Thursday . . . to sign the papers."

At the end of May I finally got my freedom—and Yuri's key to my apartment. A strange marriage had come to an end.

With both the divorce and the school year behind me at last, I looked forward to the summer. Lena and I would again go to the collective farm, perhaps take a vacation in the south. Somehow I would survive my loneliness. Then Woody called early in June to say that his own divorce was final and that he had found an inexpensive tour out of London that would bring him to Leningrad and Moscow at the end of July.

Thank God! Our luck was holding.

Woody telephoned from London on July 28. The next day I flew to Leningrad; we were to meet that evening at ten in front of St. Isaac's Cathedral. A call to BOAC confirmed that his plane had landed on schedule at 7:30 P.M. I would be with him in a couple of hours.

With nothing else to do, I walked through the Baltic twilight along the Neva Embankment near the Winter Palace. Woody had sounded unusually excited on the telephone; he could not wait to explore his favorite Russian city with me, a thoroughgoing Muscovite with no special enthusiasm for the city named after Lenin. Poking along slowly, I tried to understand why he liked Leningrad so much.

People from more southerly latitudes often come under the spell of the summer light in the north. The sun, striking the earth at a different angle, seems to blur shadows and colors. I always think of Leningrad—600 kilometers (400 miles) north of Moscow—as slightly out of focus. It lacks the black-and-white Byzantine certainties, the oriental color and barely contained chaos of Moscow. Leningrad is smaller, more orderly.

I sat for a while on a park bench. At my back loomed St. Isaac's and the Bronze Horseman, Carlo Rastrelli's equestrian statue of Peter the Great. In front of me the swift mauve-black waters of the Neva raced to the Gulf of Finland and on to the Baltic Sea; and beyond the river the soft light greens, light blues, and pale ochres of the university and the Academy of Sciences glowed gently against the delicate salmon of the twilight sky. Against that haunting backdrop the broad, low buildings reflected a serene beauty, conspiring with the river and the Bronze Horseman to declare a harmony between man and nature. Perhaps the secret of Leningrad's magic lies in the fact that such cold but awe-inspiring beauty remains on a scale that is—like Peter on his horse—only slightly larger than life-size, almost attainable, manageable.

Woody had told me he cherished the northern summer's colors, and I tried to guess what it was in those mauves and dark grays, ochres and pale blues, that affected him so deeply. I studied the twilight pastels and thought of the man I loved, trying to penetrate his soul, to remember melodies from Aleksandr Glazunov and Jan Sibelius that he said sent those colors coursing through his brain. But though I let the notes flow through my mind, I could not fully share the magic. No matter; part of love must forever be grounded in mystery.

As I retraced my steps I tried too to recall something of the history of the city, another of its great attractions for Woody. He had called me his *"Dekabristka,"* December woman: here was the square named for the rebels of December 1825—the *"Dekabristi,"* men of December—gunned down there. Then the Admiralty, echoes of Peter the Great's navy; and Nevsky Prospekt, Leningrad's main avenue, stage of 1917's revolutionary demonstrations and violence.

South along the Neva stretched the architectural ensembles of eighteenth- and nineteenth-century Italian and Russian masters, including the Winter Palace, now the Hermitage. Trying to see them through Woody's eyes, I perceived their Western order and rationality; they offer the eye what Mozart bestows on the ear. Emphasizing the horizontal over the vertical, they complement each other perfectly, and their soft pastels constitute the most mathematically related formulas in the spectrum. Had they been painters, Glazunov and Sibelius would have used such a palette.

Leningrad is the city of Glinka and Pushkin, of Dostoevsky, Akhmatova, Shostakovich. And now it would briefly be ours.

Nearly two hours went by. I became uneasy and a little chilled in my light summer dress and sandals. Looking at my watch every couple of minutes, I paced nervously in front of St. Isaac's. Then all at once someone came running toward me—Woody, sun-tanned, healthy, smiling broadly. Taking me in his arms and lifting me off my feet, he swung me from side to side, holding me close. Three times in seven months this man had flown across the ocean to be with me.

We wandered through the city to the Fontanka, the fashionable canal-street where friends of friends had put an apartment at our disposal for three days. We found ourselves in a sort of nineteenth-century Bohemian dwelling with labyrinthine corridors, oddly shaped rooms, a grand piano, paintings and bookshelves everywhere, ancient chandeliers, and antique furniture.

Champagne, kisses, excited talk about everything. We interrupted one another fluidly, finished each other's sentences, understood whole paragraphs of thought after just a word or two. Clothes came off in one swift gesture like tear-away garments in a movie farce . . . wild embraces followed . . .

We had just drifted off to sleep when a pounding at the door startled us awake. Dear God! Had my husband—it took a millisecond to correct the thought, ex-husband—again tracked us down?

"Open the door!"

"Go away! You've got the wrong apartment!"

I stood next to the door, trying to collect my thoughts. The pounding resumed.

"This is *my* apartment! If you don't open I'll call the police."

Pulling on his clothes, Woody tossed me a skirt and blouse, saying, "Ask him why he doesn't use his key!"

The man ignored my question and continued to demand entrance. It was only a matter of time before the neighbors summoned the police; we would not be able to explain our presence. I opened the door.

A young man in his mid-twenties stalked in angrily, pulled out his wallet, displayed his internal passport. The apartment belonged to him.

We left immediately; I never learned what had gone wrong. At the time I assumed that the people who had made the arrange-

ments for me had done so without the knowledge of the legitimate occupant of the apartment, who simply returned unexpectedly. I did not know anyone in Leningrad, at least not well enough
to ask such a favor, so I had relied on friends in Moscow who did
have good contacts. Later, when the KGB's implacable opposition to our relationship became obvious, I considered the possibility of its intervention that summer night. It would have been in
keeping with its methods.

We walked to the Embankment and collapsed on a bench,
Woody's burgundy plastic BLOOMINGDALE's bag full of presents
beside us. Leaning against each other, we finally dozed off, only to
be rousted by a policeman.

"You can't sleep here. Show me your papers!"

The stern commands did not accord with the kind face.
Clumsily trying to hide the bags, I produced my documents,
handed them over, and pretended to search the inert Woody's
pockets.

"We're from Moscow," I mumbled sleepily, " . . . big party
with friends. I'm afraid he passed out." I nodded at Woody, who
had not opened his eyes.

The officer leafed through my identification carefully before
returning it.

"All right," he said, grinning indulgently, "get him on his feet
and walk him around. He'll be okay."

He saluted and continued on his rounds. Alas, if there is anything everyone in our country understands, it is a man who has
had too much to drink.

The day dawned early, and we walked along the river dead
tired, yet thankful we had come safely through the night. But
daytime held danger; we could not be seen together in Leningrad.
There was no choice but to separate. Woody returned to his
hotel, I flew home to Moscow.

Three days later Woody appeared at Anastasiya Nikolayevna's
apartment; his tour was to be in Moscow three days before continuing on to the Crimea. I could have arranged to stay with

friends in Yalta, but the experience in Leningrad discouraged me. Woody told Intourist he would be back in the Soviet Union in December to do research for six months and would like to get an early start by staying in Moscow rather than going to the south. To our astonished delight, they granted his request. It never occurred to us that Lev Sukhanov and his associates at the KGB might have orchestrated everything, or that anyone outside our circle of friends could have the slightest interest in us.

Woody did spend six of the next ten days in the Lenin Library, but the nights and weekends were ours. We traveled by bus into the countryside for picnics and took long walks in the forest on the weekends, found an isolated spot on the Oka River south of Moscow where we swam and sunbathed nude, spent one night in a forest hut. Back in Moscow, in the evenings over dinner, Anastasiya Nikolayevna and Sergei Yakovlevich listened to our plans and dreams, shared our happiness. For them and other friends in the Soviet Union, what was happening to Woody and me symbolized their hopes for what our government called the "relaxation of tensions," Washington—"détente."

Soviet people play no role in politics. The Communist Party has a monopoly. But people do want peace and need to *believe* in the possibility of peace. So in 1972 and 1973 Soviet-American relations did encompass a little more than Nixon and Kissinger in Moscow, Brezhnev and Gromyko in Washington: two ordinary people, one Soviet, the other American, fell in love.

Nothing spoiled those happy August days. Though sad, of course, when the time came to part, we had a great deal to look forward to. In December we would be together again, this time for six whole months, or eight, if Woody were allowed to stay through the summer doing research. There was time to plan . . .

8

Marriage

IT WAS almost midnight, December 31, 1973: a
new year poised to enter our lives. Because they consider the New
Year the most important holiday, Russians approach it with great
hope, an almost superstitious faith that it will bring happiness and
a better life.

We were gathered around a holiday table headed by Sergei
Yakovlevich Khovansky, resplendent in his best gray suit; a new
blue shirt accentuated his bright, lively gray-green eyes. He made
some appropriately solemn remarks about the importance of the
occasion, then sat in silent, patient dignity during the final moments of the old year, composing the first toast of the new. At the
other end of the table, his wife Anastasiya Nikolayevna, dyed-
blond curls awry, passed around a new plate of *zakuski* even
though the table was already totally covered with food. Also
around the table were Woody and I, my fourteen-year-old Lena,
eight-year-old Marina, Galya, and her husband Valentin—all of
us dressed in holiday finery.

From the enormous New Year's tree that brushed the ceiling
hung old-fashioned wax candles, ornaments, toys, candy, colored
tinsel streamers. Underneath was a huge mound of name-tagged
presents: big boxes, little ones, packages, bundles, all wrapped in
gaily decorated holiday paper. The table, draped in a Ukrainian
holiday tablecloth, had been moved to the center of the room,
extra leaves added to accommodate all of us and the great feast.
Anastasiya Nikolayevna had cooked almost all night. Sergei
Yakovlevich, alone able to withstand the fumes, had heroically
grated a huge amount of fresh horseradish for the *holodets*—the

jellied beef, boiled eggs, onions, and carrots in aspic that was the centerpiece of the meal.

Midnight: on the television screen, Red Square. The fantasy-world onion domes of St. Basil's Cathedral glow as the Kremlin chimes strike the hour. The droning, monotonous voice of Leonid Ilich Brezhnev greets the Soviet people, promises them an extraordinary life. At our table, Sergei Yakovlevich raises his glass in honor of the New Year, wishing all of us happiness, looking intently at Woody and me as though willing us safely into the future together.

Lena had taken an instant liking to Woody. She chatted with him constantly and gave Marina to understand he was *her* Vadim—even though she had just met him and Marina had known about him for months. Surrounded by my loved ones, happiness engulfed me; but deep inside a worm of doubt gnawed.

With Marina, Anastasiya Nikolayevna, Sergei Yakovlevich, and Filka the cat, December 1973, shortly after Woody's arrival.

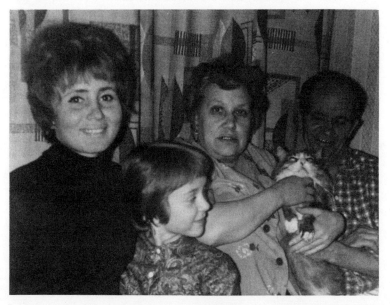

Woody had arrived two days earlier sporting a handsome full beard. He was as happy as ever to see us, but something was on his mind, and it created an invisible barrier. Anastasiya Nikolayevna felt it too; she wanted to speak to him, search out the trouble. I forbade her.

"Let's put it off until after New Year's," I said. "We'll celebrate the holiday and then you can have a talk with him."

I tried to guess his secret. Such withdrawal seemed unlike Woody; I was accustomed to complete frankness in our relationship. Over brunch on New Year's Day, Anastasiya Nikolayevna launched right in.

"Well, here we are, Vadim—the New Year! Tomorrow you'll need to start things moving, collect documents, go to the registry office and fix a date. Everything's got to be legal so Irina won't have any trouble."

His answer shocked us.

"I think we ought to live together for a while . . . get to know each other better . . . *then* talk about the future."

Anastasiya Nikolayevna's eyes bulged in astonishment. She knew Woody had proposed nine months earlier. A shudder raced through me. In principle Woody was right; we hardly needed to rush into marriage. But he had forgotten something. Live together? Get to know each other? That would never work here; the Soviet government would not tolerate it. Had Woody forgotten he was a foreigner in an unfree country? I had already lost a job; who knew what else lay ahead? And where would we live? In my kommunalka? Impossible—the neighbors would inform the police. In his hotel? Forbidden. With Anastasiya Nikolayevna and Sergei Yakovlevich? How long could we impose on them?

"Vadim," Sergei Yakovlevich said at length, "I don't blame you for being cautious. But it may be a luxury you can't afford."

"Surely a few weeks won't make any difference?" Woody seemed unsure of himself.

"Normally it wouldn't, and I'd be in favor of waiting," Sergei Yakovlevich said. "But you never know what kind of a mood the authorities are going to be in."

"You'd be wise not to put it off too long," Anastasiya Niko-layevna added. "Brezhnev and Nixon aren't cozy now like last spring."

Torn by conflicting emotions, I had not spoken. My fear of marriage was at least as great as Woody's.

"Vadim," I said finally, with more conviction than I felt, "so far we've decided everything together. No sense changing that now. We'll think it over for as long as necessary."

An uneasy sense of something new and ominous in our rela-tionship crept over me. Having looked forward with such antici-pation to Woody's long stay in Moscow, I wondered whether my dreams of happiness would founder.

On January 2, the first working day of the new year, Woody headed off to the library. I went with him on the metro to do some errands in the city center. When we returned to our gentle hosts that evening, their faces were frozen with tension. Pale and dis-traught, Anastasiya Nikolayevna bustled about the apartment. Sergei Yakovlevich stared fixedly at the television set.

"What's the matter?" I pleaded, hurriedly shedding my coat and boots. "Out with it—what's going on with you two?"

It was simple, straightforward, very Soviet: Sergei Yakovlevich had been summoned to the Lubyanka, KGB headquarters.

"They've ordered me to kick Vadim out. He's supposed to stay in his hotel." Sergei Yakovlevich sighed deeply and closed his eyes. Then, turning suddenly to his wife, he barked, "Nasya! Give us vodka!"

Anastasiya Nikolayevna had spent the afternoon nursing an attack of anxiety-induced diarrhea. Motioning to her to keep her seat, I retrieved the bottle from the windowsill and filled water-glasses half-full for Sergei Yakovlevich and Woody. Anastasiya Nikolayevna likewise resorted to the peasant remedy.

"Come on," she urged, "pour some for yourself and me."

After downing his vodka *à la russe* at a gulp, Sergei Yakov-levich told us what had happened.

"They were quite polite about it," he said evenly, "and quite firm. They want you out—quickly."

Chewing on a piece of black bread spread with hot Chinese mustard, a vodka-chasing habit learned during his exchange-student days at Moscow University in the early sixties, Woody asked, "Any special reason?"

"You're a foreigner, you speak Russian, and that's enough."

Then, as an afterthought, Sergei Yakovlevich added, "What about your country? Don't *you* watch foreigners?"

"Oh yes," Woody replied. "I'm sure we do. But I hope the FBI doesn't interfere in their private lives so long as they don't break the law."

"There are laws and there are laws," Sergei Yakovlevich mused, refilling the glasses.

"And in the Army they say," Woody responded, " 'There's no reason—it's just our policy.' "

Sergei Yakovlevich grinned.

"So your Army's the same as ours . . . Let's drink to both of 'em!"

I poured more vodka, the men clinked their glasses and, nodding politely in our direction, tossed it back. That is the way things are done in Russia: A monster lurks outside the door and threatens us. We will have to face it—tomorrow. For now let's have some vodka.

Woody and I had quickly become fond of Sergei Yakovlevich. Born in the Don River region in 1905, he had witnessed revolution and civil war as a young boy. A son of the working class, he had been allowed to attend college and had spent his life serving the Soviet state as an investigating magistrate. It was his job to assemble physical evidence for the prosecutor's office in criminal cases. He specialized in matters involving malfeasance in office.

His appearance reinforced his deceptively simple manner. Short and thin, he habitually wore a dark, rumpled suit, faded white shirt buttoned to the top, and no tie. In his too-large black 1930s fedora and dark overcoat that almost brushed the ground, he would shuffle around Moscow for hours looking for things his family needed. And more often than not, he found them. He

Anastasiya Nikolayevna and Sergei Yakovlevich in the 1960s. She wrote on the back: "These were our best years."

chain-smoked *papirosy*, cigarettes with long hollow "filters" and cheap, foul-smelling *mahorka*, shag tobacco, cocking the thing between his lips at a jaunty angle, like Popeye's pipe. All his teeth were capped in stainless steel. Because his skin was easily irritated, he usually had a two- or three-day growth of whiskers. When Woody began bringing him supplies of American razor blades, his gratitude knew no bounds.

Sergei Yakovlevich equaled his wife as a storyteller; Woody insisted he learned more Soviet history from him than from a dozen professors and a thousand books. The two men developed a warm, intense friendship right from their first meeting, when Woody asked whether Sergei Yakovlevich claimed descent from the Khovansky who is the hero of Mussorgsky's opera *Khovanshchina* and a captain of the guard at Peter the Great's half sister's palace. They went on to talk Russian history, music, and the origins of the composer's name (it means "Rubbish") until nearly five in the morning.

Woody with Anastasiya Nikolayevna and Sergei Yakovlevich, New Year's Eve, 1973.

"Well," Woody said after a while, "I'm sorry I've caused you this trouble. I wish . . . "

"Forget it!" Sergei Yakovlevich interrupted. "Not your fault. I don't want to visit the Lubyanka every day, but so far nothing terrible has happened."

The next morning Sergei Yakovlevich departed for Mahach-Kala. He would be gone at least two months investigating some local scandal. We also left the flat, Woody bound for his hotel and I for my apartment. Anastasiya Nikolayevna had tears in her eyes as she softly kissed us both, saying, "Don't be upset—everything's going to be all right." She made me promise to call.

Late in the afternoon of the following day, dazed from insomnia, we met in front of the old Moscow University complex near Red Square. Together, but with nowhere to be alone, we roamed through the cold, dreary streets and finally stopped at a sleazy, dimly lit restaurant. Gray-green wallpaper hung peeling off three walls and a "socialist-realist" painting of a blast furnace decorated the fourth. Shabby, sullen people sat hunched over greasy table-cloths looking like candidates for a night's shelter at state expense. A long time passed before an insolent waiter brought soggy meatballs and some cold, grayish macaroni.

When the restaurant closed at ten-thirty we were forced into the street. What were we to do? Woody flatly refused to leave me, insisting there had to be some way to be together.

Rather than go to his hotel, I decided to risk my apartment. We took the metro to the Lenin Library station and walked slowly the rest of the way across Red Square, up Bogdan Khmelnitsky and Chernyshevsky streets, making sure the neighbors had plenty of time to get to sleep. It was after midnight when we crept up to the door. We removed our boots in the stairway and tiptoed past the Voronovs' room. (Lena was staying temporarily with my mother.) I left my own boots and coat in the hall, took Woody's things into my room, and got a jar from the cupboard; we could not risk his going across the hall to the toilet.

We spent a second sleepless night.

In the morning the evidently unsuspecting neighbors left

early as usual. Woody and I dressed quickly, had some coffee, and fled to Anastasiya Nikolayevna, confident she would point us in the right direction.

"You've got to sublet an apartment," she said. "It will be expensive, but it's your only hope."

"Is that legal?" Woody asked.

Anastasiya Nikolayevna snickered indignantly.

"Legal! *Everything's* legal—so long as you get away with it. You can sleep here until you find something."

Woody and I stared at her in astonishment.

"But aren't you afraid . . . " Woody started to ask.

"I'm afraid of *nothing!* What can the KGB do to an old woman on pension?"

I immediately got on the telephone. Olga sympathized but knew no one with a flat to let. Galya promised to call back after checking around. My cousin Vitalik, an up-and-coming film director, responded evasively; he wanted to help but did not know of anything "at this time." But it was at this time I needed help.

Around noon Galya called—no luck. She would keep trying but was not optimistic. Over lunch, we racked our brains. Eight million people lived in Moscow; why was it so hard for Woody and me to find a corner for ourselves? I made several more unsuccessful calls and then, late in the afternoon, tried a young woman acquaintance from IMEMO who—as Milochka told me when I called her—had recently married a French businessman and planned to live in Paris.

Still in Moscow at her new husband's apartment, still the legal owner of her own flat in a cooperative building, she agreed to sublet it. The flat was ten minutes by trolleybus from Anastasiya Nikolayevna. The rent would be fifty rubles a month; Anastasiya Nikolayevna and Sergei Yakovlevich paid fourteen for their three-room place.

It took a couple of days to make the apartment livable. Unfurnished except for a table, four rickety chairs, and a medium-sized wardrobe, it consisted of one small room, with a tiny galley-like kitchen, toilet, and bath, but to Woody and me it seemed romantically cozy. We bought two mattresses and put them on the floor

Japanese-style. I fetched bedding, curtains, and a few kitchen things from my apartment. Woody moved in with his typewriter, books which he put in the kitchen cupboard, and most of his clothes. He left a few shirts and socks in his hotel room. It would not do to defy convention too blatantly.

Lena moved in with Anastasiya Nikolayevna and Marina. Now nearly nine and in a special school for musically gifted children, Marina was no less delighted than Lena to have a "sister." She had lived with Anastasiya Nikolayevna and Sergei Yakovlevich since her parents' divorce. The two young girls would be company for each other.

Love is blind, at least to physical discomfort; although our "home" had only the basics, Woody and I quickly settled in. Mornings we met Lena at the Novye Cheryomushki metro station and rode together into the city center. Woody got off at the Frunze station for the archives; Lena and I continued on to our school. In the late afternoon Woody met me at the Intourist Hotel on Gorky Street. Over a cup of espresso and sometimes a late lunch we read whatever foreign newspapers were available. At the time, non-Communist publications from abroad were never openly displayed in the kiosks; foreigners who wanted them— vendors had orders not to sell them to Soviet citizens—had to ask. Woody's daily routine was shattered if he did not get newspapers. To assure his supply, he bribed the woman at the hotel newsstand with a carton of American cigarettes now and then. In return she always kept the *International Herald Tribune* or *The Times* or *Le Monde* for him.

Afterwards our itinerary often led to the second-hand bookstores, of which there were many in the center of Moscow. A true collector, Woody regularly discovered tattered and yellowing classics, often in dusty heaps tied up in string. Concentrating on pre-revolutionary books on Russian history, he explored the crowded shelves and when he found a bargain—at that time you could often purchase antiquarian books for next to nothing—he was as excited as a child.

"Look at this!" he would exclaim, calling me over, "An original edition of Tatishchev. Five volumes—only twenty rubles!"

I knew nothing about the work but it was obviously a treasure and a steal at the price (less than twenty-five dollars). Once, at the Novye Cheryomushki peasant market, Woody spied a peasant vendor wrapping carrots in a page torn from an ancient, beautifully illustrated, calf-bound history of the Mongol rule in Russia. The astonished woman was only too happy to sell him what remained of the mutilated book for a ruble.

Two or three times a week Lena, Woody, and I gathered at Anastasiya Nikolayevna's for dinner. On the other days we cooked in our own tiny kitchen, of necessity keeping the menu simple. I prepared borscht, *pirozhki* or meat pies, potatoes fried with onions. When Woody wanted to cook, which to my delight was often, he made spaghetti or hamburgers—at my suggestion, half beef and half pork—or something I never learned to like, chili. Because they were in such short supply we rarely had fresh fruit or vegetables in the winter. When we could find it, we drank Czechoslovakian or East German beer with the evening meal, Georgian or Moldavian wine on special occasions.

We shared impressions of the day, joked, laughed, constantly embraced, often dropped everything and jumped into bed. With each passing day we built a relationship such as we had both dreamed of. We never quarreled, not once.

Over dinner three weeks after we began living together, Woody looked at me and said, "Let's collect the documents."

Our happiness did not require a marriage certificate. But without one, we had no future together. Marriage was not my goal, nor was living in the West; being with Woody was. I was relieved when he decided to take responsibility for me.

We drew up a list: birth certificate, divorce papers, release from work, medical documents, college degree, Lena's papers, document from the tenants' committee of my apartment building——and permission from my mother, which we decided to leave until last. We stood for hours in queues, and when photocopies were required Woody went to the American Embassy to make them. The very few copiers available to the Soviet public demanded endless waiting in line.

Friends began to visit us. At first they were cautious, but gradually we were accepted as a couple. One impromptu party stands out.

February 23 is Soviet Army Day, the unofficial but widely celebrated male equivalent of International Women's Day. On this day all Soviet males, even those with no connection to the Army, are permitted to consider themselves heroes. A few days before the holiday, my school colleague Ananii, a decorated World War II veteran for whom February 23 had special significance, invited me to celebrate it with him, our historian colleague Mark, Tamara the mathematics teacher, and her husband. Ananii chose the Belgrade Restaurant on the Garden Ring across from the Ministry of Foreign Affairs.

Woody had been in Moscow nearly two months. I wanted to introduce him to my colleagues, but no suitable occasion had arisen, nor could I predict their reaction. Now Ananii had provided an opening.

"Do you mind if I don't come alone, if I bring someone . . . a man?"

Ananii smiled slyly.

"Of course—it's even necessary!"

Watching his expression closely, I took a deep breath and warned, "He's an American."

There was a brief pause while Ananii sorted this out. Then, grinning, he replied, "Aren't *you* something! All right, come along with your American."

Arriving at the restaurant around 7:00 P.M., I spied the group from a distance. As I introduced Woody I gazed intently at my colleagues' faces. To my relief I saw only curiosity and interest, no discernible fear.

Ananii had neglected to make reservations, and for once the "Full" sign which is always posted at the doors of popular Moscow restaurants meant exactly what it said. We were all dressed up with nowhere to go. It was not only a holiday but a Saturday evening as well, and there was no hope of finding a table at a good restaurant. I winked at Woody, who instantly understood.

"Let's go to our place," he said. "We've got a couple of bottles . . . something for *zakuski.*"

Half an hour later we crowded into our small room. The men pushed the mattresses into a corner, put the table and chairs in the center of the room, and went about the ritual appreciating of our hard-to-find Stolichnaya.

The toasts began: to the Soviet Army, to the United States Army, in which Woody had served more than four years, to those who had died in World War II, to those who had returned safely from the front—that is, to Ananii and his comrades—and finally to men in general. We relaxed. After a while Ananii offered an unexpected toast:

"To our Irina Igorevna and Vadim—secret in the open!"

By that time the conversation was flowing freely. Ananii told us he was a Polish Jew; I had not known that. Many of his relatives had emigrated to the United States after World War I, but his Communist father had gone east to the Soviet Union. Mark peppered Woody with questions about teaching in America. Not a Party member, Mark taught Soviet history despite an unwritten rule that the subject be entrusted only to Communists. Apparently the authorities made an exception because of his outstanding record at the Pedagogical Institute and because they lacked qualified teachers. A few years later he would lose his job. Not only was Mark not a Communist; he was also Jewish.

Tamara's husband spotted the guitar someone had given me during my student years and began playing and singing the songs of Bulat Okudzhava. The rest of us joined in, a ragged but enthusiastic chorus. Later, at Woody's request, the guitarist struck up a famous song from the Russian Civil War, The Horse Cavalry March:

March tempo

Woody belted out the words in his Vologda accent, delighting everyone. Here was an American who knew the words to an old Soviet song; his inability to carry a tune did not matter. Russian sentimentalism seized them all—Woody had won them over. As the party came to an end, Ananii cautioned him, "Vadim, she's got a proud character. It's the Mongol blood."

"Ananii, what do you know of my character?" I objected, laughing.

"Not much . . . you're unapproachable. That's why all this"— he nodded at Woody—"came as such a surprise."

After the guests had left, Woody kissed me and praised my friends. Again everything seemed joyously normal, *right*. No frontiers, no ideologies—just a party with friends.

We had widened our social circle. Now we had to deal with my mother, who knew that Woody was in Moscow. Never having met an American or indeed *any* foreigner, she was both curious and apprehensive. Early in March we invited her to dinner.

I met her at the trolleybus stop near our apartment. She made no effort to conceal her unease. Squeezing my hand, she whispered, "Irochka, I'm nervous."

My own uneasiness, distinctly not ideological, was that of a daughter introducing her future husband to her mother. Trying to calm her, I said soothingly, "Mama, don't worry. He's such a great guy, you'll like him. There's nothing to worry about!"

Woody greeted us at the door in jeans and a sweater and welcomed my mother respectfully, without stumbling over the nine syllables of the polite form of her name.

"Hello, Elizaveta Ivanovna! Please come in . . . I'm delighted to meet you."

Mother was specially coiffed, wearing her best, perfectly ironed white blouse and a severe navy blue wool skirt. She had prepared herself as though to meet Nixon himself. Jittery as a schoolgirl, she smiled shyly at Woody and returned the greeting. We sat down at a table already spread with food and drink.

"Well, let's drink to your meeting each other," I proposed. Certain that Woody had made a favorable impression, I no longer felt so nervous.

"A little vodka, Elizaveta Ivanovna?" Woody enquired politely.

"Oh no, what are you saying! That's not for me," Mama demurred coquettishly.

"Mama, come on now—have a little."

She allowed Woody to pour a small glassful. She downed it, honoring my toast, and made a face—"Ugh! The strong stuff!"—but did not object to a second glass.

Woody heaped her plate with salad and fish, saying, "Have a bite, Elizaveta Ivanovna—it'll settle the vodka."

The alcohol soon melted the tension and the smiles became more relaxed. Mother watched Woody closely, trying not to be too obvious. Periodically, a bewildered look crossed her face. I could tell she was thinking, Well, it seems he's an American all right. But such a simple, normal man!

We switched to Cinzano, and Mama said to Woody, "All right, tell me, what's this you've got your mind set on? You want to take my Irochka away to your America?"

Woody outlined our plans. We would go to the United States, then come back the following summer to see her and Lena.

Woody would bring Charlie along; my mother would have a new grandson. We would have to leave at the end of August, taking Lena with us, but would return as often as finances permitted.

Mama questioned Woody at length about his son, his job, schools and housing in America, then asked about my future: What kind of job could I get? Where would we live? All sorts of practical questions which Woody patiently answered. They talked while I put the main course on the table. My mother ate with real appetite. The questions continued until finally she arrived at the main ones, advancing them confidently like the well-informed person she considered herself to be.

"Are you sure they won't kill my daughter over there? So much crime! Maybe you'll lose your job one day? All that unemployment . . . "

Woody smiled indulgently.

"Elizaveta Ivanovna, sometimes your press gets it wrong. The United States isn't like that. Leave everything to me."

At last she seemed convinced. Over dessert, my mother declared that our marriage would have her blessing. We had passed the test.

A few days later she went with us to the registry office and signed the papers. Our wedding was scheduled for April 2, four weeks hence.

During this period Valeri Tishkov flitted in and out of our lives, appearing unexpectedly at our door as though trying to catch us unaware. His unwelcome visits recalled former troubles, and the tension he brought with him lingered long after his departure. When I insisted that he not be allowed to enter our apartment, Woody replied that he shared my suspicion but not my fear.

"Let him come," he said. "Better to know the *stukach*," the informer. "That gives us at least a little control over him."

Unsure of having any control over a KGB informer, if that was indeed Tishkov's role, I had no doubt that his presence in our lives boded ill. Except for the dissidents, who have little to lose, Soviet people rarely dare to associate with foreigners. Yet Tishkov aggressively sought out Woody. Periodic campaigns in the press warn that only traitors fraternize with "spies." Every now and then the KGB demonstratively kicks a foreigner out of the country and imprisons his or her Soviet acquaintances.

Not only was Valeri Tishkov not a dissident; he was a member of the Communist Party and subject to its discipline. If he hung around Woody and me, it was not because he found our love story touching.

Another man caused us still greater anxiety. Claiming to be a "research associate," he would occasionally invite Woody to discuss research problems over lunch. In the beginning this seemed natural enough; all foreign researchers are assigned someone whose job it is to assist them with their work. But this man wished to discuss a lot more, notably politics, and soon he turned the conversation to West Point, where Woody—while on active duty in the Army—had taught in the early 1960s. And then the man, whose name I never learned, asked about William Odom, the assistant military attaché at the American Embassy and Woody's successor at West Point.

The questions, and the man's wheedling, ingratiating manner, left no doubt as to his mission. Refusing to take Woody for an ordinary professor of history, the KGB apparently suspected him of working for American intelligence.

Woody always came home exhausted after meeting this man. He discussed the matter with Bill Odom; they decided that the best solution was to ignore it. If they did *not* see each other, the KGB would wonder how they were meeting without its knowledge.

The KGB did not ignore us. Over lunch one day, Comrade No-name attempted to convince Woody not to marry me. At first he acted friendly.

"Why get married again? You've had two failures. What's the hurry now?"

When Woody insisted that he knew what he was doing, that he loved me deeply, his companion attacked.

"You know who you're planning to marry? A whore."

Stunned, Woody mumbled something, trying to collect his thoughts. Then he said savagely, "This conversation is ended. Leave my private life to me."

With that, they parted. Woody came home in a foul mood that evening, and though it was cold and rainy insisted we go for a walk. On the street where we could not be overheard, he described the episode.

The man's words did not bother me. They merely recalled Sukhanov's formula: Any man we don't like is a spy, any woman a whore. But I was upset by what I believed to be Woody's equivocal reaction. Had the KGB managed to plant a seed of doubt? For some time we walked along without speaking while I tried to calm myself, then I explained how I felt.

"I'm not going to salve your ego or defend my reputation. You let this man insult me . . . "

"But I *didn't!* What do you want me to do—beat up a KGB agent and get expelled from the country? Would that make you happy? The point is not what he said but that they're playing a rougher game than I anticipated."

"You could have been more vigorous . . . "

"Now what does *that* mean? You know we're in an awkward situation—one false step and we'll never see each other again."

Still not satisfied, still half-convinced that Woody had let the accusation get to him, I asked: "Why do you doubt me?"

"I *don't.* There was nothing I could do but break off the conversation and hope the bastard leaves me alone."

"Do you think *I* found it pleasant when they told me you're a spy?"

We walked home in silence, deeply agitated; never before had harsh words passed between us. Late at night Woody embraced me and said, "Come on. We mustn't let them spoil our happiness."

After this Woody managed to avoid the man for a few weeks, but then he turned up again at the archives all smiles, full of apologies for the "misunderstanding," and insisted on taking Woody to lunch. Despite the tension, Woody and I allowed our-

selves to hope that, as soon as we were married, Comrade No-
name (against my will, Woody referred to him that way to protect
me) and the KGB in general would leave us alone.

Three days before our scheduled wedding on April 2, Woody
came home with his overcoat soiled by a bird. At the sight of the
stain I gasped; it is a widespread Russian superstition—one of
many involving birds—that such a thing foretells bad luck.
Woody laughed at my fears and promised that no Communist
sparrow could ruin our day. As if to reinforce his words he took
me that evening to the excellent Yakor Restaurant, known for
its fish.

Returning home relaxed and happy, we found a strange, hast-
ily scrawled note from my mother tacked to our door: "Come at
once. We have to talk."

My mother never went anywhere alone. She knew only the
way to and from work and from her apartment to the nearby food
stores. But she had made her way late in the evening to our apartment on the far western side of Moscow. Mystified, we hailed a
taxi.

Parked as usual in front of the television with *Pravda* on his
lap, my stepfather was surprised when I barged in around 11:30
P.M. In the past few months he had seen me only rarely and knew
nothing of Woody's existence. My mother had told him that I
was to be assigned to the Soviet Embassy in Washington to teach
English to the children of diplomats. She embellished the story,
adding that only the most deserving teachers were so honored.
Woody waited outside in the darkness while she cooked up some
excuse to go for a walk.

On the street, Mama began to sob hysterically. It took us
some time to calm her; then she confessed to having gone to
ZAGS to withdraw her permission for our marriage.

"I got scared," she protested. "What will become of Irochka?"

"Elizaveta Ivanovna," Woody scolded, "why didn't you talk
to *us?*"

The question only brought forth a new flood of tears. Disgusted, I looked on silently, certain the KGB had made my mother go to the registry office. Even in retirement, she would never be free. But what in the name of God did they want from Woody and me—two people who asked for nothing but each other?

Patiently, Woody calmed my mother down. He assured her she had nothing to fear and to our surprise extracted her promise to return to ZAGS the next day and withdraw her objection. When she gave in I realized that, for its own reasons, the KGB had authorized her in advance to reverse her position again if Woody and I insisted on getting married.

Neither then nor later did Mama discuss this episode with me. Always subject to KGB discipline, she obeyed orders.

Only civil marriage is recognized in the Soviet Union; religious ceremonies do not have the force of law. For that reason, the Griboyedov Street Wedding Palace, the only registry office in Moscow where foreigners are permitted to marry, is under direct KGB control. As befits an agency of the richest service in the country, it occupies an expensively restored turn-of-the century townhouse.

The director, a tall, dignified, well-dressed woman, received us like the humble petitioners we were and listened as Woody explained the situation. She spoke to him, and me, civilly enough, but when my mother begged her to permit the wedding to take place on schedule, the director, who presumably knew nothing of the charade, responded icily: "Citizeness, you should have thought about that earlier. This couple will have to wait another month now, until May 4. If you or anyone else tries again to block this marriage, the application will be annulled and they'll have to start from the beginning."

My mother's face reddened as though she had been slapped. As we passed through the waiting room, she suddenly produced a piece of paper and a pen, put them on a table, and directed me sternly, "Write a statement. I'll dictate."

"*Now* what do you want from me?"

But she was already dictating:

"I, Irina Igorevna Astakhova [my second husband's surname],

swear to my mother that I will never under any circumstances divorce Vadim McClellan."

I signed. She solemnly folded the piece of paper, placed it in her purse, and said in a hostile, satisfied voice, "So."

Spring came to Moscow in April. Winter's gray skies broke at last into glorious blues. Buds opened on the trees, Muscovites began to dress in brighter colors and spend more time outdoors. The city is delightful in the spring. Nature's noisy, colorful awakening gladdens and sharpens the senses, the days grow longer, and one can walk anywhere in total safety. But for Woody and me, April was a cruel month, a tortured wait for May. Like prisoners counting the days of their sentences, unable to think of anything else, we stopped going out, invited no one to our apartment. After work we went directly home, had dinner, took long walks, talked much less even to each other.

Then, out of the blue, the Academy of Sciences offered Woody an apartment, quite a large one by Moscow standards, for the three of us—himself, me, and Lena. Our hopes soared: we were not yet married, but the Academy was recognizing us as a family!

The new fourteen-story brick building on Gubkin Street belonged to the Academy and was used to house foreign visitors. Our top-floor apartment consisted of two large rooms, one for Lena and one for us, with a large eat-in kitchen, bath, and balcony. Lena and I especially admired the kitchen; Russians like to spend a lot of time in their kitchens with family and close friends. We received some standard, boxy, government-issue furniture and brought our own linens, dishes, and kitchenware to the new apartment.

At last the day came: May 4, 1974. Our excitement stemmed not from joy but from apprehension. We made our way to the Wedding Palace as though to Golgotha: my mother, Lena, Anastasiya Nikolayevna and Sergei Yakovlevich, Olga, who was my witness, Galya and her husband, Valeri Tishkov—who had insisted on acting as Woody's witness—and his wife Larissa. We rode in several taxis from our apartment to Griboyedov Street.

Russia is sometimes whimsical: taxis lined the street in front of the Wedding Palace, many with large toy dolls—fertility symbols—tied to the hood. Inside the Palace, several young Soviet couples waited their turn. The brides were clad in white frilly dresses fringed with lace, and some even wore veils. The grooms looked uncomfortable in dark, ill-fitting suits. Flowers were everywhere. A tape of Mendelssohn's "Wedding March" played constantly in the background.

Presenting their witnesses, bride and groom were ushered up to a plump auntie on whose imposing chest the red polyester sash of Soviet Power reposed in solid dignity. This woman recited the same civil ceremony to everyone:

"Dear Bride and Groom! Today your young family begins a new *life!* Know, dear friends, that the motherland regards your welfare as its own. The Government of the great Soviet Union, and our glorious Communist *Party,* wish you every happiness. Be faithful to each *other,* to the State and the *Party!* In the name of the Bauman District *Soviet* of Workers' Deputies, I *congratulate* you on this significant day in your *lives!"*

The banal solemnity deeply impressed my mother. Eyes brimming with sentimental tears, she leaned over after the ceremony and whispered in my ear, "Irochka, you'll remember everything? Such important words!"

The young couples embarking on their first matrimonial venture had only normal human problems to prepare for, not the opposition of the KGB. After the ceremony they filed out of the Wedding Palace and headed for the Aleksandrov Garden along the north wall of the Kremlin to lay a wreath at the eternal flame honoring the unknown dead of World War II. As respectful of the war dead as anyone, but emotionally drained, Woody and I returned directly to the new apartment with our friends and witnesses to celebrate our hard-won marriage. Taking a door off its hinges, we improvised a table and set it up in Lena's room.

It was not a night for sleep. As though spiting our enemies, we teased each other repeatedly with *"Now* it's legal . . . "

9
Torn Apart

FRIDAY, May 24, twenty days after our wedding, Woody and I held our *svadba,* or wedding feast. Repeatedly calling out *"Gorko! Gorko!"* (Bitter! Bitter!), our guests obliged us to kiss and make it sweet.

Given the difficulties we had experienced in getting married and our checkered marital past, we saw little reason for such a celebration, but my mother and our friends insisted. Several dozen people—mostly Soviet, with a few embassy people and a couple of visiting American professors—crowded into our apartment on Gubkin Street around a banquet table composed of three doors on sawhorses borrowed from the building superintendent, the kitchen table, and Woody's desk, all covered with white sheets. Salads, champagne, vodka, cold cuts, smoked fish, flowers. Toast after toast to our happiness, to parents and friends, to peace in the world—and endless raucous cries of *"Gorko!"* Woody and I kissed again and again.

That afternoon we had submitted my application for a foreign-travel passport to OVIR, the emigration office, an agency of the KGB; an officer there told us to expect a decision in two months. We were sure it would be favorable. Because Lena wished to complete high school in Moscow, she would stay with her grandmother for a year, then join us in America after graduation.

Two weeks after the *svadba* we traveled on the Red Arrow train to Leningrad. Under the terms of the Soviet-American exchange agreement, the Academy of Sciences gave Woody a trip around the country; he decided to make it our honeymoon. Lena

and Mama came along to Leningrad. It was an unusual honeymoon quartet, but a long separation loomed, and we wanted to
share those last days together.

During the day Woody took us sightseeing, in the evenings to
the best restaurants, gallantly entertaining the three women in his
new family. Only the White Nights—when the sun sets for just a
few brief moments—were his and mine alone, the real honeymoon. Leaving babushka and granddaughter in the Evropeiskaya
Hotel, we made our way on foot to the Neva Embankment, where

"At last it's legal!" Our *svadba*, May 1974.

groups of young people with guitars gathered in the prolonged twilight that almost imperceptibly metamorphoses into dawn. We listened to their songs, watched the drawbridges majestically open and close their gigantic steel maws, swayed back and forth on the park swings, gazed across the Neva, shared dreams of the future . . . and in the early hours of the morning returned to the Evropeiskaya to make love and sleep.

After three days Lena and Mama returned to Moscow. Woody and I stayed on in Leningrad another forty-eight hours, then spent a week in Estonia and Latvia.

Woody had received a two-month extension of his visa and now raced to complete his research by the middle of August. Because history courses had bored me so thoroughly, I could not share his enthusiasm, but his excitement touched me and I did my best to help him. He pored over archival materials and obscure published sources, taking thousands of notes which I typed and filed. He was studying the nineteenth-century Russian revolutionary movement, and with Sergei Yakovlevich's help, began a long-term project, a social history of the Soviet Union from the end of the Civil War to the Nazi invasion. Sergei Yakovlevich, who knew the period intimately, directed Woody to archival treasures in Moscow and the provinces, and helped him find rare books.

I gave clothes and other belongings to friends for both practical reasons and as mementoes. We stockpiled supplies of canned and dried food from the Beriozka shops for Mama and Lena. A few at a time, Woody mailed home hundreds of books. Having spoken only Russian from the beginning of our relationship, early in August we switched to English at mealtimes to attune my ear to American speech.

In the late afternoon, when he returned from the archives, Woody and I played tennis. There are only a few courts in Moscow. We bought passes to one near our apartment building and went there almost every day. After several enthusiastic sets we walked home tired and sweaty, showered, drank some beer, then had an early dinner. To my delight Woody had come to like our custom of soup with meals: cold borscht, mushroom soup, fish soup, and sorrel, his favorite.

Every weekend that summer began with a treat for Lena and me: Woody cooked us a southern American breakfast. We were not permitted in the kitchen until ten, when he called out, "Please come to the table!" Standing in the door with an apron around his waist, a clean white dishtowel on his left arm like a waiter, he bowed to me, saying, "Madame, kindly be seated," then went through the same routine with Lena. On each plate was a big helping of steaming snow white grits—something we had never head of; Woody bought them at the embassy commissary. He decorated the grits with crisp slices of bacon and a perfectly poached egg. A large plate of fresh raw vegetables stood in the middle of the table next to a pot of coffee; beside each napkin lay a list of errands and tasks for the next week. We lingered over those breakfasts.

I was preparing myself emotionally for life in a new country. For a Russian born and raised in one place, educated in a closed society, unaccustomed to change, the prospect of being uprooted is terrifying; my eyes often filled with tears as fear of the unknown rushed through my mind. Woody comforted me.

"Irko, don't be upset, don't worry. I'll plant some birches in our garden . . . in a year we'll come back to get Lena . . . "

Friday, August 2, 1974. Downtown errands accomplished, we were about to enter the Dzerzhinsky Square metro station when with a plop! bird droppings streaked down Woody's blue blazer. To Westerners nothing but a banal annoyance; to Russians, an omen.

A postcard from OVIR was waiting at home; Citizeness McClellan was to call. From a pay phone I dialed the number. A stiffly polite female voice answered.

"You're McClellan, Irina Igorevna? Just a moment please. Oh yes, here it is. You've applied for an exit visa? Your application is denied."

A bored clerk might say in the same tone of voice, "We don't have your size."

I could only stammer, "What? What?"

"If you have questions, come to see the chief Monday." The line went dead.

In that quintessentially Soviet moment, my lovingly assembled world fell apart. Paralyzed, I couldn't say a word. Shock quivered through me to Woody, who seized me by the shoulders and demanded, "Honey, what's happened? *What's going on?*"

"They've denied me a visa," I said helplessly.

He held me tightly, both of us trembling. In the elevator, he said over and over, "Don't worry, it's just a mistake, we'll get it sorted out."

In January and February we had read Solzhenitsyn's *Gulag Archipelago* in bed, under the covers, with a flashlight. A tourist friend of Woody's had smuggled in a copy of the Russian-language edition published in Paris; if the Soviet authorities had discovered it we could have been sent to prison. The first reaction of innocent people arrested by the secret police, Solzhenitsyn had written, never varied: It's a mistake, someone has erred, higher authority will promptly *straighten it out.*

I have only a fragmentary recollection of the first few hours after that telephone call. Disaster . . . complete surprise . . . profound shock. It was like going to the doctor for an upset stomach and hearing: "Terminal cancer. You'll be dead in a few weeks."

Why in the name of God had they let us get married if they were not going to permit us to live together?

Monday morning at ten we went to OVIR, the Office of Visas and Registration, near my kommunalka in the center of Moscow. Formerly the townhouse of a rich merchant, the two-story, turn-of-the-century building was located on Kolpachny Lane, its beige façade distinguished only by an arch in the middle through which the bourgeoisie had once driven in carriages and sleighs. The inner courtyard abuts the garden of the building behind and as a child I used it as a shortcut to school, blissfully unaware of the turns life would take before it led me back through that arch on Kolpachny Lane.

A policeman stood guard in a small entrance hall. In the first-floor lobby, straight wooden chairs surrounded a large rectangular table; more chairs lined all four walls. In opposite corners two closed-circuit television cameras perched like wingless birds of prey on metal swivels. They moved in slow, wide arcs, continuously surveying the lobby. Here, everyone was suspect.

The door to Room No. 24 bore a small bronze plaque: "Director of Municipal OVIR Colonel Fadeyev." The chairs nearest the door were occupied. People bustled about awaiting their turns, while every few minutes a female voice over a loudspeaker repeated: "Comrades, don't stand in front of the door! Be seated!" The same voice announced the names of those invited to enter Room 24.

Woody and I had to wait nearly an hour and a half, and as we sat in the lobby we watched the despairing, embittered, faces of those who emerged from Colonel Fadeyev's office. Our hopes that the decision in my case had been a mistake fell further with each crestfallen supplicant who emerged, tearful eyes to the floor, and passed silently through the lobby into the street.

The summons over the loudspeaker startled us: "McClellan, Irina Igorevna!" We entered.

Perhaps twenty meters square in size, Room 24 had the high ceilings of most pre-revolutionary buildings. It had but one window and was paneled in dark wood. Because the only light came from a small, green-shaded brass lamp on the director's massive desk, one felt trapped at the bottom of a well, an impression heightened by the portrait of Feliks Dzerzhinsky on the wall behind the desk. A native of Poland, Dzerzhinsky joined the Bolsheviks and on Lenin's orders created the Soviet secret police after the Revolution. It was he who established the principle that it is better to shoot ten innocent people rather than allow a single guilty one to escape.

Heavy-lidded and jowly, Colonel Fadeyev sat at his desk

dressed in the uniform of the Ministry of the Interior; OVIR does
not advertise its connection with the KGB. Fadeyev recognized
none of the conventional social reasons to treat us politely. His
face was partially obscured by the lamp, the only thing on his desk
besides two black telephones. He gestured contemptuously toward two chairs positioned in front of the desk.

We sat down, and Fadeyev peered into my eyes for a long
moment as though deciding his form of torment. At last he asked,
"Well, what do you want?"

"An explanation of your refusal to let me go to the United
States with my husband," I said boldly but politely.

Again Fadeyev glared at me in silence.

"We do not give explanations."

Someone in Fadeyev's office had told me to come to him if I
had any questions. What lay behind this game?

"Why was I allowed to marry this man if I can't live with him
in America?"

Fadeyev brightened up and replied in smug tones, "Ah, had
you come to *me* before you got married, *then* I would have explained everything . . . "

Again the executioner's stare bored into me. I shrank in-
wardly, but on the surface I refused to give up.

"But where's the logic?" I demanded. "Three months ago I
had never even heard of OVIR!"

"Well, *now* you know all about it," he responded triumphantly, relaxing his shoulders in a gesture of finality. There was
nothing more to talk about.

I felt trapped. I had lost my job, my mother had been forced
into retirement, my husband was about to leave the country—and
I would remain behind. Indeed, there seemed nothing else to say,
nowhere to turn.

Suddenly I was aware of Woody's voice.

"Excuse me, Colonel—I was under the impression that Soviet
law permits a husband and wife to live together."

Turning for the first time to Woody, Fadeyev said sharply,
"In this office there are no laws, only instructions."

The audience was at an end. We could not draw KGB Colonel Fadeyev into a civilized dialogue.

He had his instructions.

Our thoughts whirled crazily as we dragged ourselves home. Where to turn for help? What to do? Many questions, no answers.

At the Institute of History, where he went to say goodbye, Woody's Soviet acquaintances expressed astonishment: How could this be? Surely a mistake! But then, one by one, the people who had been so cordial all year found reasons to leave the room; soon Woody was alone. In the corridor he encountered Comrade No-name, who had urged him not to marry me.

"Hello, Woody!"

He and Valeri Tishkov were the only two Soviets who did not call my husband Vadim.

"Haven't seen you for ages! How's family life?"

"It seems it's coming to an end," Woody answered bitterly.

"But why?"

"Your friends have denied my wife an exit visa."

"Really? There must be some mistake! I'm sure I can help . . . call me in a week."

Comrade No-name did not react to "Your friends." Woody never called him.

When Woody told me about the encounters at the Institute of History, I recalled another episode there. Late in May, he had given a talk before an audience of Soviet historians, describing his research in the archives of Western Europe. As his wife, I was invited to attend.

They introduced him as "Vadim Vadimovich McClellan," an American professor. Everyone in the audience grinned good-humoredly at the highly unusual name, which rings a little like *Catch-22*'s Major Major Major; it is unlikely that another "Vadim Vadimovich," that is, Vadim, son of Vadim, exists in all the USSR.

The American professor with the funny name and the engaging Vologda accent began to speak, outlining his research in Switzerland on Russian revolutionary émigrés. He reported some of his finds in Zürich and Berne, then said, "Now let's go on to Geneva." After Geneva, it was "Let's go on to Paris"—and Brussels and Amsterdam and several other cities. He meant it kindly, of course, and his Soviet colleagues appeared delighted by the combination research tour and travelogue, but as I looked on from the back row I knew Woody's friendly "Let's go on to . . . " must strike a melancholy note. Only a tiny handful of Soviet scholars would ever be allowed to do research abroad.

Warm applause greeted my husband when he finished, and people crowded around him at the reception afterward to pursue various topics he had raised. Many of them congratulated me on our marriage.

Now, three months and the denial of an exit visa later, all that changed. Those same colleagues fell away.

For the first time since the *svadba*, Valery Tishkov appeared at our door. He too insisted that someone had merely confused the issue. Everything would be made right. His eyes boring into us to gauge our mood, Tishkov tried to question us about our plans. Woody told him to leave.

Unexpectedly, there came a second postcard. In the middle of the week I was summoned to OVIR to see other officials.

UNAUTHORIZED PERSONS NOT ADMITTED: the notice on the second-floor door promised nothing good. A secretary emerged, glanced at the "invitation," ordered Woody away.

"You, citizen, will wait downstairs."

The situation left no room for appeal. Woody embraced me, whispered encouragement, and left. They were already separating us.

Two men. One with a pale, expressionless face behind tinted glasses, the other a diminutive, ratlike lackey.

"We're your *friends*, Irina Igorevna," the lackey said, "from the *KGB.*"

He inclined his head to the side and looked at me expectantly. "Would you like to smoke?"

He extended a pack of cigarettes. The words broke through my torpor; in the face of danger, strength came surging back. No one ever had a friend in the KGB.

"How can you be my friends when I don't even know your names, *gentlemen?*" I ignored his cigarettes.

The little one answered,

"I'm Ivanov, and . . . "

"And your friend's Petrov, of course," I interrupted. Ivanov and Petrov are the two most common Russian surnames. "And tomorrow you'll be Sidorov and Kozlov, as the situation dictates."

The lackey appeared to take offense; his colleague looked at me sternly. They expected a despairing citizeness to leap at their offer of "friendship."

"I am here," I said firmly, "only to learn why I'm not allowed to go to the United States with my husband. We were legally married. What right have you to deny me permission to emigrate?"

"You have some information . . . " lackey "Ivanov" said, voice trailing off into obscurity.

"What kind of nonsense is this!" I erupted. "I graduated from college, I'm an educated person, read all the time"—my voice rose higher—"and *of course* I have 'information'—tons of it! Is that a crime?"

He began to enumerate the jobs I had held, and again I interrupted.

"I'm ready to discuss my work record," I announced, "but we start with this: I never had a security clearance, never even applied for one."

He fell silent. His colleague, the boss, did not take his eyes off me.

"The Afro-Asian Solidarity Committee—it's a public organization, isn't it? And I was only a secretary. The map of Africa has changed a lot—I don't even know the names of the new countries."

Would they like to talk about Intourist? I had worked as a secretary in the automobile repair section, since abolished for lack of business. IMEMO? My area was the protocol section and I did not deal in secrets. I traced my professional history out loud, wondering how the two *KGBeshniki* would produce something out of nothing.

"You're a very smart person," the little one said. "Unfortunately you wear rose-colored glasses."

"And you hide behind dark ones," I retorted.

A long pause. It was absolutely clear that they hoped to back us into a corner of desperation. Comrade No-name offered "help," Valery Tishkov "hope," these two "friendship," certain that drowning people would grasp at a straw. I looked at them and thought to myself, You measure everyone by your own principles. I rose to leave.

Raising his hand to stop me, "Ivanov" asked, "Any more questions?"

"Only one," I responded. "When will you let me go to my husband?"

Speaking for the first time, the tinted-glass boss leaned forward to pronounce sentence in a guttural, sinister growl: "You need a year to clear your mind."

"It would be interesting to know of *what,*" I replied.

"A year to clear your mind."

On the street, I thought I would faint. Woody was dejected. For the first time we noticed a "tail," a young man who made no effort to conceal his mission. We ignored him.

Woody decided to go to the American Embassy. He asked to see the ambassador; surprisingly enough, the request was immediately granted.

Ambassador Walter Stoessel—as Woody later told me—promised to take up the matter with the Foreign Ministry. Could he intervene quickly, Woody asked, perhaps induce the Soviets to reverse their decision? We wanted to leave together.

The ambassador smiled at such naivete. He could not simply

call up Andrei Gromyko and ask a favor. Embassy staff would make enquiries. The "McClellan case"—Woody's heart sank when he heard the term—would be added to the State Department's "representation list" of divided Soviet-American families. When was the list presented to the Foreign Ministry? Regularly. The number of families currently on it? Hundreds, most separated by World War II. How many cases were favorably resolved each year? Half a dozen. What did the ambassador think about bringing the matter to the attention to the press? Stoessel immediately signaled his preference for "quiet diplomacy," pointing out that the people who did eventually receive permission to leave were those who kept quiet.

Someone—we never learned who—had already alerted the American journalists in Moscow. When we came home from the meetings at OVIR and the embassy, we found taped to our door a note asking us to call the Associated Press correspondent. The KGB prefers to operate in darkness; we decided to force the issue into the light.

We will never know whether our decision was the best one. We instinctively followed Solzhenitsyn's advice to people in the clutches of the KGB: Fear nothing, expect nothing, believe nothing. Except for the fear part—we could not suppress fear, but we were defiant. With all the cards on their side, they might well win; but we would give them a fight.

The Associated Press despatch merely stated the fact of the refusal of an exit visa and quoted Woody as saying, "This is a cruel, monstrous injustice. I have no explanation for it."

Then we went to see Christopher Wren, the *New York Times* correspondent. After a lengthy interview, Wren filed an accurate, sympathetic story that reported the scene in Colonel Fadeyev's office. Wren indicated that "a U.S. diplomat expressed surprise . . . that Mr. McClellan's wife had been rebuffed at a time of improving Soviet-American relations."

Peter Osnos of *The Washington Post* published an article noting that the number of mixed-marriage cases in which the Soviet spouse had difficulty obtaining permission to leave has been increasing at a faster rate recently, probably, the [American] embassy believes, because improved relations between the United States and the Soviet Union have brought more Americans here in contact with the Russians. . . .

A few Soviets who have married Americans have gotten out, but invariably with difficulty.

Why do couples like the McClellans have so much trouble? Why do the Soviets risk adverse publicity in the United States on such a straightforward humanitarian issue when they are seeking support in Congress for improved trade legislation? No one seems to know for sure.

Some Americans speculate that the Soviets want to discourage too many Russians from leaving by making the process unpleasant and occasionally even dangerous. (The prospective groom of an American woman was attacked on the street last spring and received a fractured skull.)

In those nightmarish last days of August 1974 Woody sent a letter to Leonid Brezhnev, with copies to other Soviet leaders and to *Pravda:*

OVIR's decision, if it is allowed to stand, will ultimately begin to poison Soviet-American relations. Both sides will be able to deal with the irritant, of course, but it will distract your officials and ours from more urgent business and as it festers it will complicate contacts.

This is not remotely a political issue. I married a Soviet citizen on Soviet territory, and all I ask is that we be allowed to live together like any normal couple. I respectfully request your personal intervention to reverse OVIR's decision so that my wife may leave the Soviet Union with me next week.

Needless to say, no answer ever came.

Moving like zombies, we cleaned the apartment on Gubkin Street and took our remaining household goods to my kommunalka, where Lena and I would have to return. We tried not to let our last days together deteriorate into emotional chaos, but sometimes, unable to keep up a brave front, we sank into depression. At night we clung to each other like prisoners without hope. Physical desire had vanished; we were fighting now for survival.

August 28, 1974, was a warm and sunny day, Woody's last in Moscow. His bags were packed, friends had come to support us in those last painful moments, to have a drink *na pososhok,* one for the road, and wish my husband a safe journey.

An hour before leaving for the airport, we sat alone in our bedroom near the open balcony. As we talked quietly, two pure-white doves, a male and a female, settled on the railing and gave themselves over to courtship, paying no attention to us. For what seemed a long time we watched them groom each other's plumage and gently rub their heads together. We called everyone to see them. This must be a *good* omen!

Transfixed by those birds and perhaps by her guilt, my mother was inconsolable. Lena, Anastasiya Nikolayevna, and Sergei Yakovlevich all had tears rolling down their cheeks. When we rose to leave, the doves flew away together, soared gracefully through the summer Russian sky, and finally disappeared into the distance, still together.

Only a decade later, having become a believer, did I learn that a white dove is a symbol of the Holy Spirit. And still later did I realize the double augury of that August afternoon. Only through reunion with God could I be reunited with my husband.

Book 2

Our separation is illusion;
You and I cannot be parted.
My shadow is on your walls,
My reflection—in your candles.

—*Anna Akhmatova, "Poem Without a Hero"*

10

Life in a Kommunalka

WOODY went away and with him the fairy tale my new life had been. So deeply did I love him, so enormous was my sense of loss, that I had a terrifying sense of beginning a posthumous life in a strange state called Limbo.

The trip from Sheremetyevo Airport to the center of Moscow takes an hour, but on August 28, 1974, it lasted a lifetime. My mother, Lena, and my friend Alisa talked about this and that while I sat silently, crushed by the weight of emptiness. Their conversation pained me; I wanted to be alone with my void. As the airplane carrying my beloved faded into the sky, I thought despairingly—I will never see him again.

A voice, my mother's or Alisa's, broke through, trying to cheer me up.

"Never mind, you'll soon be together. Don't be upset."

The words rang no less hollow for being well meant. I nodded as if in agreement. Eventually the taxi would drop me off at home . . . and indeed here we were at Chernyshevsky Street, at our entryway on Potapov Lane, then the door to the apartment . . .

Lena at my side, I stepped into the tiny hall with its seven doors: to the outside stairwell, the kitchen, bath, toilet, my room, Lena's room, and the neighbors' room. A naked 25-watt bulb hung by a frayed, dusty cord from the high ceiling, barely penetrating the gloom. We had been away since January, when Woody and I had moved to our tiny apartment and Lena had gone to live with Anastasiya Nikolayevna.

The Voronovs greeted us with looks that said, *You* here? Thought we were done with the likes of you . . . They blocked the way insolently, body language proclaiming, We're the bosses here! It was as though the apartment had grown smaller, the Voronovs bigger. As before they were only three—husband, wife, and daughter—but now they seemed to occupy the entire space, leaving no room for Lena and me. I was soon to learn the reason for this puffed-up arrogance: the KGB had recruited them to spy on us.

Our home was no longer a place safe from the world. We were under surveillance, without escape.

Dust covered our two rooms. Boxes containing relics of my life with Woody were strewn about; we had brought them to Chernyshevsky Street only yesterday. I had controlled my emotions during Woody's last few days in Moscow, not wanting him to remember me in tears. Now I collapsed in an armchair, lit a cigarette, and began to cry.

Lena, no less lost and confused, comforted me.

"Mama don't cry . . . please don't. Everything will come out all right. Come on, let's clean up."

I looked at her gentle, troubled face.

"Lenochka, please . . . leave me alone for a while . . . I just don't know what to do . . . it's frightening. . . . "

One cigarette after another; the ashtray overflowed. Time crept by. Lena cleaned, unpacked boxes, put things in their places, now and then spoke. I only half heard her.

Trying to make sense of what had happened, I reviewed the events of the past two years: meeting Woody; losing my job and career; struggling to get married, then the marriage itself; the granting of the Academy of Sciences apartment and the honeymoon on the Baltic, virtually arranged by the Academy. Why the protracted, complicated charade if Woody was to be forced to leave Moscow without me? What had I done? Where was my guilt?

No answers, no logic, only questions. Colonel Fadeyev's words rang in my mind: "In this office there are no laws, only instructions."

The English say that one's home is one's castle, but Lena and I had to share ours with the Voronovs. They were a sorry lot. Into their single thirteen-square-meter room they had wedged their three-quarter bed, their daughter's cot, a small table and three chairs, a tiny refrigerator, a wardrobe, a school desk and chair, a couple of lamps, assorted boxes and crockery, and all the rest of their possessions. They had nailed their one window shut, and a stable-like odor wafted through the apartment whenever they opened the door.

Voronov *père* was a thirty-year-old alcoholic with a pot belly. Though somewhat handsome, he behaved like a monster within the confines of our communal apartment. Several nights a week he staggered home drunk to rage at his plump, dark-eyed wife, with whom he was perpetually at war, and at us, witnesses to his addiction. He would try to slip in so we would not see him. Then when his wife began to scold, he would curse her; there would be sounds of a scuffle, her screams, someone or something falling, then silence.

In a way, however, the Voronovs were not unhappy. They understood each other, saw the world through the same eyes, belonged to the same social class, and carried on the class struggle conscientiously in the communal apartment. At the KGB's bidding they reported everything: who came to visit, my end of telephone calls, mail, my moods, and so forth.

Life in the kommunalka, tense at the best of times, became one long battle set in our tiny shared kitchen. Along one wall, underneath a narrow window, stood our little table and an identical one belonging to the Voronovs. Jammed between the tables was a four-burner gas stove. A communal cupboard hung on the opposite wall. There was no room for a refrigerator; each family kept a small one in their own room.

According to the unwritten law of communal living, families divided the stove: the burners on the left were ours, those on the right the Voronovs'. The friction between rose to such an absurd level that the Voronovs would clean only "their" half of the stove. We could not split the oven but in theory could take turns using it; the theory did not work. When I wanted to bake or roast something, I would light the oven early to warm it up, then go back to my room for a few minutes. The oven would be in use when I returned. I tried to reason with Voronova, whose response never varied: "I have a family to feed. You can wait. You have more free time." She did not consider teaching school work, nor Lena and me a family.

Husband and daughter would dart into the kitchen discussing the menu greedily, stomachs agrowl. When dinner was ready, the family would carry their pots and dishes to their room. The slurping and chomping of the nightly orgy penetrated to every corner of the apartment. Lena and I would turn up the volume on our television.

The Voronovs bathed less often than they cooked, washing themselves and doing their laundry only once a week, on Sundays. Then it would be next to impossible to get in to brush your teeth, let alone do anything else. Tub and sink would be full of washing. More than once I proposed that we be given an hour on Sunday to take showers. Voronova invariably responded, "Oh no, we're working people! You've got the whole week to shower. Wait a while, it won't kill you."

On Sunday evenings the gloom lifted briefly. Woody called me regularly at 8:00 P.M. The first time he telephoned, I had been waiting for hours near the door of my room so as to be first to the phone when the call came. The telephone rang with startling suddenness. I grabbed the receiver, palms sweating in excitement, heart thumping. In metallic, disembodied tones, the operator demanded, "McClellan? America is calling you."

And then that dear, passionate voice:

"Irko! Darling! How are you? I love you! I miss you! I think about you every minute . . ."

I took the telephone by its long cord into my room and closed the door. Struggling to hold back the tears, I began to talk. Now only the telephone could join us.

"Vadim, I'm lost without you . . . how am I going to live? I love you so much. I don't understand why we aren't together . . . "

When I could not continue, Woody spoke tenderly. As his voice conquered the distance, my troubles slipped away. He told me of his plans. He would go to the State Department, seek out friends and acquaintances in Washington, bring pressure to bear on the Soviet government. He spoke confidently, refusing to accept even the *possibility* of defeat. Alas, I could not share his bright vision.

Forty minutes flew by in an instant. Our next meeting on the telephone would be the following Sunday. The calls, and letters, were all we had.

The telephone went dead. I remained sitting on the sofa, feeling Woody's physical presence. It was as though he had gone out of the room for a moment; his touch was still on my skin, his breath warm against my neck. Then reality reasserted itself and I knew that he was thousands of miles away in Charlottesville, Virginia, only a point on a map to me, seeing friends I knew only by name, leading a life I could not share. I ached to fly to him.

The Voronovs had lived in the kommunalka much longer than I—nine years—and it would be another six before they finally got a new apartment. Several weeks after Woody left Moscow, something unprecedented happened: they refused to let Lena and me in.

We had been to visit some new acquaintances. The wife, Alina, had applied three times for a visa to visit her father, a "nonreturner" from World War II; he had refused repatriation from a German POW camp. He now lived in Baltimore. Alina and I were both petitioners at OVIR. We talked long into the wet October night, cozy in her little flat. Around eleven, Lyonya, her husband, drove us home and escorted us to our door. All Moscow was nervous. In recent weeks a psychotic escaped convict had murdered half a dozen women in the central city.

My key would not open the door. The neighbors had thrown the inside bolt. Dumbfounded, I rang the bell, rang it again, held the button down for several minutes, pounded on the door, called

out. No response. Inside, the Voronovs' television blared. As Lyonya and Lena took turns ringing, my anger mounted: I was unable
to enter my own home!

After twenty minutes I headed for the precinct police station;
on the way I encountered two policemen on foot patrol. On hearing my story, one of them reluctantly accompanied me to my
door. The Soviet police routinely shun communal apartment dis-
putes.

The policeman rang, also without results. By now it was midnight. In exasperation he offered a solution.

"If you like, I'll break down the door."

"Then what?" I asked.

"Let the neighbors fix it."

"Hah! They don't even repair what *they* break! They'll sue me
for hooliganism."

"Then I can't help you." He turned and walked down the
stairs.

Lena, Lyonya, and I went to the station, where a couple of
bored, drowsy sergeants declined to assist us. "File a complaint,"
one suggested. We wrote out something; when we finished the
foot patrolman happened to return to the station and agreed
to countersign our complaint. The duty sergeant, however, remained adamant: nothing could be done until morning.

Lyonya drove us back to his flat, where an astounded Alina
found extra blankets and sheets and made us a bed on the floor. I
lay there trembling, angry and afraid.

The next morning I appeared in the kitchen with dark circles
under my eyes after a sleepless night. Alina called Anna Markovna, the principal of my school, and explained that I would be
unable to teach that day. She also telephoned the precinct police
captain, who agreed to meet us at the apartment that evening.

The encounter with the Voronovs took place at 6:00 P.M. in
the tiny, dark hall. I was supported by Lyonya, Alina, Tamara, my
school colleague, and my friends Igor and Alisa, who knew
Woody. A few minutes after our arrival, the precinct police captain strode in. A rosy-cheeked, flaccid little man in his forties
accompanied by a sergeant, he knocked on the Voronovs' door.

Sullenly, Citizen and Citizeness Voronov appeared. The second act of the drama began.

My friends presented identification: Lyonya, a rather introverted man with a Van Dyck beard, displayed his membership cards in the Artists' Union and the Union of Cinematographers. The vivacious Alina, towering over her husband by a head, boldly announced her credentials: "Housewife. Mother of two children." In his polite, friendly way, Igor, who looked like a sandy-haired cowboy, showed his papers as senior researcher at the Institute of Ethnography. His wife Alisa, a short, stylish woman, merely stated her name in a thin tremolo. Finally Tamara, a gypsy-like woman with long black hair and dark, exhausted eyes, the last soldier in my little army, presented the workbook all adult citizens must carry listing every job one has held.

The Voronovs displayed nothing. She was a bookkeeper, he a stock boy and alcoholic.

The captain asked for an explanation. Pandemonium erupted as everyone spoke at once. Voronova attacked Alisa, the quietest, smallest person in the company, rudely using *tu* instead of *vous*.

"Get out of here and mind your own business, hag! Go take care of your children! We'll settle this without you!"

Meanwhile, Voronov launched into me. He announced that I was a drug addict and demanded that the policemen arrest me. I smoked only in my room; he could not have seen me. But menthol cigarettes were then practically unknown in the Soviet Union. The smell of the Salems Woody had bought for me at the embassy commissary aroused his suspicion.

The police captain tried to question Voronov. Lyonya asked for my cigarettes and showed the policemen the green and white package. What Soviet law forbids smoking in the privacy of one's room? Would the captain like to try one? No? Lyonya lit up and puffed away. Changing direction, Voronov screamed that I was a parasite who did not work and should be interrogated on *that* count. Coming in at all hours, I disrupted the peaceful lives of good Soviet citizens, honest workers who were in bed by 11:00 P.M.

Now Tamara jumped in.

"What's this? Teaching school isn't considered work? We work as hard as anybody! Irina Igorevna finishes teaching at two. *Of course* she's home earlier than someone like you who comes home drunk every other day!"

Voronov glared at her angrily but before he could reply it was Lyonya's turn.

"What law says an adult citizen has to be home by eleven P.M.? You have your schedule and Irina Igorevna has hers—what right have you to lock the door?"

I stayed outside the fray, saying nothing, and wondered what the police would do. They had trouble getting a word in. Voronova would not stop yelling. Finally they directed her husband to calm her down. Then the captain gave the Voronovs a lecture on respecting the rights of neighbors in a communal apartment. The two listened glumly, frowned angrily at us, occasionally smirked.

My triumphant forces and I went to my room to celebrate. I fixed coffee, and we women—the men did not smoke—lit up Salems. We had won a small victory, but not the war.

Letters from Woody stood out against this dark background like rainbows. Early in November 1974, he wrote:

I'm so sorry you continue to have all this trouble with the neighbors . . . as if you didn't have enough to worry about, they lock you out! This is unbelievable. What kind of savages are they? And who is backing them up in all this?

At least your friends came to your defense. I'm deeply grateful to them—but I should be the one to defend you. Sitting here thousands of miles away helpless while people are making your life miserable is the most frustrating experience I can imagine. And why does it have to be this way? I wish I knew.

But like all his letters in that first year of our separation, this one ended on a defiantly positive note:

Always keep faith in our certain reunion, my darling: we shall *win*!!! I love you, Irko, with all my heart.

11
The Struggle

THE STRUGGLE to be reunited with Woody obsessed me. The KGB's explanation for denying me an exit visa—the mysterious necessity for me to "clear my head"—was preposterous. I soon stopped trying to understand and fought instead to leave the country—not my beloved Russia but the Soviet Union the Communists had created in its stead.

But how? I knew only a single path, the one to OVIR, the emigration office just around the corner on Kolpachny Lane. I would have gone there every day had there been any point in doing so, but OVIR made its own rules. Once denied an exit visa, I had to wait a full year before petitioning again. Even so, I visited that hated office regularly, trying to learn how to appeal its decision. On my fourth visit, a surly clerk informed me that Lieutenant General Sorochkin in the Ministry of Internal Affairs reviewed such appeals.

I made an appointment and on Thursday, September 12, 1974, walked the few blocks from my apartment to Petrovka 38, an address associated in every Soviet citizen's mind with crime films: MUR, Moscow Criminal Investigation. An odd place to plead for a wife's right to live with her husband.

General Sorochkin personally received a limited number of petitioners once a month. I found myself among the favored few in a large, paneled reception room furnished with a wooden table, chairs lining the walls, and the obligatory portraits of Lenin and Dzerzhinsky.

A young woman near the end of pregnancy caught my attention. I approached her and, trying to break the ice, asked why she had come to Petrovka 38 instead of a maternity hospital. Her reply chilled me.

"They won't let me go to my husband. He's Polish . . . lives in Krakow."

My God! I thought. If they won't let this woman go to "fraternal" socialist Poland to join the father of her unborn child, what hope do I have? I was searching for something to say when a clerk appeared and gruffly announced that the general would see her. The rest of us—a dozen or so petitioners—watched anxiously as the door to the general's office closed behind the young woman.

The minutes dragged by, and I began to wonder whether she had decided to have her baby in General Sorochkin's office. But then she emerged pale and shaking, escorted by the general himself. She sat down beside me. She had indeed told him she would not leave without an answer; if need be she would give birth on the floor of his office. Alarmed, the elderly, distinguished-looking officer assured her he would investigate and reach a decision promptly.

But not today. The pregnant woman left, in and out of my life so quickly. Such is Russia.

Finally my turn came; my interview was short, sharp, and totally negative. General Sorochkin insisted he could do nothing and advised me to return to OVIR to see Comrade Inspector Akulova, who was in charge of "American affairs." The woman's name did not inspire optimism: *akula* means shark in Russian.

The next day, Friday, September 13, I hurried to OVIR right after school. A guard at the door directed me to the second floor, where Akulova's office lay behind a door marked UNAUTHORIZED PERSONS NOT ADMITTED. That door also led to the office of the two KGB "friends" who had interrogated me in August. In response to my knock, a thin woman in her mid-fifties appeared on the landing. Dressed in modish Western clothes, Akulova began sternly.

"Why have you come? Were you not told clearly that your case will only be reviewed after a year?"

I attempted to explain that I did not know what "information" I was supposed to clear out of my head. Maybe there had been a mistake?

She turned back to her office saying, "I've got a lot of work to do. Why are you taking up my time?"

"And why do you address me so rudely?" I demanded, determined to give as good as I got. "Isn't my case your business?"

This brought a sinister response.

"See here, Irina Igorevna," Akulova hissed, motioning toward a man at the head of the stairs, "decent Soviet people are waiting for me."

Turning away, she moved swiftly over to the man, a benign new mask on her face. A polite exchange, and he had Akulova's assurances he would soon have his visa.

Distraught, I looked on, witness to the bestowal of the state's blessing on a citizen in whom it had faith. Akulova brushed by me without so much as a glance.

The decent citizen was a man of about fifty, neatly dressed in a stylish, most un-Soviet three-piece suit, carefully knotted silk tie, expensive-looking foreign shoes with tassels. He came up to me and said condescendingly, "You know, it's best not to quarrel with Akulova. She's an influential lady. A lot depends on her."

Perhaps he meant to be civil, but I had not quarreled with Akulova.

"Well," I replied after a moment or two, "probably we have different reasons for wanting to leave the country. That's what this is all about."

Woody's letters and his Sunday telephone calls underlined the difference in our situations. As a citizen of a free country he had not needed anyone's permission to marry a Russian, and now, forcibly separated from his wife, he received the support of the American government and press. He worked feverishly, constantly visited various offices in Washington and New York, wrote letters, made telephone calls, enlisted friends and colleagues, did his best to keep my spirits up. In the beginning he rarely mentioned the names of those who had promised to help. He wrote

regularly but enigmatically to keep the KGB censors off balance.
We wanted them to know Woody was pursuing our cause actively, but not the details. In his September 30 letter he wrote:

> . . . many Senators and Congressmen are intensely concerned about
> the matter and . . . are genuinely worried about your safety. [They] are
> doing everything possible through diplomatic channels and so forth.
> . . . [This] case . . . gives many people food for thought: what kind of
> uncivilized behavior is this, keeping a woman away from her husband?

It was Woody's assumption, and mine, that the decision to
deny my request for an exit visa had been made at a fairly low
level, and that exposure of such criminal bureaucratic arbitrari-
ness might led to its reversal. That was why he had written to
Brezhnev, sending copies to other leaders and to *Pravda;* but the
ten days specified by statute for a response elapsed with no word
from anybody. A few days after my encounter with Akulova, however, I received a telephone call.

A female voice enquired, "Are you McClellan, Irina Igorevna? Yes? Your husband wrote a letter to *Pravda?* We will not
give you a written reply, but you can come to our offices to speak
to someone."

A secretary conducted me into the *Pravda* office of Comrade
Abramov. Behind a solid desk sat an unremarkable civil servant, a
faceless Fadeyev—"no laws, only instructions"—type. He stared
at me icily. On his desk, in plain view, lay the envelope Woody
had addressed in huge, bold letters. I returned the stare in silence
and after a moment sat down without invitation.

"Well, what brings you here?" He threw the question at me.

"Didn't you invite me?"

"But what can I tell you? I don't know English . . . what does
he want, this husband of yours?"

I felt myself grow suddenly angry: had I traveled an hour
across Moscow to hear such a question? I wanted to overturn his
desk and dump the container of meticulously sharpened pencils,
two telephones, and carefully positioned notepaper on his head; in

a minute I would scream. With difficulty I restrained myself and asked calmly, "Can't *Pravda* find a translator?"

"Why should we?" Abramov replied. "We've got Yuri Zhukov. He knows English well, of course, but why bother him with this? He has important government matters to attend to."

Zhukov, a vitriolic, passionately anti-American journalist, conducted a weekly television program, "Your Letters." In it he answered enquiries from workers and peasants—written in their names by the KGB—about the junta in Chile, the situation in Angola, the American threat to Cuba, and so on.

"Excuse me, but what are 'government matters'?" I asked. "Do they not involve people and their problems?"

Abramov's expression made it clear he had no wish to continue the conversation, but I pressed him.

"Why did you ask me to come? Why waste my time?"

He looked at me with something between a leer and a bureaucrat's arrogant grimace and said, "To have a look at a woman bold enough to marry an American."

I rose and walked out.

Soviet bureaucracy is consistent. It does its business abroad in the same way it does it in Moscow; foreigners who challenge it suffer the same treatment as Soviets do at home. Early in October 1974, Woody wrote that he had called the Soviet Consulate in Washington in an attempt to speak to someone about our case. The man who answered refused to give his name and declared that the consulate did not deal with such matters. Woody should call the embassy. "I called the Embassy; some outraged woman said that the Consulate had no business telling me to call them and that the Consulate itself should speak to me (!). I called the Consulate back . . . no answer."

Frustrated, Woody sent a letter—the first of many—to Ambassador Anatoli Dobrynin, only to have the Soviet Consulate return it in a hand-addressed envelope along with an unsigned form letter in which all blanks remained blank:

EMBASSY OF THE
UNION OF SOVIET SOCIALIST REPUBLICS
CONSULAR DIVISION
1825 Phelps Place, N.W.
Washington, D.C. 20008

Dear Sir:

In reply to your letter of   we would like to inform you that
unfortunately we are not in a position to help you on the matter you are
interested in because such matters are out of our Embassy's competence.

Sincerely,

[The form was never signed]

These cold lines made me miserable for days. Along with fear
and despair, I felt shame—shame for my country, whose representatives abroad could not even pretend to be civil.

But as always my husband was there, cheerful, hopeful
Woody, with his letters and Sunday calls. He told me in the
middle of October that Senator Edward Kennedy had responded
positively to his appeal for assistance; the Kremlin's well-publi-
cized respect for the late President's brother might help us. Senator Hugh Scott, the Republican leader of the Senate, and Senator
Harry F. Byrd of Virginia also promised to raise the matter with
both Soviet and American authorities. Later, more than sixty
senators would become involved in our case; Hubert Humphrey
tried to help from his deathbed, Birch Bayh did all he could,
Abraham Ribicoff and Barry Goldwater were extremely sympathetic, and later Claiborne Pell, Paul Simon, Richard Lugar, John
Warner, Dan Quayle, J. Kenneth Robinson, and others offered
assistance. Woody wrote to me about the unusual political coalition taking shape as American officials sought to bring us together. The good news that many high-ranking Americans had
agreed to help us would not, however, outweigh the stony resistance we met in our dealings with the Soviet authorities.

When he called me on Sunday, November 3, Woody seemed
about to burst with excitement.

"Honey! Great news . . . I've received a letter from . . . a *very*
high official. He promises to press our case."

He refused to name the individual in question and I did not push him; I would learn soon enough. Terribly agitated, full of optimism, Woody bombarded me with plans for our reunion, which he was sure would take place soon. I was caught up in the wave of enthusiasm.

A few weeks later, a friend of Woody's who was visiting the Soviet Union brought me a copy of the letter.

Dear Professor McClellan:

Thank you for your letter of September 2. I found it profoundly moving. . . .

I want you to know that I shall take a direct and personal interest in the plight of your wife. Indeed, I plan to discuss this case fully with Ambassador Dobrynin in the near future and shall press his government to issue your wife the necessary Soviet exit papers.

I, of course, cannot guarantee a favorable outcome. I shall do my best and shall keep you informed of any major developments.

Best regards,
[signed] Henry A. Kissinger

There were to be several more Kissinger letters, each more cautious than the last. This first one sustained our hopes through that dark winter of 1974–75. Kissinger was well thought of in the Soviet Union because of the cordial relations he had cultivated with Soviet leaders. I allowed myself to hope that, liking the American Secretary of State as they did, those leaders might do him a favor and let me go. Those hopes proved fruitless.

Our moods and hopes swung in response to external forces. Unwilling to wait passively for events to take their course, we did everything we could think of to hasten our reunion. I went to OVIR with a new idea: I would invite my husband to visit me in Moscow. He would have a vacation at the end of December. What could be more natural than for him to spend Christmas and the New Year holiday with his wife?

In November 1974 I sat again in the crowded reception hall

waiting to be admitted to Room 24. The overwhelming majority of those on the same mission were *otkazniki,* refuseniks, people denied the right to emigrate to Israel. Although my status was that of a divided spouse, the state treated me the same as it did the refuseniks, whose sad faces I could easily recognize. They talked among themselves in undertones, occasionally making bitter jokes about their fate. Having rejected the state's embrace, all had lost their jobs: biologists and physicists now worked as elevator boys and street cleaners. Deprivation of state sanction of their normal existence, however, had given these people a measure of freedom, a spiritual life beyond the state's control—in Limbo.

Once again I received a refusal in Room 24: my husband would not be permitted to come to Moscow. The explanation?

"His visit is undesirable."

"How can that be? He came to the Soviet Union many times before we met . . . visited *me* several times before our marriage. Now that we're married you refuse to let him come?"

The *nachalnik,* the boss, remained silent. In anger and frustration I continued to bombard him with questions, my voice rising higher and higher.

"Undesirable? To *who-o-m!*"

No answer.

"Why these games? If you were going to refuse him a visa, why did you make me stand in line for hours?"

No answer.

The queue system in Soviet offices, the unethical behavior and illegal decisions of officials, the policy of refusing to answer petitions or explain refusals—all this reflected the Brezhnev regime's attempt to revive the Stalinism of the 1930s. The system worked as of old, on the same principles: the state decides who is an enemy, who is one of its own.

To cope with the disappointment, Woody and I created our own little illusions. Exhausted by separation from my husband, depressed by my failures at OVIR, suffering from insomnia, I decided to embroider a poncho during the long nights. I made the poncho from a soft beige blanket that had lain useless in a closet for years. Every night I completed a large cross-stitched tulip, telling myself that, when the last tulip was shaped, my exit visa would appear.

Woody had his own dreams. Late in the autumn of 1974 he wrote:

Yesterday before going to Washington I repaired one of those ceramic beer mugs you gave me in Moscow; it was broken in shipping. At first inclined to throw the pieces out, I decided, no, let's put it back together as a kind of symbol of our determination to overcome obstacles. So for a couple of hours I glued and dried the thing and finally managed to restore it. It is not perfect; but it's whole again.

12

Outcasts

A FESTIVE AIR invigorates Moscow on September 1, the first day of school. Schoolgirls wear white starched aprons instead of the everyday brown, boys white shirts and gray trousers. Younger pupils of both sexes tie crimson Young Pioneer kerchiefs around their necks and nearly all the children carry bouquets of flowers for the teachers. First graders preen nervously, full of importance but grateful for the presence of their well-dressed mothers, fathers, and even babushkas. In the glorious late-summer sunshine, on freshly hosed-down streets and sidewalks, amid children's cheerful laughter, there is a sense of purpose, of renewed dedication. Under the watchful eye of principal and teachers, pupils assemble by class in the courtyard in front of each school. The principal addresses a welcome to the new first graders, some particularly distinguished member of the senior class speaks, a parent says a word or two, then another pupil rings a bell. Each tenth grader, or senior, takes a first grader by the hand and leads the child to the proper classroom. School is in session.

Despite family problems, or maybe because of them, Lena and I looked forward to the renewal of the school routine in September of 1974, her next-to-last year. When I awoke early that morning, the first thing that flashed through my mind was, Thank God I still have a job! People around me, Lena nearby, a salary coming in. Late in August I had called Anna Markovna, the principal, to be sure the job was still mine; it was. I had not been deprived of that vestige of state support.

I had gone to the school in July to obtain the workplace reference OVIR required to process my visa application. As always in summer, the school was unnaturally empty and quiet; what is a school without children? A few teachers worked in their classrooms, preparing for the fall semester before going on vacation.

In no hurry, Anna Markovna discussed my future life in America sympathetically, giving me all sorts of advice. Like many single middle-aged women, she was sentimental about love stories. When I handed over the key to my classroom, she spotted an elegant French pendant on my key ring and without a trace of subtlety hinted I should give it to her as a memento.

"You can get another one in the West."

Before I could react she continued, "Don't forget to send others for my collection. And some visual aids for the school. Don't worry about Lena and her studies—I'll personally look after her."

But much had changed since July. Now Anna Markovna greeted me coldly, saying, "Well, Irina, why did you not go to America?"

"They didn't *let* me go."

She feigned surprise.

"What are you saying? Husband and wife kept apart? That's *impossible!*"

It was all a sham. The situation at school changed the minute I was denied permission to leave the country with my husband. Neither Anna Markovna nor my fellow teachers had any experience with such matters, but they all recognized an outcast and like most Soviet people immediately thought of their own skins. Since the Revolution our people have suffered terribly for having the wrong friends. From the first day of school my colleagues distanced themselves, speaking curtly or simply avoiding me. Only Ananii, Tamara, and Mark remained friendly.

My colleagues' behavior compounded my sense of isolation, and a few days into the semester I counterattacked. After a snub in the hall, I would approach the person, force eye contact, and politely say hello. If that failed to produce a response I simply blocked the way and demanded, "Why, what's going on? Aren't

people greeting each other this year? How will we teach good
manners if we ourselves don't act civilized?"

In spite of themselves they began at least to acknowledge
greetings. The grudging resumption of civility made my precarious standing less uncomfortable.

But it was the children who saved me. They hailed me excitedly at the start of the new school year and crowded around to talk
about their summer vacations. Ignorant of politics but sensitive to
injustice, they quickly felt my ostracism, supported me in their
childish way, came to my room during the breaks, often with
flowers. Once some tenth graders brought a puppy, a funny black
dachshund. Frightened by the children's raucous laughter, it ran
frantically around the room. I was apprehensive lest the uproar
disturb Anna Markovna.

After my last class each day I sat down to correct papers,
surrounded by the student art that decorates language classrooms
everywhere: collages of photos of Great Britain and the United
States, British and American flags, dust jackets of books by British
and American authors, a poster with a quotation from *Hamlet,*
Polonius's advice to his son: "This above all, to thine own self be
true." The simple reminders took me back to the hopes and romantic dreams of my youth.

In the summer of 1962, when my three-year-old Lena was at
summer camp with her nursery school class, I took a month's
leave from my job at the Afro-Asian Solidarity Committee, gathered up stacks of books, and imposed an iron discipline on myself.
I studied from early morning until midnight, with only brief inter-
ruptions for lunch and dinner, to prepare for the entrance examinations to the Institute of Foreign Languages.

I had graduated from high school six years earlier and had
forgotten a great deal of English grammar. I had a family to care
for and a full-time job, but I could not put off my application to
the Institute any longer. It was now or never.

Moscow State University, the Institute of International Relations, and the Institute of Foreign Languages are among the most

prestigious institutions of higher education in the USSR. In addition to good high school grades and a spotless Komsomol record, one must ordinarily have *blat,* connections, to gain admission. Lacking those, I had to rely on my own abilities and hope for a miracle.

When the testing period came in August, I passed the written composition exam and the oral examinations in literature and history with high marks, but the last, most important hurdle—English—remained. Many of my competitors had gone to special schools where several of their subjects would have been taught in English. For others, parents had engaged private tutors, and a few, the children of diplomats, for instance, had even lived in English-speaking countries.

In ordinary high schools like the one I had attended, training in foreign languages is generally mediocre. Moreover, I had had almost no chance to speak English since graduation. My pronunciation, however, had always been good, and in preparation for the exam I memorized little speeches, answers to potential questions on my personal history, work, Komsomol activities, Communist Party history, and so forth.

My future depended on that exam.

We were tested in small, separate classrooms, summoned in pairs from the large hall where the finalists waited. My examiner was a frail and dignified elderly woman with still beautiful hands and carefully arranged hair. Her severely elegant black dress was so many decades out of style it seemed the height of fashion. Instinctively I knew she was a member of the *byvshie,* "has-beens," the pre-revolutionary upper classes.

I was paired with a tall and pretty seventeen-year-old girl from a special school; the examiner called her first. The girl had fluent English, but in an attempt to show off she frequently interrupted with an answer before hearing the entire question. The examiner became more and more irritated with each interruption. Finally the old woman said sternly, "Kindly allow me to complete the question."

No matter how well one has learned a foreign language, an

expert can find gaps; that is what happened to the girl. The examiner gave her a 3, or C, dooming her chance for admission to the Institute. I later learned that she was admitted only as a correspondence student.

Addressing me in English, the examiner summoned me to the table at the front of the room and briefly outlined the examination procedure. The first part involved retelling an assigned passage from a book, in my case a work by Jack London. I kept my account as simple as possible, trying to avoid mistakes. Her face a blank, she listened in silence, then proceeded to the "free talk" section of the exam, questions and answers. Desperate to answer her questions, I became confused. The more I struggled, the worse my confusion. There was nothing for it but to confess.

"I can't speak English."

Looking her in the eye I added, "But I want so much to study at the Institute . . . and this is my last chance."

Obviously surprised by my candor, she did not reply. After an awkward silence I made her a timid offer in the form of a question.

"I can . . . tell you about myself?"

When she nodded assent, I launched into a memorized autobiography, telling her about my husband, who was taking night classes at the Institute of Economics; my daughter; my own work; and my longstanding dream of entering the Institute of Foreign Languages. Slowly the examiner's expression began to soften. Her mouth relaxed slightly, her eyes seemed to sparkle. When I finished, she stared intently at the card with my grades on the previous examinations, as if weighing her decision, then looked at me for a long moment. A warm smile crossed her face. She said gently, "I think you are capable of doing the work. You ought to be in our Institute. Your grade is a four [B]."

That would do it: I was in!

Thunderstruck, I stammered thanks and shot out of the room exhilarated. The future seemed bright.

In later years I have often thought about that former aristocrat, wondering why she passed me. Maybe it was her way of protesting the *blat* system by which children of the Soviet elite are admitted to prestigious institutions. Or perhaps, seeing in me someone willing to sacrifice for an education, she decided to clear a path.

Five years later, in 1967, I graduated.

Happy memories; but in the autumn of 1974 reality lay in the school where I had once been thought a good teacher. The pupils liked me, and my personal conduct—aside from having married an American—was above reproach. Nevertheless, Anna Markovna would gladly have sacked me, but she had neither received authorization nor found a replacement. Because my husband was abroad, it was always possible that any action against me would become public knowledge. The state's campaign proceeded slowly and deliberately.

By the middle of the fall semester, members of the District Education Board and the District Party Committee, even fellow teachers behind my back, referred to me derisively as *"Amerikanka,"* the American woman. This was like labeling someone a Communist in the United States. Anna Markovna was repeatedly asked when the *"Amerikanka"* would leave the school.

Lena's situation also changed dramatically. The teachers shunned her, and the students who were not in my English classes took the cue and excluded her. Suffering from the isolation, she began to visit my room during breaks between classes. I did my best to protect and comfort her, but there is little a mother can do against the outside world's determined savagery. Frightened and bewildered, my fifteen-year-old daughter began to pay for her mother's "crimes" against the state.

Either under instructions or her own initiative, Anna Markovna carried out a campaign among the pupils. She summoned them to her office individually and in groups to warn them about Lena and me. Some told me of these sessions: their admission to college would be blocked, the principal warned, and their parents' careers jeopardized, if they continued to associate with us. Irina Igorevna's apartment was "bugged," she informed them. The au-

thorities knew everything that went on there; the children were
not to visit us. She had little success among my own students,
more with those whose foreign language was German and thus
did not know me personally.

The campaign climaxed in March 1975 on the last day before
the spring vacation. Someone scrawled YANKEE GO HOME! in English on Lena's schoolbag, a group of older "German" boys threatened to beat her up unless she left the school, and a crude
handmade poster appeared on the door of my classroom: it de-
picted the Soviet flag dominating a defaced American one and
bore the inscription: DOWN WITH AMERICAN IMPERIALISM!

The vacation week gave us a breathing space from school, but
no rest from the outside world. I was summoned to OVIR, where
an official stunned me with the news that I had three days to get
the documents for myself *and Lena* in order.

"There will soon be a decision on your case," the woman
assured me. "Be prepared to leave on short notice—maybe two
weeks!"

Overjoyed, I flew home. Lena and I hugged each other deliri-
ously, then I called Woody. It was noon in Moscow, 4:00 A.M. in
Virginia.

"Honey, wake up! I've got good news!"

Always a light sleeper, he was instantly alert.

"What is it? They've given you a visa?"

"Not yet . . . but I have to file the papers quickly."

"My God! That's wonderful! What about Lena?"

"Lena too. Tomorrow we hope to get permission from her
father for her to emigrate."

"When do you think you might leave?"

"There is a lot to do. They said maybe two weeks."

"Come as soon as possible! Don't waste any time. Just throw a
couple of toothbrushes in a bag and *come!*"

There would have been no time for celebration even if we had
been so inclined. A crucial step remained: Lena and I had to get
her father's permission.

Now a man of status, Volodya, or Vladimir, was a factory manager and a deputy to the Moscow Soviet, the City Council. He had his own chauffeured state-owned Volga sedan and lived in a splendid apartment building reserved for the elite. He traveled abroad on business trips and took vacations in Bulgaria and Romania. The only country forbidden him was the United States, home of his ex-wife's husband. Every time he saw Lena he complained bitterly about this, and when he did Lena—despite her tender age—lectured him.

"Papa, you can go to Europe. Look how many countries there are! Life isn't long enough to visit them all. Let Mama go to America . . . her husband's there."

Irritated, her father would reply sarcastically, "I don't like all this about 'America' and 'her husband.' And as for you, *you* have to live in your own homeland, study here, work."

As Lena and I made our way to Volodya's factory, situated in a little lane a few metro stations from our apartment, my courage began to fade. Surrounded by a high black wrought-iron fence, the plant was protected by an armed guard who emerged from his sentrybox to check identification at the gate. If he approved, visitors went through a turnstile into a small courtyard and then the building. I had no official invitation and would never get one; my plan was to catch Volodya unawares, back him into a corner.

The factory made ice skates. In the Soviet Union, with its mania for secrecy, even trifles are considered state secrets.

To postpone the moment of truth, Lena and I crossed to the opposite side of the street. She looked at me forlornly. As far as she was concerned, it was hopeless. But there was no alternative. I had to get Volodya's permission to take my child with me to the United States. Like a high jumper preparing to spring, I took a deep breath, gathered my strength, took Lena's arm firmly, and strode across the street toward the turnstile without a glance at the sentrybox. I pushed the bar. Ordinarily it is locked in place, but this time the guard had forgotten to do his duty. The bar turned smoothly at my touch.

Lena and I were already in the little courtyard, making for a door marked OFFICE. My heart thumped loudly. I heard the guard shout, "Citizeness! Where are you going?"

The words were lost in the breeze as we disappeared behind the door. I had only one desperate thought: to reach Volodya's office as quickly as possible. We passed a dumbfounded secretary and burst in.

The spacious, carpeted room had paneled walls and, naturally, a large oil portrait of Lenin. As manager, Volodya bore responsibility for ideology no less than production. At a massive desk, the "skates director" himself sat arguing loudly with a visitor.

We halted just inside the door. Volodya rose from his chair suddenly and stood staring at us, mouth slightly open. His handsome face had gone pale, but his astonishment did not diminish his imposing, dignified presence. He recovered enough to excuse himself to his visitor, whom he escorted to the door. Still confused and obviously apprehensive, he turned to me and asked, "Why have you come to my office?"

Emboldened by his uncertainty, I took a seat opposite the desk, beckoning Lena to sit next to me. Volodya stood awkwardly for a moment, then settled in his brown leather executive's chair. I stated my business frankly.

"Listen, we've got to have your permission for Lena to emigrate—today. I'm not leaving without it. Write it out and have your secretary notarize it."

He repeated the familiar objections, and I heard him out to the end. Then, out of his sight across the huge desk, I squeezed Lena's hand and replied, "All right. You don't want Lena to go to America. Will you take her to live with you?"

Volodya had a new family, a wife and daughter. My proposal frightened him; it did not figure in his plans. I could almost read his thoughts as he struggled to find a decent excuse.

"A child has to live with its mother," he pleaded.

"*Exactly*, Volodya. Quite right. That's why we need your permission—so Lena can live with me."

Again he began to ramble. People poked their heads into the office; Volodya asked them to come back later. He talked some more while I remained silent. At last I stood up and said, "Well, I've heard all this before. Now you listen to me. Either you write out the permission immediately or I'll go to your Party Committee."

I had noticed the sign on the adjacent door when we entered the office.

"I'm sure those Communists can settle all this."

Those people would never help me and I had no intention of turning to them, but their mentality is well known in our country: a Communist fears his own Party above all else. Volodya produced a piece of paper from a desk drawer, wrote as I dictated, then summoned his secretary to witness his signature.

As Lena and I were leaving, Volodya's parental instinct resurfaced for a moment. Almost plaintively, he called out to her, "Lena, will you come to visit me?"

"If you invite me, of course I will," she replied.

We left, satisfied.

Documents in hand, we hurried to OVIR and gave them to the clerk. The next day, I went to the school to submit my resignation. Relieved, Anna Markovna accepted it on the spot without insisting on the customary two weeks' notice. For the second time Lena and I said goodbye to friends and disposed of household goods we could not take with us. I bought three large suitcases.

As he waited for OVIR's decision, Woody's initial euphoria gave way to suspicion. He wrote urging caution:

. . . it is quite possible that the OVIR people are playing an even more cruel game with you and Lena, all in an attempt to break your spirit. By getting your hopes up now . . . [and] leading you to believe that things might work out soon, they . . . [may] be preparing to hurl you into the abyss once more. Let us hope that this is not the case. But until I meet you and Lena . . . in Washington or New York, I cannot help but remain anxious . . . and skeptical about OVIR.

Neither Woody nor I said anything to the American press about OVIR's promises. Having failed in August 1974 to embarrass the authorities into reversing their initial refusal, we considered such a tactic even less likely to succeed in March 1975. Our judgment was confirmed by Marshall Shulman, a Columbia University Kremlinologist then in Moscow.

Dignified and soft-spoken, blessed with a gentle smile, Marshall frequently visited IMEMO, where we met in 1971. Woody knew him slightly through academic circles in the United States. Delighted when he came to see me early in 1975 despite my new status as a divided spouse, I readily agreed with him that there was no point in seeking publicity. When he returned to the United States a few days later, Marshall called Woody, whose next letter reported their conversation: "Marshall is even more optimistic than you and I, and that too is a good sign because he is a cautious man. In his view, there is now no question that they will soon let you leave. I just hope he is right, that he has read all the signs correctly."

Woody and I had been separated nearly eight months, and we wanted to believe the ordeal would soon end. His hopes soaring again, Woody wrote in his next letter, " . . . take Aeroflot Flight 243 on Friday . . . to London. You leave Moscow at 0815 and arrive at 0855 London time. In London, you change planes and take PanAm 107, leaving at 1050 London time, arriving Washington 1400 our time. And you can be sure your husband will be there!".

At the end of two weeks I received a postcard from OVIR. My heart stopped when I saw the message: Come to Room 24. They gave nothing but refusals in Room 24.

A middle-level OVIR official, who said his name was Zolotukhin, received me. Sitting next to him, a stony-faced, red-haired man stared intently at me as though making a psychological evaluation. Zolotukhin announced that my request for exit visas for myself and my daughter had been denied.

Outraged, I jumped out of my chair and yelled, "Why did your accursed clerk give me three days to collect all my documents and tell me I'd be leaving in two weeks? I've lost my job!"

Zolotukhin's face remained expressionless as he intoned, "You must have imagined this."

I lost control.

"What are you doing?" I shouted. "Are you all crooks?! Ruining people's lives . . . you know everyone's calling me 'American woman'! They make the children write 'Yankee Go Home!' on my daughter's book bag and threaten to beat her! I'll never let her go back to that school! Why do you keep us here? Let us go!"

"What are you saying?" the anonymous one demanded. "Have you lost your mind?"

He fumbled with something under the table, and suddenly I was on my guard—maybe he had pressed a button, and a police car was on the way to take me to a psychiatric hospital? My natural defense was an attack.

"And you, Comrade Anonymous, why do you interfere in this conversation? First you'd better identify yourself! I have the right to know with whom I'm speaking."

An unexpected attack startles anyone, especially Soviet officials who base their power on the cowering, sheeplike behavior of the people they rule. If one stands up to them, they are at least momentarily confused. The anonymous one leaned back in his chair and relaxed his shoulders slightly. I continued my tirade.

"There's some question as to who is out of his mind," I said. "The school principal has poisoned the children with her campaign against my daughter. What kind of values are you instilling in the younger generation?"

I turned and left. The people in the waiting room, evidently having heard the loud exchange in Room 24, gaped at me in astonishment.

The game had been carefully planned. Deceived again, this time I had been tricked into quitting my job.

I decided to keep Lena home. Even though there were only two months until summer vacation, anything might happen. We agreed that, if we were not allowed to leave the country by September, she would resume her high school studies at an evening school. A day or two later, Anna Markovna called and begged me to let Lena return. When I objected that the school had become dangerous for my daughter, she declared that she would personally be responsible for Lena. I remained adamant.

After my outburst at OVIR, Anna Markovna had evidently been warned that she had gone too far in her campaign against Lena. She telephoned repeatedly over the next few days and urged me to reconsider. Finally Lena said, "Mama, come on—let me go back. Anna Markovna is so scared now she'll probably want to carry me around in her arms!"

The principal kept her word. Two months later, Lena passed her exams, not with high marks, but that did not disturb us. We were simply relieved the nightmare had ended. We prayed we would no longer be in Moscow for her final year of school.

Woody's 118th letter since he left Moscow reached me in the middle of April:

... I was too shocked—though I should not have been—to write yesterday. It was the shock of anger and disgust and dismay at the barbaric treatment accorded you and Lena....

... As soon as we hung up ... I was on the telephone to Washington ... my phone and typewriter are smoking. I gather that the State Department and our Moscow Embassy are stunned and surprised by the OVIR game. Several officials to whom I spoke voiced ... shall we say, strong opinions.

Darling, never doubt that I shall fight with every ounce of strength. I shall keep after the American officials, take the matter to the press, go anywhere and do anything that might conceivably bring this to an end. I'll never rest until we are together.

13
Lena in Pain

LAVA-LIKE, a destructive force swept down on us. We were isolated and rejected, and Lena became a victim.

The illness appeared in June 1975, near the end of that terrible school year. Lena was sixteen and a frail child anyway. Now, with the tension in our lives and her apprehension about her final examinations, she fell ill. She complained of stomach pains, slept fitfully, became sluggish, apathetic, ill-tempered. After a superficial examination, an overworked physician at our neighborhood polyclinic cocked his head to one side, peered over hornrimmed spectacles, and rendered his diagnosis: "Young lady, I can't find anything wrong. Perhaps you just imagine pain before your period—or maybe don't like taking exams?"

The pain persisted.

A major attack struck that fall. This time, after giving Lena a thorough physical and analyzing the results of various laboratory tests, a different doctor, a woman, discovered the perforated ulcer.

My own experience with doctors had made me skeptical of the medical profession. But Lena, perpetually exhausted and losing weight, needed treatment. Home remedies—herbal infusions and bland diets—did not help. We went to a woman, a Jewish refusenik who practiced "Chinese medicine," a kind of "laying on of hands" except that the hands never actually touch the sufferer. This likewise proved worthless.

One day Lena said, "Mama, please take me to the hospital. I can't stand the pain any longer."

It was not only the pain. Exhausted and subconsciously resentful, Lena needed to escape. Beset by guilt, I checked her into a

University of Virginia photo

September 1975, after a year of separation.

hospital with a good reputation. They placed her in a twenty-five-bed female ward, a huge room atop a two-story building known to patients as "Kazan Station" after Moscow's largest railway terminal. Sounds reverberated off high ceilings that were stained, like the walls, with dark streaks of ancient water damage. The original green-gray paint had almost disappeared under a film of dust and time. Spaced a couple of meters apart, metal beds with sagging horsehair mattresses stood perpendicular to the walls. Repeated washings had turned the bed linen—always in short supply in our hospitals—to a dingy gray; it was hard to imagine the sheets had ever been white. Sad-eyed, pale-faced women of all ages sat on the beds, clad in shapeless, sand-colored flannel gowns. They looked like prisoners. Some of them, evidently veterans on the ward, greeted us warmly.

In the middle of the room were two large tables covered in green plastic, the kind found in cheap cafeterias. We had arrived at dinnertime. Perspiring profusely, a hefty woman from the kitchen staff appeared, dressed in a stained blue smock and knee-length gray hose full of runs. She rolled a heavily laden metal cart into the ward and, reaching underneath, flung thick white plates on the tables as though dealing cards. She dipped a huge wooden spoon into a steaming kettle and heaped the plates with sticky mounds of stew, calling out good-naturedly, "*Devchata* [Lassies]—Come and get it while it's hot!"

There were not many takers. Most patients rejected the stuff from the kitchen in favor of food brought in by relatives or friends. Patients called the hospital's "dietetic cutlets," rubbery disks of meat well mixed with cereal, "hockey pucks." These almost always went back to the kitchen. When some years later I got a dog and a cat, Lena would collect these hockey pucks as a treat for them. Kasha, or buckwheat groats, the dietetic staple of Soviet hospitals, was so claylike and beige-gray in color it was impossible to determine what grain it was made from. The greasy mass slid around on a plate like a slick pancake; patients dismissed it as "Spackle."

In one corner of the ward stood a huge refrigerator where

patients kept food packets wrapped in cellophane and marked with their names. Most ulcer sufferers were hospitalized for a month or more at a time and naturally became friends. At mealtime, gathering in small groups in various corners of "Kazan Station," they had little gourmet parties, sharing parcels from home. Each meal ended with tea, also brought from outside; no one could drink the "urine"—as they called it—made from the hospital's cheap tea leaves.

The absence of decent hospital food does little to cure the ailing patient. A much worse problem, however, is the lack of medicines. For a long time I kept the news of Lena's illness from Woody, but then one of her doctors, who knew our story, advised me to ask my husband to send us certain drugs not available in the Soviet Union. In November of 1976 Woody wrote:

The news that Lena has an ulcer is extremely disturbing. She probably got it at least in part because of our troubles. . . . God knows she has seen her mother through some terrible times.

The "Dicavdosil" you asked for is called "Camalox" in this country. I didn't need a doctor's prescription, and had a local apteka [pharmacy] send 400 tablets. That should last several months, enough time to determine whether it's effective. Now we wait to see whether Soviet customs inspectors will pass it . . . after the way you have been treated I won't be surprised at anything.

The pharmacy sent the medicine air mail. Five months later, in May 1977, the undelivered package came back to Charlottesville, Virginia. Soviet customs had opened it, removed a few tablets, resealed it, and marked it with the notation IMPORTATION INTO THE USSR FORBIDDEN.

Lena spent time in several hospitals during the years of her illness. The doctors treated her with drugs of dubious value and a special diet, made sure she rested, and gave her what passed for psychological counseling. All in vain. Twice a year, in spring and autumn, she spent four or five weeks in the hospital. I scoured Moscow for decent food, assuaging my guilt in the hated queues. I made chicken soup; boiled beef and vegetables; made cranberry custard and Lena's favorite "zephyr" cookies with marmalade. None of the ingredients was remarkable, but the inadequacy of Moscow's food supply system meant I could never count on finding what I needed.

Sometimes Lena came home feeling better. The pain was less. She gained a kilogram or two, and her mood improved. Back in our communal apartment, however, her condition inevitably deteriorated. Regularly as clockwork, she returned to her hospital bed.

We learned that Soviet medicine considers ulcers virtually incurable. Aware that emotional stress can cause them, physicians counsel victims to reduce the tension in their lives and urge them to develop "more positive emotions." An easy prescription to write but so difficult to fill.

When Lena was well, I tried to keep her happy, to maintain her "positive emotions." I took her to play tennis, a sport we both loved and which let us relax together. When she decided to take up the expensive sport of skiing, I somehow managed to buy second-hand equipment. Woody sent her a fashionable sky blue ski jacket, and she went to the mountains.

Together we attended plays, concerts, and exhibitions, and I gave her books to read. My goal was to help her mature intellectually so she could come to understand the world around her and our country—and in part, perhaps, our situation.

Finding the right balance in our relations proved difficult; Woody and I both tried to make her happy despite the circumstances. He sent her fashionable Western clothes through friends who visited the Soviet Union. She enjoyed dressing differently from her peers, whom she entertained with tales of our unique family situation. All this made her somewhat mysterious to her friends and lent her a special identity.

At the same time, Lena fought for emotional independence. She wanted to be rid of my problems and influence, to get out from under my shadow. The more she attempted to break free, the harder I clung to her. A sword of Damocles hung over us;

those who held it made no distinction between parent and child. To leave her behind, should I ever receive that precious exit visa, was unthinkable.

Though he knew relatively little of our precarious existence, Woody instinctively shared my concern. In January 1976 he wrote, "I fear the KGB might decide to release you but keep Lena there to ensure your silence when you are free. I'm sure you think of this nightmare often . . . you *must* bring Lena with you."

As my situation vis-à-vis the Soviet authorities steadily worsened, Lena's patience with the struggle grew thin. Feeling trapped, she naturally wanted a life of her own.

A boyfriend appeared: Misha was a pleasant young student at an aeronautics institute. Not a bad singer and guitarist, he was several years older than Lena, obviously more experienced, the center of attention in the circle of friends where she met him. Flattered by his courtship, Lena became more self-confident.

Long straight hair carefully combed and brushed a thousand strokes; high exposed forehead creating an aura of attraction and openness mixed with childish innocence; slightly slanted dark brown eyes and high cheekbones on a faintly oriental face, legacy of our Tatar ancestors—thin, svelte, and elegant, armed with high expectations, Lena went forward to meet life.

The expectations involved Misha, now her alpha and omega. She quoted him constantly, pronounced him right in everything. There was little that Misha did not know. Lena was in love. Seeing marriage as the only way to escape and create her own life, she made plans—but without consulting Misha.

This was in the spring of 1977, shortly before we were to make another request to leave the country. Two months before her birthday in May, OVIR directed Lena to submit a separate application: after reaching eighteen she could not go to the United States as a dependent child. Woody sent the necessary formal invitation, but Lena refused to file the papers. As soon as her Misha graduated from the institute, she informed me, they would go to Leningrad to live.

It seemed I would lose my daughter. Even as a student Misha

had a security clearance, and he would certainly have one after graduation. He would be forbidden to associate with foreigners.

Misha of course knew of our family situation; I urged Lena to have a serious talk with him. If he were to marry her, he would have to inform his state employer that his wife's stepfather was an American. That would close many doors in the Soviet Union, certainly those connected with aviation.

A few days later Lena came home in tears. Misha would go to Leningrad without her.

One reflexively shares a child's pain, but that makes it no easier for the child to bear. I felt deeply sorry for Lena: she had again suffered because of me. Gently, I pointed out that Misha's career was obviously more important to him than his love. She was not ready to hear that.

Trying to deal with her difficulties, Lena spent hours with her girlfriends and held incessant whispered telephone conversations, all the while barely speaking to me. Not wanting to make things worse, I kept out of the way. She saw Misha only rarely; the affair seemed to be coming to an end.

After a couple of weeks I had to raise the matter of the documents for OVIR.

"I'm tired," Lena replied sharply to my question. "This has gone on for nearly three years. I can't go on."

Friends invited her to dinner and tried to persuade her to submit the documents.

"What would I do in America?" Lena retorted. "Let Mama go to her husband—I'm staying here."

I pleaded with her, cried, told her I could not leave her alone. We both knew she would be lost. The talks led nowhere.

A solution materialized from an ominous quarter. On a warm April day Lena went to see a girlfriend. When she returned after several hours, she reached into her bag, an open duck one she had sewn herself for the beach, withdrew a piece of paper, and with a puzzled expression silently passed it to me. The paper bore the emblem of the Hotel Bucarest, a second-class establishment just across the Moscow River from St. Basil's Cathedral and Red

Square. It served foreign tourists; that meant the KGB served *it.*

In an over-precise hand, someone had written: "Lenochka, Call me at work. I need to talk to you." The signature, also carefully penned, was Vladimir Vsevolodovich Shchukin. We knew no such person.

When Lena had left our courtyard that morning, a well-dressed man in his mid-forties began to follow her. He jumped aboard the trolleybus after her, pushed his way near, bustled about in an obvious way trying to catch her eye. Several times he attempted to speak to her, but Lena turned away. I had repeatedly warned her that any stranger might be a KGB agent.

"Obviously he threw the note in my bag," Lena said. "What can he want?"

I paced the apartment. After a couple of bottles of beer to subdue my fury, I decided to call—pretending to be Lena.

"Hello, Vladimir Vsevolodovich. This is Lena."

The trick was to try to sound like a naive eighteen-year-old girl.

"Lenochka! I'm glad you called. I really want to see you. Come to the hotel and just ask at the desk . . . I'm in Room 1. Everyone knows me."

"And then?" asked the innocent "Lena."

"We'll have a talk . . . " He let his voice trail off into a suggestive silence.

"But about what?"

"Well, you're ill . . . I can get medicines for you, the very best! Relations with your mother are probably tense . . . I can help there too."

This man knew a great deal. Here was the KGB at its worst, going after a mother through her child . . .

"But why are you so concerned about me?" I tried not to show sarcasm, to keep my voice young and beguiling.

He kept trying to convince "Lena" to come to the hotel, and at last I said, "All right. I'll talk to my mother and call you back."

"No, no!" he exclaimed hurriedly. "You must *not* say anything to your mother. Let this be between us!"

I had heard enough. Speaking in my normal voice, I said as venomously as I could, "You see, dear Vladimir Vsevolodovich, my mother and I don't have any secrets. And if she can't get medicine her husband will send it from America. Good luck to you!"

I slammed down the receiver. Stunned, Lena gaped at me, suddenly aware that the KGB would never leave us in peace.

My first impulse was to march on the Hotel Bucarest and tear Room 1 to pieces. I called several friends and gave full vent to my feelings about the swinish Comrade Shchukin for the benefit of the KGB tap. My friends begged me to let the incident die.

This brought Lena and me closer. A few days later she submitted her papers to OVIR. Needing my protection and support, she would remain with me.

The Shchukin episode outraged Woody:

The horror of it all . . . more KGB torment. As soon as we finished our telephone conversation I wrote three of the Moscow correspondents who have followed your case actively. They cannot give you any direct protection, but at least they'll know what's going on.

Needless to say, you won't want to let Lena go out alone at night. The tradition of Comrade Beria lives on at the KGB, and no one is safe.

I wrote still another letter to General Secretary Brezhnev, asking him to put a stop to the KGB harassment and let Lena and me go to my husband. Woody turned to the United States Senate. Senators Birch Bayh, Hubert Humphrey, and Claiborne Pell drew up a letter to Brezhnev and within a couple of days persuaded thirty-four other senators to sign it. As Woody wrote to me, the senators "asked Brezhnev to release you and Lena and mentioned the fact that you have been harassed. . . . [It] was hand-carried to the Soviet embassy in Washington late in the afternoon on May 4 . . . our third anniversary."

In 1977, as in 1975 and 1976, Woody and I celebrated our anniversary on the telephone, the main topic of conversation OVIR's "present": another refusal. As always, he told me he loved me deeply. But after nearly three nerve-racking years during which our moods and hopes swung violently up and down, he was beginning to sound less optimistic. Woody was tired. In his closed university town no one understood the nature of his fight to get his wife out of Moscow: "Everyone is sympathetic, of course, but no one knows anything about the Soviet Union. It's like a Chinese puzzle: people get bored with things they can't solve quickly."

This telephonic anniversary did not bring even the brief happiness that always clothed my talks with Woody. His tired, disappointed voice betrayed his sense of helplessness. The feeling of being protected by his love waned. For a long time after we hung up I sat numbly . . . three years of separation . . .

Russians say, "Trouble has come . . . so open the gates." As if the gates to my life were always open, one worry tumbled behind another.

Of my old friends, only Zoya and Maria stood fast. Zoya and I went back fifteen years. A farm girl who had graduated from a top institute and now worked in a secret laboratory, she almost came apart under the stress of my fight with Soviet power. She did not want to break off our friendship but feared being called to account for it.

Through Zoya, I met her colleague Maria. Also an intelligent, highly educated woman, Maria's blue, slightly crossed eyes and thick glasses accented her reserved manner. We took to each other instantly and began spending a great deal of time together; the friendship soon crowded out any fear on her part. Lena and I frequently visited her and her family—she had a husband and a small son—and they came to see us on Chernyshevsky Street.

Toward the end of the summer of 1977, the KGB interrogated Zoya and Maria.

They came to the laboratory for Zoya, summoning her unexpectedly to Room No. 1—the security office. She knew instantly that it had to do with me. The two zealous young KGB agents started out cordially enough.

"We want to talk to you about your friend Irina McClellan," one of them said. "How is she getting along?"

Zoya instinctively defended herself.

"Why don't you ask *her?* I don't see her very often."

"But what happened?" the second one asked, feigning astonishment. "You've been friends for *such* a long time!"

They used the standard KGB tactic of indicating they knew *everything*. Frightened people often believe them.

"That's our business," Zoya said coolly, trying to conceal her turmoil.

"Do you think her marriage to the American is a real one—or is she just trying to get out of the country?"

"So far as I know they're very much in love. But again—ask *her*. She can speak for herself."

"Did you meet any foreigners when you went to her apartment?"

They were trying to get their hooks into Zoya. Like Maria, she had signed a pledge to have no contact with foreigners as a condition of employment.

"As you say, Irina and I have been friends for a long time. She would never do anything to harm me and doesn't invite me when she has foreign guests. Now, is there anything else? I have work to do."

"Why are you so nervous? We've enjoyed talking to you . . . we'll be back!"

The smile on the young agent's face only magnified the threat. Zoya stood up to go.

"I haven't enjoyed the conversation at all. Please do not come here again. I will not tell you anything about my friend."

Returning to her office, Zoya beckoned to Maria to follow her to the women's room. Once there she broke down in hysterical sobs. Maria turned on the sink faucet full force to conceal the sound and tried to calm her.

Zoya's instincts had served her well: determined to protect both of us, she had refused to answer questions about me. But she became a nervous wreck, her sleep ruined by a recurrent nightmare in which the KGB came to arrest her. Not long after the encounter, she broke off all contact with me. Through Maria, I begged Zoya to see me one last time. She declined.

A few weeks later the same men returned to the laboratory to question Maria. She too refused to tell them anything and suggested they go to the source. But the agents had a new question. "What kind of literature does Irina Igorevna read? Does she lend you books?"

This did not come out of the blue. In my apartment were several dozen *samizdat* and *tamizdat*—published abroad and smuggled into Russia—materials from various friends, including an American colleague of Woody's then in Moscow: Solzhenitsyn's works; Nadezhda Mandelstam's memoirs, a favorite in my circle; books on the KGB; Svetlana Alliluyeva's reminiscences; Roy Medvedev's *Let History Judge;* Gulag literature; poetry by Joseph Brodsky.

Always worried lest the KGB pound on my door with a search warrant, I naively hid the most sensitive works under my mattress. I shared books with friends. We devoured them hungrily and invented transparent codes for telephone conversations: "Come to see me, I've got a new blouse to show you," or, "I found some lace and got some for you too. Come over and I'll give it to you." The KGB must quickly have grown suspicious about the number of blouses and pieces of lace we were buying. From time to time we changed our "codes."

This literature became the intellectual sustenance of my life in Limbo. Through it I learned about the country where I had lived for thirty-eight years in almost complete ignorance. The books helped me understand the Soviet system and to a certain extent eased the fear of the unknown; they also liberated me from the system, which had offered nothing to believe in and for its own reasons had made me an outcast simply for falling in love with a foreigner.

Frightened by the interrogation, Maria decided she must get the books out of my apartment; she and her husband came without warning that same evening. They walked the last few blocks on opposite sides of the street, looking constantly over their shoulders to be sure they were not followed. Maria scribbled a note telling me about the KGB visit.

Silently, we packed the books in two large bags. Astounded and deeply moved by my friends' determination to help me, I wrote on a piece of paper, "Where will you hide them?" Maria wrote back, "On our balcony."

What a place to hide books from the KGB! On top of all my fears came a new one: What would become of my friends?

The crisis now embraced my daughter, my husband, and my friends, and it was aggravated by the tension with my mother. When I needed someone older and wiser who knew everything about my life and loved me—and Woody—without reservation, I fled to Anastasiya Nikolayevna, whose love and concern enveloped me in a warm embrace. She was my refuge.

My mother and I now saw each other only on the state holidays she celebrated so diligently: the anniversary of the Bolshevik Revolution on November 7; May 1, International Labor Day; Soviet Army Day on February 22; March 8, International Women's Day; the anniversary of our victory in World War II on May 9; and New Year's Eve.

Holiday dinners never varied. On a beautifully washed and ironed cream linen tablecloth stood a bottle of champagne and one of vodka and a holiday food package from special stores, my stepfather's due as a war veteran.

Usually there were just the four of us, my mother and stepfather, Lena, and me. In high spirits, Mama shuttled between the kitchen and the main room with plate after plate of salads and *zakuski*, delighted to show off the abundance and to spoil her husband and her "girls."

The toasts began, offered with great solemnity by my stepfather. The first depended on the occasion: to the Revolution, to the victory over Germany. Then came liquid homage to the Communist Party, our leaders, world peace. When my stepfather appeared to run out of ideas, my mother would urge him to think of another cause, another hero, worthy of recognition.

To honor them on their holidays, I always drank a toast to parents, with all my heart wishing them health and happiness.

And in their own way they *were* happy; they simply closed their eyes and souls to the lie they lived. Life was easier that way. Lena and I hid our pain and smiled.

When the toasts ended and we had eaten our fill, we would get ready to leave. Further conversation might bring up a sensitive topic, and that was always forbidden, not only on holidays. But it would have been impolite to depart so quickly; my mother proposed a game of Lotto. We cleared the table and Mama got out the cards. She usually won, happily raking in the coins—five kopecks a game.

At last we could make our exit. Pressing carefully packaged leftovers on us, my mother would say, "Don't forget to kiss Papa!" as we put on our coats. On the street, Lena expressed her adolescent indignation: "Mama, I can't stand this comedy!"

My answer to this was that she was my mother. I did not choose her, nor could I remake her. My devout grandmother had raised me to respect her not in the sense of approval but rather of acceptance. And something else was very important to me: I wanted to maintain the family ties that preserve a sense of connection between one generation and the next.

My stepfather knew nothing of Woody. The longer I stayed in Moscow, the more he worried about my supposed teaching job at our embassy in Washington. On a day in the spring of 1977 I found him alone in their apartment; my mother had stayed longer than usual at a Party meeting. He insisted I tell him why they were not letting me go to America. Taken aback, I dropped my gaze and stammered something, trying to think of an answer.

"I know," he said sorrowfully. "It's because of me."

"What do you mean, Papa?"

He shook his head and stared out the window for a long time, then said, "It's because I was taken prisoner. They'll never forgive that."

I gazed at his kind, troubled face. What a remarkable country we lived in! More than thirty years after the end of the war, a man who had fought heroically was still made to carry a deep sense of guilt for having been captured by the Germans, as though he had

had a choice, as though he had not tried to escape three times.

"What are you talking about, Papa? They rehabilitated you ages ago! And besides, the application form doesn't ask about stepparents."

I went on talking for a while, but he remained upset. Something else was bothering him, something he could not speak of. Unsure where to steer the conversation, I fell silent. After several moments my stepfather unburdened himself.

"People from the KGB come regularly to see your mother . . . they take her into the street and talk quite some time. She never explains anything to me."

"How do you know they're from the KGB?"

"I found out recently, by chance. A couple of young guys came when she wasn't home and asked, 'Where's Elizaveta Ivanovna?' I got angry: 'What are you up to, bothering my wife all the time? Have you no shame?' They showed me their identification—KGB agents. Then they tried to calm me down. 'Don't worry, everything is all right . . . we're just here on business to see our former co-worker.'"

He paused for a moment and gazed into space. My mother was now merely the director of a neighborhood lending library; she had been there when the men came.

"They took the address of the library and left. Your mother did not come home until late that evening, and when she did she refused to answer my questions. The only thing she would say was, 'It's business.' But what kind of business can it be? She retired several years ago!"

His question hung in the air. Who was to tell him that the KGB never frees anyone from its service?

I could not speak freely with my stepfather, could not point out the obvious. For all the pain his Party had inflicted on him, he remained a dedicated Communist. If he knew the truth, he would condemn *me*. But that, ultimately, was his problem. Mine was how to get out of a country run by the KGB.

Run! I told myself, run away quickly, let them all live as they wish and not suffer because of me . . .

14

In the Same Boat

TO RUN AWAY was not so simple. A snippet of refusenik gallows humor had it right: Soviet power loves you so much it cannot bear to let you go. Woody understood. In the summer of 1977 he wrote, "People often ask why you don't simply go to Helsinki or Vienna and then come here. It's almost impossible to convince them that foreign travel is an extremely rare privilege . . . they just do not understand."

In October 1977 the signatories to the Helsinki Accords met in Belgrade to review the record. Two years earlier, the European powers plus the United States and Canada had signed a sweeping three-part agreement. The first pledged them to recognize each other as equals, refrain from violence, and respect each other's territorial integrity; this constituted the long-delayed treaty ending World War II. The second part involved trade, scientific and cultural exchanges, cooperation on environmental issues, and tourism. The third in effect called on all nations that had signed the Universal Declaration of Human Rights and the United Nations Charter to honor those commitments. The right of all people to leave any country, including their own, was specifically mentioned. And the Helsinki signatories pledged to work for the speedy reunification of divided families.

The Soviet Union had almost totally ignored its own promises concerning human rights. As the Belgrade review meeting approached, however, on a sudden impulse I retrieved the issue of *Pravda* that had published them, cut out the section on "Reunification of Divided Families," marched down the street to OVIR, and thrust the clipping and a petition on the desk of the *nachalnik*, the boss in Room 24.

My petition read:

On the basis of the Helsinki Pact, signed by the heads of the European states, the United States, and Canada, and by Comrade Brezhnev,
General Secretary of the Communist Party of the Soviet Union, I request to be permitted to go to my husband in the United States.

Glancing quickly at the heading of the clipping, the *nachalnik*
declared, "This document does not concern you in the slightest.
Your departure would be contrary to the interests of the state."

"But how can that be? Where's the connection?"

Either he did not know or was not authorized to discuss the
subject. In any event he refused to answer. The audience ended
abruptly.

Mulling over my limited options, I recalled an article I had
read in *Pravda:* after more than thirty years, the Soviet Red Cross
was continuing to track down and bring together families separated during World War II. Joyous reunions regularly took place.

A fashionably dressed Red Cross official ensconced in a well-
appointed office in downtown Moscow read my request. I compli-
mented the organization for its excellent record in finding
families separated by war, and asked it to reunite me with my
husband, U.S. citizen Woodford McClellan, last known address
Charlottesville, Virginia. Through no fault of our own we had
been forcibly separated more than three years.

The cordiality disappeared. Lips taut, the man shoved the
piece of paper back at me.

"We don't deal with such problems—our charter is quite specific. Go to OVIR."

"So," I said, "you're not interested in family members who
lose track of each other in peacetime. My husband and I don't
want *war.* Just to live together."

"There is no way I can help you."

End of interview.

Another article in the Communist Party newspaper spurred
me into further action: the Soviet Women's Committee was helping the women of Angola and Chile in their struggle for emanci-
pation, and so on. I decided to pay the Committee a visit. Again

that hallmark of Soviet agencies that deal with foreigners, a chic office. A female functionary's politely indifferent smile vanished as she read my petition:

In despair I turn to your Committee as a woman who is neither Chilean nor Angolan but Soviet, your compatriot. I have not seen my husband in three years. Please help reunite us.

She turned on me coldly. No doubt the Committee's charter did not call for civility toward fellow citizens.

"We only assist women from underdeveloped countries."

"Is our country so powerfully developed, when cases like mine exist?"

The question hung in the air unanswered. The woman shuffled papers on her desk, shot a frosty look at me, and said in that hostile bureaucratic voice, "Don't interfere with my work. Leave this office."

My attempts to negotiate with Soviet authorities on the basis of articles in *Pravda* came to nothing. On the street again, I vowed to go on, seek another door.

One Saturday in November 1977 the Jewish refuseniks and I found each other. By now I was well known among this newly created "nationality" in the Soviet family of nations; the "McClellan case" had been aired on the Voice of America and the BBC. Many had seen me respond when my name blared over the intercom at OVIR and approached with expressions of sympathy. Naturally they had problems unique to them as Jews, but the authorities drew no distinction between people denied visas to emigrate—stripped us of our jobs, tapped our phones, kept many under surveillance, frightened friends and even relatives away. In ancient Russia people like us were called *izgoi,* those cast out.

In the 1970s, at the maize-colored Arkhipov Street synagogue, both devout Jews and Jews seeking to emigrate—together a small fraction of Moscow's several hundred thousand—gathered on Saturday afternoons. The synagogue is located in the center of Moscow, a five-minute walk from the Kremlin, three from KGB headquarters on Dzerzhinsky Square. Around 4:00 P.M. the area seethed with a vibrant life unsanctioned by the authorities. Where Jews gather in the Soviet Union there is danger. Today I was the only Russian in a large crowd.

In the innermost circle were middle-aged and elderly Jews dressed in old-fashioned but expensive clothes, believers who regularly came to worship, sustain the faith, carry on the traditions of their forefathers. After services they gathered on the sidewalk in front of the synagogue to discuss worldly matters and arrange marriages between their children and grandchildren. No matter what the obstacles, these Jews were determined to maintain their Jewish identity.

Across the street from the synagogue milled the middle circle—Jewish refuseniks. Generally much younger and certainly far more numerous than the believers, they were from other cities as well as Moscow, people seeking release to Israel or another country. Bearded, dark-haired men with piercing black eyes, lively women, all of them agitated. Most knew each other, and when a stranger appeared in their midst he or she was quickly introduced. They discussed the latest news and gossip about exit permission—who got it, who did not, what the authorities said; which Soviet officials or agencies to visit in connection with visa applications; international developments, especially Soviet-American relations; which conferences where foreign specialists would be present—and might be approached for assistance. Like me, they had all been turned down many times when they applied to leave the country. Now they stuck together in their own *aliya,* their unofficial Jewish-refusenik community.

On the fringes stood little groups of KGB agents. We knew their faces well—blank, wholly unremarkable faces, with dull, dangerous eyes. The men usually wore brown nylon jackets. Each held a rolled-up newspaper in his left hand as a kind of badge—and a weapon, if it came to that. The KGB never tried to conceal its identity.

The *KGBeshniki* watched and rarely interfered. But sometimes, when a high-ranking Western (especially American) visitor or delegation was in Moscow, they would become aggressive and try to provoke fights, looking for an excuse to make arrests and pull potential troublemakers off the street. If this tactic failed, they would simply round up individuals considered "ringleaders" and keep them in jail until the visitors departed.

Western diplomats and tourists did not play a specific role in the Saturday afternoon street theater; they came as interested observers. Often the tourists brought greetings, news, gifts from relatives. Most importantly, they brought hope, and the assurance that the fight for the right to emigrate had wide and growing support beyond Soviet frontiers.

A new friend, a Jewish woman named Irene, had invited me to the synagogue. We met at OVIR; hearing my name over the intercom, she introduced herself when I emerged, dejected as usual, from Room 24.

Irene and I were almost exactly the same age. Thin and a bit above average height, the curly-haired woman was indomitably energetic. During that first encounter we walked around Moscow for several hours, relating our stories to each other. Aware of my isolation, she appointed herself my guardian.

"Come to the synagogue Saturday," she urged. "At least you won't be alone."

And so in our anti-Semitic country, the Jewish refuseniks, themselves *izgoi*, began to help me. The better I got to know them, the more their ability to survive impressed me. In their tiny *aliya* they jostled and bumped each other on occasion in the struggle for influence and authority, formed groups and cliques like people anywhere. But when it came to helping and supporting each other, they displayed an astonishing unity. They organized scientific seminars for people kicked out of their institutes and laboratories; found jobs as elevator boys or night watchmen—anything to survive—for physicists and mathematicians; established an unofficial medical network; and helped people trace relatives in Israel who could send family reunification invitations. They arranged Hebrew lessons for children and adults, helped each other with visa applications.

Irene put out the word that I needed paying students. Almost overnight I became a teacher of English in the Jewish refusenik community. The students were a teacher's delight: goals clearly in mind, they applied themselves diligently. I taught them English, adults and children alike, sometimes entire families.

Although not Jewish, I began to feel myself part of this collective. These new friends frequently came to my kommunalka for coffee after congregating at the synagogue, stopping on the way to buy rolls or bread and sausage. Sometimes they invited me to their own apartments to share family dinners. When an influential Western visitor—a congressman or senator or businessman—appeared at the synagogue, friends would introduce me, relate my story, and insist that I ask for help. "Speak up! Don't be silent," they would prompt. We would ask the visitor to call Woody and to intercede on our behalf in the United States. When I objected that these people had come to help Soviet Jews, I was invariably overruled. My friends insisted on pushing my case to the forefront.

All of my new friends were relatively young, and we had not lost interest in life beyond our struggle. Between our periodic campaigns we played tennis, went to the public baths and saunas, hiked, skiied cross-country in winter, and picnicked. One summer day Irene asked me to go with her to the village of Gzhel, known for a small ceramics factory where inexpensive, attractive china is produced.

Gzhel is an hour east of Moscow on the elektrichka, but light years away in spirit. Irene and I strolled along the one dusty, quiet street, admiring the small, brightly painted wooden houses with intricately fretted eaves and scalloped gables, some Slavic, others Finnish, no two alike. The gables were frequently crowned by a carved Scythian horse or stag. In the private plot behind each home, villagers raised vegetables and kept chickens, rabbits, sometimes a pig. In front, ramshackle picket fences, beds of flowers, and blossoming apple and pear trees greeted visitors from Moscow with the color and warmth we ached for after the long winter.

Little shops scattered around the factory sold Gzhel's china. Even then each shop offered very few pieces for sale. A few years later the suddenly fashionable Gzhelware would be sold only in "Beriozka" hard-currency shops for foreigners.

Irene and I had brought along bags of everyday items scarce in the village, and during the morning we visited the shops to meet the saleswomen. Having taken each other's measure, we joined in a typical Soviet barter after lunch. We produced sausage, soap, and other ordinary things; the shopkeepers reached under the counter for the best pieces of Gzhel.

We returned to Moscow that evening laden with boxes. I put the Gzhel on my shelves, rearranged the pieces many times, drank in their Russian beauty. Deep in my mind, everything I did led to Woody: this collection would be my dowry.

The 1970s witnessed a burst of activism in our country, especially in Moscow. Andrei Sakharov and Valeri Chalidze led the struggle for human rights; Yuri Orlov and others founded the Helsinki Watch Group to monitor Soviet compliance; Aleksandr Ginzburg managed the fund established by Aleksandr Solzhenitsyn—expelled from the USSR in 1974—to aid political prisoners; Anatoli Shcharansky and others spearheaded the fight of Soviet Jews for the right to emigrate; various religious groups demanded the state let them worship without interference. Masses of people directed petitions to the authorities and confronted them in their offices, held innumerable meetings to discuss strategy, aired grievances and hopes to foreign correspondents and diplomats.

Jewish emigration rose steadily. Thousands received visas, sold belongings, bade farewell to family and friends, and left to begin a new life. But most of the lucky ones were poor Soviet Jews from the Caucasus and Central Asia. The number of refuseniks, many in the scientific and technological intelligentsia, increased faster than those allowed to leave. Room 24 at OVIR worked overtime issuing denials.

In the beginning the authorities responded patiently. They usually accepted the Jewish petitions and even admitted group representatives into their offices, talked to them, sometimes made vague promises. Irene and other friends convinced me to accompany them on these marches even though I did not figure in their petitions.

"Come anyway," Irene urged. "Leave your own petition at each office and demand to see someone. If they turn you down tell them, 'Here you're receiving Jews, and you reject a Russian woman?' "

We paraded through the streets of Moscow under a banner that blared: LET US GO TO ISRAEL! Passers-by reacted as one would expect; unauthorized demonstrations and marches had not been seen in our country for half a century. People gawked in fear or anger; some jumped skittishly aside. A few yelled out, "Look at the blasted yids!" Hateful anti-Semitic remarks followed on all sides: "What's the matter with them—they don't like it here?" "They want to go to Israel? Let them get out and leave us in peace!"

After these demonstrations, we frequently came back to my apartment, less than ten minutes on foot from the Party Central Committee on Old Square. There we drank tea and discussed the next step. The reaction of my neighbors matched that of the crowds on the street. Voronov would look on angrily as these Jewish women barged noisily through the hall into my room. His malevolent expression made me think of the *pogromshchiki*, those who organized anti-Jewish riots (pogroms) in czarist times.

Once Voronov's frenzy got the better of him.

"You Yid!" he yelled. "You've kikefied yourself! All you do is hang around with Yids! I wouldn't even *shit* next to you!"

In fact, Voronov's mother was a Jewess, albeit Russified and wholly assimilated. Such assimilation is common in the Soviet Union, where all religions are restricted. Nevertheless, according to Judaic law, my neighbor, like his mother, was a Jew.

Controlling my anger, I reminded Voronov of his heritage. He dropped the subject forever.

Aware of my mother's anti-Semitism, I had not mentioned my Jewish friends to her. When she learned about them—it was easy to guess from whom—rage overpowered her. She soon found an occasion to express it.

There seemed no reason to celebrate my thirty-ninth birthday
in September 1977; Maria and I decided that she would just stop
by for a drink. But then Irene called and said, "Get ready—we're
coming over this evening." Around six o'clock quite a little crowd
appeared: Irene and her husband, Maria, Anastasiya Nikolayevna,
Alex and Rosa Ioffe, Lena Dubyanskaya, Rima Yakir and her
husband, and several others. The guests had brought bottles and
presents, and the toasts began: to me, to happiness, to my reunion
with Woody. As always, the conversation turned to familiar
themes—how to accelerate our struggle to leave the country.

Then the doorbell rang: it was my mother. For years she had
made it her habit to come the day *after* my birthday for a quiet
dinner with Lena and me. She never liked to visit when we had
friends. Something special had brought her that evening. Silently
laying claim to a place of honor, she took a seat in the middle of
the group and eyed my guests. She knew only Maria and Anastasiya Nikolayevna. I watched her face tighten as she noticed that
almost all the rest were Jewish.

We had changed the subject of conversation immediately
upon her appearance, and as soon as she sat down someone proposed a toast to parents. The diplomatic Irene chattered engag-
ingly about this and that, but nothing worked. After an hour, my
mother excused herself.

I took her to the elevator. As soon as we were out of earshot,
she turned on me.

"*This* is why they don't let you go to Vadim—you've surrounded yourself with Jews! They're against the Soviet Union.
They're using you for their own purposes!"

I tried to reason with her.

"Mama, what have Jews got to do with it? I only met them
recently. I've waited *three years* for an exit visa."

"No," she responded, shaking her head, "I've talked with *my
people*. They told me the reason."

"All right," I said. "We'll talk about this another time. I'm
going back to my guests. Don't ruin my birthday."

Returning to the room, I could not conceal my distress. The
others tried to cheer me up, but the evening was spoiled.

Early in 1977, Rabbi Gedalyah Engel, director of the Hillel Foundation at Purdue University, read an article about me in the *New York Times*. As he later explained, it suddenly dawned on him that everyone who wanted to leave the Soviet Union encountered difficulties. The emigration nightmare did not belong to Jews alone. Long active in the struggle to assist Soviet Jewry, he decided to expand his efforts: he called Woody and offered to "adopt" Lena and me. Frustrated by the Carter administration's indifference to our case, and to that of human rights in the USSR in general, Woody gladly accepted. Rabbi Engel sensed that an ecumenical human rights movement might bring greater pressure to bear on the Kremlin. It would perhaps thwart the Brezhnev regime's crude exploitation of Russian anti-Semitism.

The rabbi and the people in his community began to write regularly to me and to various Soviet and American officials. They called me and two Jewish families they sponsored at least twice a year. From Indiana, they would arrange a three-way conference call between themselves, Woody in Virginia, and me in Moscow. The rabbi always spoke first, enunciating carefully so I could understand him. He invariably pointed out that the Indiana group had only humanitarian goals and requested only that Lena and I—and the two Jewish families—be allowed to leave the USSR. Several representatives of the group, students and clergy, spoke briefly to convey their concern and determination to help. Two members of the rabbi's committee came to Moscow, paying their own way and bringing us messages of love and support.

After meeting Rabbi Engel and the people in Greater Lafayette later in the year, Woody, a nonbeliever, wrote to me,

This is a real man of God. He genuinely feels our pain and has imbued a whole community with his sensitivity. I don't know whether they can actually do anything although they have succeeded in enlisting their Congressman [Floyd Fithian] and Senators Birch Bayh and Richard Lugar in the fight. At least we are no longer alone.

As the years passed it would become more and more difficult for Woody to participate in these conference calls, in which he was expected to appeal to my patience and courage to continue the struggle. He suffered in his own way, but managed it better in a free country. His inability to bring my ordeal to a solution nonetheless produced enormous feelings of guilt that were compounded every time he urged me to persevere.

Rabbi Engel understood his dilemma. Through those long years when there was little reason to hope, he reminded Woody that I needed to hear voices from America. I needed reassurance that there were people who would never forget me. No matter what, the calls must continue.

In the summer of 1977 tension between the authorities and the human rights movement heated up. The state conducted a series of trials, some open, others secret, and sentenced the activist leaders Orlov, Ginzburg, Shcharansky, Marchenko, and many others to long prison terms. The KGB grabbed the male refusenik demonstrators and clamped many in jail for fifteen days on charges of "hooliganism." A sense of danger pervaded the movement as once polite officials turned hostile and threatening overnight. In these new circumstances, the Jewish women decided to leave their husbands at home and continue the demonstrations alone. A group of twenty emerged as leaders. Many were my friends, and as before I joined them on their rounds. Up to that time the authorities had generally refrained from arresting the women. We continued along that well-worn path to state and Party offices with our petitions.

Months went by with little discernible progress; the nervous strain intensified. Early in 1978, the twenty leaders decided to celebrate International Women's day on March 8 with a major demonstration in front of the Lenin Library. At secret meetings we drew up detailed plans. As the day approached, everyone grew extremely jittery. On March 7, to calm myself I called the brothers of a friend in the movement and asked them to go to Gzhel with me for the day. They agreed.

On my street in the early morning darkness, five KGB men and one woman waited, making no attempt to conceal their mission. Recovering from my initial shock, I took the long way to the metro, cut through familiar courtyards, made several random turns, and doubled back trying to escape. The six stayed close, never letting me get more than twenty or thirty meters away.

"The hell with them," Lyonya said when I met him and Zhenya at the railway station and indicated the multiple "tail." "We won't change a thing. If they want to follow us in this miserable weather, so much the worse for them."

Thick, wet snowflakes fell as we boarded the elektrichka for Gzhel. The female agent's heavy mascara ran down her face in long black streaks. Muttering curses as they shook the snow from their damp brown jackets, the men took seats at the opposite end of the nearly empty railway car and played cards, using a briefcase as a table.

It was not an ideal day for an excursion to the country. The late winter storm developed into a blizzard, driving the villagers into their homes and leaving us almost without spectators. The few people we encountered appeared bewildered by the strange procession.

Early in the evening we returned to Moscow, dragging our "tails" behind us. Lyonya and Zhenya's mother, Bronislava, and their sister Liliya were to participate in the next day's demonstration, so I had decided to spend the night in their apartment; Lena was waiting for me there. Liliya told me that everyone who planned to demonstrate had been kept under close surveillance all day.

Our conspiracy was known. The KGB had learned not only the day of the demonstration but also who was to take part.

After a sleepless night, we awakened on March 8 to find three black Volgas waiting at the entrance to the apartment building, one each for Bronislava, Liliya, and me. The KGB honored us with a privilege normally reserved for the *nachalniki*, personal automobiles. Three men in business suits stood by each vehicle. Expecting only to be followed, we went downstairs and out onto the sidewalk. The moment we appeared, the men by the Volgas rushed up to us and, violently twisting our arms behind our backs, shoved each of us into the back seat of a separate car and sped off in different directions.

Wordlessly, my captors took me to the Interior Ministry office on the second floor of my own apartment building and pushed me into a small room. Two Komsomoltsy, decent-looking young men from the Communist Youth League, waited to guard me. They seemed perplexed; I hardly resembled a criminal or a prostitute. They talked to each other quietly, trying to conceal their confusion. Suddenly I remembered that the signs I had intended to display at the Lenin Library were in the large cloth shopping bag at my feet: GIVE ME MY HUSBAND and I'VE WAITED FOUR YEARS FOR A VISA. They could have been evidence against me . . . but no one asked to see my bag.

At eight o'clock that evening, having held me without charge or explanation all day, they let me go.

For the first time in my life I did not greet my mother with flowers and gifts on International Women's Day. When I finally called she was irate: "What happened?"

"I spent the day at the police station."

"Good God! Why?"

"Ask your KGB!"

Furious and exhausted, I could not continue.

Two days later she called back in a fury: "You anti-Soviet-chitsa! You've sold out to the imperialists, given yourself to the Jews! They've ruined you—I'm through with you!"

I listened silently to the tirade, then replaced the receiver.

Three years would elapse before I saw my mother again.

They arrested all the women that day. A few who had gone into hiding before the demonstration actually got to the Library, but KGB agents seized them as soon as they arrived. That evening, March 8, the Voice of America, the BBC, Deutsche Welle, and other foreign broadcasts received in the Soviet Union carried reports of our aborted demonstration. The announcer invariably began, "Today, twenty Jewish women and a Russian woman, Irina McClellan, were arrested by KGB agents as they tried . . . "

Distressed by the singling out of my name, the activists demanded that their movement henceforward be purely Jewish. Despite my friends' protests, the majority voted to exclude me from future demonstrations.

Rabbi Engel's actions stood out in striking contrast. He not only "adopted" Lena and me but found a way to unite an entire American community in the struggle for our liberation: Catholics, Protestants, Jews. Thousands and thousands of people in Indiana signed the petitions, sent postcards the Soviet authorities rarely permitted us to receive, wrote and called their representatives in Washington. Religious differences receded into the background as these people shared our suffering, sought to bring us hope.

But that was in America. In Moscow, I was once again alone.

15
Into the Streets

A LETTER Woody wrote late in February reached me three days after my arrest on March 8. Like most letters after 1975, this one came through one of the erratic nonofficial channels we had arranged.

Everything points to one agonizing conclusion: the only way to save yourself, the only way for you to have any chance of leading a normal life, may be to denounce me, to go to the authorities and tell them you made a mistake in marrying me.

You must know that this is as terrible a prospect for me as it is for you. We fought the KGB with everything we had; alas, we had very little.

I know you feel desperate and trapped, but you must go on, you must think of Lena and your friends. . . .

It's obvious that the protracted separation has changed our relationship; it would be foolish to deny that. But I have done everything in my power, and I'll continue to do all I can to help you no matter what relations are between us.

He did not propose divorce. Rather, he gave me *carte blanche* to make my own decision. I read and reread the letter, not believing my eyes. Now almost four years long, our separation had taken a heavy toll. For both financial and emotional reasons we now spoke only a few times a year by telephone and wrote much less often. Our letters reflected a growing estrangement. Woody no longer knew what to say to me, and I was inhibited by my inability to describe the Moscow nightmare adequately.

My first reaction was that I had reached the end of my rope. I thought of suicide: *That,* I said to myself, is the solution, the way to liberate everyone. Let others live as they wish and be happy; no one needs me. As though possessed by demons, for several consecutive nights I paced back and forth in my apartment and finally decided on self-immolation in Red Square. The Kremlin chimes rang clear in the still night. I imagined myself aflame on the square as those familiar sounds marked the last seconds of my life . . . or maybe a noose. For hours I stared at the heavy light fixture in the ceiling. Would it hold . . . ?

Lena was asleep in her room, my only child, who had already suffered so much because of my untidy, convoluted life . . . Dawn came and reason returned. Suicide was not the answer—it would be too great a stigma for Lena to bear. But I had to do *something*, act before it was too late.

Then, rather abruptly one morning, a plan came to me. I hurried to Irene's apartment to tell her of my idea. She made suggestions, I refined my plans. Gradually my energy returned; with a plan, there was hope. If only my nerves did not collapse. Twenty days to go. My thoughts feverishly raced back and forth . . . to Lena, Mama, but above all my husband.

April 10, 1978: opening day of the Supreme Soviet (parliament) session. In the warm weather, delicate young leaves pushed out on long-bare tree branches. People were dressed in brighter clothes, and springtime shone in their eyes as they strolled through the sunny streets. Slowly, I made my way on foot to the Lenin Library, carrying a bag with the signs I had never displayed on International Women's Day. Looking at the happy faces on the street, I too wanted to bask in the sun. But inside and out, I was cold with fear.

At last, the well-known steps. I mount them, stop on the landing, turn to face the street, pull the signs from my bag and— arms shaking—hold them high. Passers-by hesitate, consternation on their faces as they read the signs hand-lettered in Russian and English: DAITE MUZHA—GIVE ME MY HUSBAND and ZHDU VIZU 4 GODA—I'VE WAITED 4 YEARS FOR A VISA. Fear quickly triumphs over curiosity, however; no one stops longer than a few seconds.

I recognized a few faces in a little group that closed in on me: correspondents. Flashbulbs, cameras, notebooks, shouted questions. As I tried to summarize my story quickly, I spotted someone striding purposefully in my direction, a very angry young man in civilian clothes, bursting with authority. Everything about him bespoke KGB. During important Party or government meetings, hundreds of such people patrol central Moscow. He came up to me, grabbed my signs, and whirled to face the journalists.

"There's nothing to photograph! Get out of here immediately!"

The correspondents withdrew a few steps. Clutching my elbow in a powerful grip, the man said rudely, "And *you*, citizeness, will come with me."

At the curb stood a black Volga. Someone pushed me into the back seat and men jumped in on either side of me. The agent who had made the arrest got in front next to the driver and the automobile tore off up Kalinin Prospekt. Brakes screeching, we pulled up in front of a police station. They hustled me roughly inside to the main office; our unexpected appearance startled policemen assembled for a shift change. The arresting agent dumped my signs on the duty sergeant's desk and rubbed his palms together a few times as if to clean away the filth. Accustomed to dealing with ordinary criminals, hooligans, and prostitutes, the policemen appeared bewildered when the KGB agent told the sergeant in a loud voice, "This little citizeness tried to demonstrate at the Lenin Library. Keep her here—we'll send someone to interrogate her."

Sizing me up as neither dangerous nor likely to flee, the sergeant motioned toward a bench to the right of his desk. There was a great deal of coming and going, and now and then a policeman would stop and whisper, "What's this, you want your husband? Where is he? In *America!*" There was a pause, then a final question: "Why don't you go there?"

After a while a thin, bespectacled, middle-aged man with an intelligent face appeared, escorted me to a small room, pointed to a straight chair, and sat down behind a battered gunmetal gray desk. He introduced himself: KGB. Polite and cordial, he seemed as perplexed as the policemen. Looking at me with a faint but kindly smile, he asked, "All right, what is an attractive young

woman like you doing making a commotion on the streets of
Moscow?"

He listened patiently to my story, which ended with my attempt to get the attention of the Supreme Soviet.

"I want to go to my husband before I get old," I said half-
jokingly.

"See here," he said when I finished, "go to OVIR. Settle the
problem there. Don't do anything else foolish."

"But it's OVIR who keeps me here!"

"Go back and try again."

I looked into his eyes and said evenly, "It's useless. Maybe
you'll believe me when I set fire to myself in Red Square."

He flinched. His instructions would not have covered such a
threat. There was a long moment of silence, then, ignoring my
words, he let me go.

That evening I went back to Irene with a new plan. In ten
days, Secretary of State Cyrus Vance would be in Moscow. Six
years had gone by since President Nixon had come to Moscow to
sign the SALT I Treaty; now President Carter and General Secretary Brezhnev looked forward to the early conclusion of SALT II.
Both sides had great expectations for the Vance visit. Determined
to make them take *my* hopes into account, I would chain myself
to the fence outside the American Embassy at noon on April 20.

Irene immediately offered to tip off the correspondents. She
would meet them on the street with a note indicating the details.
Under no circumstances would she speak out loud—the offices
and living quarters of foreign journalists are "bugged" with sophisticated listening devices. To preserve the secret, she and I
would not meet again before the demonstration.

Invisible chains are part of daily life in Russia, but an ordinary
metal chain is a scarce commodity. Clerks at one hardware store
after another barked *"Nyetu!"* (We don't have any). I began to
wonder whether the plan was feasible. Then Liliya, with whom I
had been arrested on March 8, recalled a small shop in the countryside near the family dacha. It sold chains of the sort used to
restrain watchdogs. She would help.

Liliya and her husband drove to the village, bought a chain, and delivered it to my closest friend, Maria. Seven days to go.

Lena became extremely concerned for my safety.

"I'm going with you," she declared. "With two of us it won't be so bad, Mamochka."

I did not oppose her firmly. There would be time to talk her out of it.

On April 14 I dropped out of sight. Even though all my accomplices understood the gravity of the situation, so many people were involved that I feared my plan might leak out. The KGB had ways of ferreting out information, and I dreaded another failure. I took the elektrichka to the village of Peredelkino outside Moscow, to a dacha belonging to the mother of an acquaintance. Living there alone, the elderly lady, writer of patriotic stories and novels, was accustomed to her daughter's friends appearing from time to time and welcomed the company.

Peredelinko is a writers' colony. Boris Pasternak lived there for many years, next door to the dacha where I would hide. It had once belonged to Aleksandr Fadeyev, an aggressively Stalinist writer who shot himself in an upstairs bedroom after Nikita Khrushchev denounced Stalin. On Fadeyev's death the huge cottage was divided into two apartments; the first floor passed to my hostess, who seemed delighted to see me. Setting a table far beyond my feeble appetite, she chattered away about television. This woman was a loyal Party member living out her days in solitude. With nothing but television for company most of the time, she believed every word of it.

I was thankful that the last few tense days would not be spent alone; however, they would evidently be spent watching television. Although the propaganda about the wonders of life in the USSR grated, I smiled and nodded as though in agreement with whatever flashed across the screen. When I could, I strolled along carefully tended paths through the pine woods to Pasternak's grave and sat on a nearby bench. The walks cleared my mind and reassured me: no one was watching the dacha.

Four nerve-racking days passed. At last, late in the evening on April 18, I thanked the old woman, walked through the village to the depot, and caught the nearly empty elektrichka back to Moscow. A young couple prated loudly in the far corner, laughing uproariously at shared jokes, paying no attention to me or anyone else. Spring was in their souls. I could think of only one thing: Let the hour come, quickly!

At 1:00 A.M. I knocked softly on Maria's door. Having waited up, she silently let me in. Lena was already asleep, as were Maria's husband and young son. The chain was waiting: when I saw it on the kitchen table, my heart skipped a few beats. This was it. We sat down to drink tea. Trying to calm us both, Maria brought me up to date on her family's doings over the past few days. Her presence and the calm sound of her voice gradually relaxed me.

In the morning, Maria and her husband went off to work, leaving their child at a day-care center. Lena headed for school, declaring that her mind was made up—she would go with me. My gaunt appearance had upset her deeply. We agreed to meet that evening at another apartment.

Wednesday, April 19, was spent alone in Maria's apartment practicing with the chain. I wound it around my waist, then snapped a clasp through two links. The clasp had a strong spring in its hollow shank. By pressing down hard with my thumb on a little knob, I could just barely open the "question mark" enough to run the hook through the links. Then I threaded the two meters of so of the chain's slack through the back struts of a kitchen chair and closed a padlock through two links. I timed myself; it took far too long, almost a minute. I could not do it without Lena's help. She would have to fasten the chain to the fence. After a while my thumb ceased to obey and I could not open the clasp. My hands shook uncontrollably; I had to stop for coffee, which only increased my anxiety. But I had to keep practicing.

Late in the afternoon I slipped out and walked to the metro, took a train to nowhere and got off. I strolled a few blocks, boarded a bus, rode half an hour, ambled around the unfamiliar

neighborhood, then boarded another train, again traveling aim-
lessly around the city passing time, losing myself in the crowds.
Reasonably certain no one had followed, I appeared at my last
headquarters around ten o'clock that evening. The building stood
directly across from the American Embassy. Lena was already
there. With a warm greeting the young woman occupant and her
husband ushered me into the kitchen and produced tea and jam.

My lips were parched. I sat down, unable to talk. Lena tried
valiantly to help, but she too could think only of the next day. Our
hosts' efforts to cheer us up and take our minds off the coming
ordeal unsuccessful, they discreetly said goodnight and retired.
Lena and I shared a bed, clinging to each other tightly. Every now
and then we looked at our watches.

Much earlier than necessary the next morning the whole
apartment stirred. We all started moving around and conversing
with unnatural cheerfulness in an attempt to hide our anxiety
under the cover of meaningless words.

At eleven-fifteen I put the chain around my waist as tightly as
I dared. With some difficulty Lena fastened the clasp through two
links behind my back, then wound the slack. I placed the padlock
shackle through the last link of the slack end, turned the shackle
away from the slot and put lock and chain end into my jeans
pocket. Then I checked the placards one last time, stuffed them
under my raincoat, straightened Lena's sky blue ski jacket—the
one Woody sent her—and stroked her hair. Then I kissed her
three times . . .

We sat down. It is a Russian custom to meditate briefly before
embarking on a significant journey. After a few moments, our host
took some photos and blessed us:

"God be with you!"

Two small women in blue did not look like conspirators bent
on challenging the Soviet state. Certain that everyone could dis-
cern our intentions, however, we dared not look across the street
at the embassy. Counting our steps, barely breathing, we reached
the corner of Tchaikovsky Street and Kalinin Prospekt and de-

scended the steps to the underground pedestrian passage. It was 11:25 A.M.

Tchaikovsky Street is ten lanes wide at that point, not counting a center corridor reserved for the highest Soviet dignitaries—who often glide through the city in chauffeur-driven limousines at extremely high speeds, all cross-traffic stopped by the police. The long pedestrian tunnel was nearly empty. Our footfalls echoed ominously off the white-tiled walls.

The distance from the street corner to the point where I planned to chain myself to the fence was almost 500 meters. As we emerged onto the sidewalk, we saw three distinct crowds in front of the American Embassy: more uniformed police than usual, KGB agents in civilian clothes, and correspondents, several with television cameras. Flanking the correspondents, who were grouped directly in front of the building beneath the American flag, the Soviet security types were watching *them* rather than the passers-by.

My knees shook as we marched along the sidewalk with forced smiles. Lena kept repeating, "It will soon be over . . . soon be over . . . soon be . . . " We made ourselves walk slowly. In the West one may saunter to protest against governments, but not in the Soviet Union, where such affairs usually come to a bad end. Any demonstration can be one's last. But we went on as normally as we could.

Past the uniformed Soviet police. Now the knot of correspondents. Several familiar faces full of unfamiliar apprehension glanced at us. I was afraid their anxiety would give us away, but they averted their gaze to the street, the police, the embassy—everywhere but in our direction.

We were just beyond the correspondents now, almost directly beneath the flag. Lena and I suddenly spun to the left, mounted the low stone curb to the meter-wide patch of grass, and crossed to the wrought-iron fence. In a convulsive gesture I pulled open my raincoat, ripped padlock and chain end out of my pocket, hurriedly unwound the slack from around my waist and—stepping over the loop—passed lock and chain to Lena. I retrieved the signs and held them above my head.

Shaking almost uncontrollably, Lena could not bind me to the fence. She dropped the chain, picked it up, got it around a bar, accidentally pulled it back as she fumbled with the padlock.

"Lena, hurry!" I pleaded in a desperate whisper. "Please hurry!"

Almost paralyzed by fear, voice breaking, she whispered back, "I can't . . . I can't . . ."

Thrusting the signs into her hands, I grabbed the chain, looped it behind two iron bars, pulled it back, snapped the lock through the links. Then I threw the key behind the fence onto American territory and seized a sign, held it high—upside down.

As though on command, the correspondents wheeled in our direction and began to snap photographs, roll videotape, shout questions. I answered as calmly as I could but my mind was on the security people: Why hadn't they come? Who closed their eyes? Suddenly the security forces swung into action. Uniformed police shoved the journalists and cameramen aside and swooped down on us. Snatching the signs, they hurled them to the ground, grabbed me by the shoulders, and pulled vigorously. Only then did they realize I was chained to the fence. Enraged, a policeman jerked my arm violently. I screamed out in pain. Lena began hitting the policeman on the back, yelling: "Don't hurt my mother!"

Yanking at the heavy chain with curses and shouts, the men discovered the "question-mark" spring clasp that bound the chain behind my back, forced me to the ground, and opened it. Though still padlocked to the fence, the chain dropped away from me. Someone twisted my arm behind my back and attempted to pull me to my feet. Nearly fainting, I sagged back to the ground. Lena pummeled my tormentor until others pulled her off and frog-marched her toward the sentrybox a few meters away. As they dragged me behind her, a correspondent with a German accent ran up and began taking pictures, asking, "Tell me, what do you feel? Does it hurt?"

I shot him a malicious look.

A thin plywood partition divided the police kiosk near the southwest corner of the embassy into two little cubicles. Each cubicle was just large enough to hold a small wooden table, chair, bench, radio, and lamp. They brought us in and we collapsed on the bare bench. A policeman stood guard. Through the partition came sounds of frantic activity. Several telephones rang at once; voices interjected "Right!" and "Yessir!" into what was obviously a high-speed stream of words from the other end. People slammed the door in the other cubicle, ran in and out, cursed, scraped chairs. They were waiting for orders—what was to be done with us? Lena and I sat quietly, arms and legs trembling as the tension floated away. Mission accomplished.

I began to gasp for air. The guard, a middle-aged uniformed policeman with a sad, sympathetic face, looked on silently, his back to the closed door.

"Would you mind opening the window a little," I asked. "There isn't enough air."

Anticipating a rude reply, I was surprised when he stepped to the window and opened the small hinged pane used for ventilation. As he turned to face me, we made eye contact; his unexpectedly decent, humane expression emboldened me to ask whether I might smoke. Still silent, he pulled an ashtray from the table drawer and pushed it in my direction.

The nicotine made my head spin for a moment, but my nerves calmed almost immediately.

Another policeman suddenly opened the door. Seeing me smoking, he blew up—at the guard.

"And what is *this?* Aren't you watching her?"

Our keeper looked calmly at the intruder and said in a whisper, "Shut up."

The second policeman stared at him in confusion, looked again at me, turned on his heel and left.

The little radio was on, and I became aware of a voice singing a "popular" song good Communists love: "I don't know any other country, Where one breathes so freely . . . " My nerves twitched again. I looked at the guard, gestured toward the radio, and asked, softly so as not to be overheard, "Could we turn it off? It doesn't seem to fit the situation . . . "

More silent eye contact, then he reached over and clicked the set off.

Finally plainclothes agents barged in and dragged us out of
the kiosk. I glanced one last time into the eyes of the man who
had guarded us, silently thanking him. Two men pushed us into
the back seat of a black Volga and got in on either side. Moving
away at high speed, the car cut across the westbound lanes of
Tchaikovsky Street, accelerated east to the Square of the Uprising, then left on Barricades Street, and pulled up in front of a
police station.

Lena and I demonstrating outside the American Embassy in Moscow,
April 20, 1978. *AP/Wide World Photos*

Sitting on benches along the wall were Irina, Liliya, and her brother Lyonya. They had watched the scene from directly across the street. Seconds after Lena and I raised the signs, agents had rushed up and arrested them. My circle of friends was evidently well known to the KGB.

A group of perhaps ten KGB agents confronted Lena and me. One of them held the chain and padlock. We were not permitted to speak to our friends. Forming a ring around us, the agents took

us to a room down the hall. Two straight chairs were drawn up in front of a large desk; similar chairs lined the walls to the right and left. Hunched over behind the desk sat a youngish man with Uzbek—Turkish-Mongol—eyes and thick, straight black hair. He arrogantly motioned us to sit. One of the agents deposited our chain on the desk.

The atmosphere puzzled me. For a long time no one spoke. The boss and the agents—who had taken seats along the walls— simply looked at us, evidently unsure where to begin. At last the boss broke the silence.

"Irina Igorevna, why are you doing this? Why don't you take your problems to OVIR?"

A broken record.

I responded as usual—for nearly four years OVIR had given me nothing but one unexplained refusal after another. The inter-rogation ended with astonishing swiftness; there was simply noth-ing to talk about. The Uzbek boss shook his head wearily and said, "You're free to go."

There was no sign of our friends in the entrance hall. Back on the street, Lena and I were at first bewildered by our freedom, but then we noticed the black Volga full of KGB agents which fol-lowed us down the street to the metro. Near the station two men jumped out and continued after us on foot.

They were to keep us under close surveillance for the next three weeks.

Our demonstration in front of the American Embassy created a sensation. Front-page photographs and news accounts appeared in most Western countries and also in Japan, India, Australia, and elsewhere. To my dismay, however, in the United States a contro-versy arose over the reporting of the demonstration, obscuring the point Lena and I had tried to make. The Soviet government refused CBS permission to use satellite facilities to transmit film of the incident, and it blocked the efforts of print journalists to send still photos. News organizations were obliged to fly their material out to Frankfurt or London.

Some time later, Woody wrote that Walter Cronkite, whose name meant nothing to me, had concluded the CBS Evening News on Thursday, April 20, with the audio transmission—our screams, the security men's shouts and curses—against the background of a blank screen. Cronkite informed the audience that the Soviets refused to transmit the picture. The next day, the same program repeated the segment—with video that came out by plane.

In an effort to justify the denial of facilities, the Foreign Ministry condemned the reporting as a "deliberate provocation by the American press." TASS, the official Soviet news agency, called the satellite-use furor an "anti-Soviet hullabaloo," aimed at creating "a certain negative background" for the Vance mission to Moscow. No mention of the demonstration appeared anywhere in the Soviet press or on radio or television.

The United States government accused the Soviets of violating their Helsinki Conference promise to guarantee the free flow of information. My friends heard on the Voice of America and other foreign broadcasts that Vance intended to raise that matter with Gromyko. The news infuriated me. Why didn't Vance ask the Soviets about *us?* The hell with the photos and videotapes . . . Vance's spokesman declared that neither the demonstration nor the journalistic dispute would have the slightest impact on the negotiations.

Concerned for her safety, I had warned Maria not to communicate with me until we saw which way the wind was blowing. She did not call, but a telegram came that evening:

DEEPLY ADMIRE YOUR COURAGE. WISH YOU STRENGTH AND FIRMNESS. MARIA.

The next day Woody telephoned. Extremely agitated, he almost shouted, "I'm so proud of you! I'm with you . . . don't ever doubt me . . . I will do everything I can to free you . . ."

It seemed he was his old self. Moments after we hung up a cable arrived:

I LOVE YOU. VADIM.

Another cable came from Woody's Washington friends Sam Berner and Lynn Crane, whom I had never met:

DEAR IRINA WE JUST WANT YOU TO KNOW WE LOVE YOU. WE SUPPORT AND ADMIRE YOU.

My telephone rang incessantly—Jewish refuseniks, Russian friends and acquaintances, even people I did not know who had heard the news on foreign radio broadcasts. Everyone congratulated me, wished me strength. But my reserves were exhausted. I needed Woody, not celebrity.

The day after the demonstration, a group of Western journalists came to my apartment. The Voronovs, against their custom, were at home. The KGB had unquestionably asked them to carry on the surveillance inside the apartment, but nothing could have prepared them for the TV cameras, lights, cables that snaked down three flights to a special truck on the street. Because of the cables the door to the apartment would not close, and the door to my room also remained open as people went in and out. "Jupiter" lights made the whole place look like a movie set. Lena and I sat watching, more spectators than participants; I repeatedly answered the same questions.

Cyrus Vance left some days later, and slowly life returned to normal. Or near-normal: KGB agents in a black Volga sat parked outside our apartment building, and wherever we went they followed.

A week later Woody wrote that Vance had denied his request for a ten-minute appointment to discuss my situation.

Friends at the State Department urged me to settle for a meeting with Marshall Shulman; I took their advice.

It was a mistake to go at all and to walk from downtown: I got caught in a rainstorm and arrived looking like a drowned rat. Marshall received me cordially enough but had an assistant present, evidently to protect him against . . . what, I don't know; maybe he was afraid of being misquoted.

Marshall insisted you will shortly be released and to make his point demonstratively bet the assistant a dollar you'll be out in six months or less. It's only human to want to believe him, but we must not get our hopes up too high. . . . My impression was that he and his boss are not really interested in problems such as ours, which they consider minor irritants in the grand sweep of American-Soviet relations.

On April 26 I had business of another kind at the American Embassy. Woody had decided to buy a house in Albemarle County outside Charlottesville and needed my power of attorney to complete the transaction; my name would be on the deed. The American Consul, Bob Pringle, who had become a friend over the months he and his family had been in Moscow, promised to take care of everything and agreed to meet me on the sidewalk.

More or less at ease, I strolled along Tchaikovsky Street, trying to enjoy another beautiful spring day. As I approached the main entrance, Bob and I spotted each other and I increased my pace in his direction. Thinning blond hair, a little chubby around the middle, he came toward me with a warm smile. No more than ten meters separated us. Suddenly, out of nowhere, two men pounced and hauled me to a black Volga waiting at the curb.

I was too shocked to resist. As on April 20, the car pulled rapidly away, cut across the traffic, and shot eastward toward the Square of the Uprising. In five minutes we were back at the police station on Barricades Street. Another KGB interrogator, another warning:

"Your behavior has exasperated the police. They will not let you get near the American Embassy again. If you have any business with the Americans take care of it at the consul's apartment or your own, on the street if you like. Not in the embassy."

The brief interview was now over, and the KGB agents, more civil, accompanied me back to the Volga. To my surprise it headed not for the metro or my apartment, but pulled up in front of OVIR on Kolpachny Lane. April 26 was a Wednesday. OVIR is closed on Wednesdays.

The KGB men rang the bell. A uniformed policeman appeared within seconds and conducted us not to Room 24 but to an unmarked door on the second floor. One of the men knocked. After a few seconds someone called out gruffly, "Come in!"

A huge wooden desk; a couple of telephones; a small lamp with a green conical shade. Behind the desk sat a jowly man in a dark business suit. One of the KGB agents said in a respectful voice, "Comrade Zotov." Clearly a big boss, Zotov motioned me toward a chair in front of his desk. The agents stood.

"Write out new applications for exit visas," Zotov said.

"Aren't all the applications in my file enough?" I asked angrily.

"All right, all right," he answered in almost fatherly tones, "it's just our procedure. Please—behave properly. Don't do anything to spoil Soviet-American relations." A pause, then he added, " . . . and you'll be going to your husband in a month."

Simple Russian words, clear. Downstairs, I struggled through my mounting excitement to fill in the blanks on the application forms.

Three holidays fall early in May: International Labor Solidarity Day on the 1st; Radio Day on May 5; and the anniversary of the victory over Germany on May 9. The KGB maintained round-the-clock surveillance over me, apparently afraid I would somehow mar the holidays. They established their headquarters in a small utility room near my entrance to the apartment complex and kept a Volga parked on the street nearby. It was impossible to come or go without their seeing me; wherever I went, at least three men followed. I soon ceased to pay attention. Lena and I lived our lives, the agents did their work and drew their salaries. As the days went by we became sort of friendly, so accustomed were we to each other.

On May 1, Lena and I went to see Maria, who, wanting to put weight on us, had made enough pirozhki and other delicacies to feed half of Moscow; her husband had bought some first-rate Moldavian wine. Naturally the surveillance followed. Two men kept their eyes on us in the elektrichka and radioed directions to the Volga. The car was waiting outside Maria's apartment.

We ate, drank, laughed, and shared anecdotes about the

events of the past couple of weeks. Now and then we looked out the open window to make sure our escorts were there; they never disappointed us. Whenever I appeared at the window, the men would smile and pointedly tap their wristwatches as if to say, Isn't it about time to go home?

I had promised Bob and Mary Pringle to stop by their apartment for a drink that evening, but it was getting late and I went down to a pay phone in the courtyard to call them. The agents came up to the booth and waited at a polite distance. When I hung up they approached and one said in a cajoling voice, "Well, Irina Igorevna, let's be going. It's a holiday for us too! Our families are waiting. We want to drink a little . . . "

The ride back into Moscow took more than an hour. It was after midnight when we tried to hail a taxi outside the Savelovsky Station—not an easy task late on a holiday night. Edging toward the middle of the street in the painted pedestrian crosswalk, I waved at every car that passed, hoping someone would give us a lift. One of the surveillance team ran up, solicitously took my elbow, and steered me back to the sidewalk, saying, "I'll find a ride for you . . . standing in the road is dangerous!"

Like a magician with a maroon KGB identification document for a wand, he strode resolutely into the stream of traffic and halted the first car. He showed the driver his ID and politely ordered him—an ordinary citizen, it seemed—to "Take these citizenesses to Chernyshevsky Street."

The nonplussed driver could not refuse. As we drove along, he kept turning to look at me. His confusion overflowed when he noticed the black Volga tailing us.

"Who are you?" he asked. "You don't look like a criminal. Haven't those guys got room in their car?"

"They only chauffeur people they arrest," I said with a grin. "Now they're just following."

The holiday period ended and with it the surveillance. Lena and I waited impatiently for the visas Zotov had promised. We had kept quiet, as the KGB asked, and had done nothing to "spoil" Soviet-American relations.

In mid-morning on Thursday, May 25, I went back to see Comrade Zotov—now a totally different man.

"Well, what are you doing here?" he snapped.

"It's been a month. I want to know when you are going to give us exit visas."

Zotov began to shout: "I didn't promise *anything!* What have you dreamed up? What's this about a month?"

"Shall I bring a tape recorder next time?"

He shot me a look of hatred. Jaw clenched tightly, he replied, "Just *try.* We'll have you stripped and searched."

My face told Lena everything: deceived again. But we were not going to take it passively. We got out a bedsheet; Lena sketched Soviet and American flags diagonally opposite each other, and in the center—my usual slogans. I tacked wooden rods across the top and bottom for stability, then made a cryptic call to a refusenik activist, Vitya Yelistratov, who alerted several foreign correspondents and hurried to our apartment. Everything was ready.

An hour and a half later, at precisely 1:00 P.M., the sheet hung evenly in the sun when Lena, Vitya, and I lowered it outside our window, boggling the minds of the passers-by on Chernyshevsky Street. Directly beneath our third-floor apartment was the precinct office of the Ministry of the Interior. The banner hung right above their heads.

The sidewalks were crowded with people scurrying in and out of the street-level stores. Many who lived and worked in the neighborhood were on their lunch hour. In the apartments above the stores, windows were open to take advantage of the fine weather. A crowd gathered on the street. Mystified citizens craned their necks to stare. The group of onlookers grew steadily; for every one that left, two new ones arrived. Foreign journalists took photos.

After perhaps ten minutes, two KGB men burst in, rushed to the window, confirmed that they had the right apartment, and dashed to our telephone. They paid no attention to the three of us. The number they wanted was busy.

The banner we hung from our window on Chernyshevsky Street.
AP/Wide World Photos

The men hung up, went back to the window, came back and called again: still busy. They would need to photograph the banner if higher authority decided to prosecute, and they would need the names of witnesses. On the other hand, if there were to be no trial, then the banner ought to come down immediately.

At last the agents got through. The instructions were unequivocal: Take the banner down. More agents arrived.

They took Lena and Vitya to one room in the Interior Ministry offices downstairs, me to the director's office. A red-faced man in an Army captain's uniform, he did not ask me to sit. Striding back and forth on the thick red runner that decorated his parquet floor, he screamed, "Why are you shaking? Afraid? I'll throw you in your blue jeans to that crowd and they'll tear you to pieces! Do you hear me?"

Soviet officialdom regarded the wearing of blue jeans as an unpatriotic act.

"Comrade Captain, where do you get the right to scream at me? And why do you address me as *tu* instead of *vous*?"

He bared his teeth to reply but at that instant his telephone rang. Speaking in low tones, he began to calm down. Replacing the receiver, he looked at me and ordered, "Go to the waiting room. The KGB's coming. Too bad it's not my job to deal with you—I'd have fixed you long ago!"

Finally the KGB man came, a small, rather mousy, middle-aged type. He sat down next to me in the little anteroom. His questions and advice differed not at all from what I had heard many times, and I gave my usual answers. We talked for a while, no more than a quarter of an hour, then he left, his seat taken by an unsmiling guard.

Late in the evening the captain appeared and curtly dismissed all three of us.

Once again they had let me go, free to continue my existence in Limbo. A terrible physical weakness overtook me. My temperature fluctuated. I lay in bed spent. No thoughts, no future. Perhaps, I wondered wearily, this is the end?

Book 3

I've learned to live simply, wisely,
To look to heaven and pray to God,
And stroll at length before evening,
To set unnecessary anxiety at rest.

Anna Akhmatova, 1912

16

Grannie Sanya

THE PHOTOGRAPHS of Woody that had hung on my walls for nearly four years were now hidden behind books on the shelves. It had become too painful to look at them. I stopped talking about him, tried to put thoughts of him away in the recesses of my mind. No longer did I anticipate letters that came through our private channels, or the rare ones he sent through the regular mail. They came less often now anyway, uneven in tone, reflecting our ups and downs. There would be a flash of hope, only to be followed by despair and emptiness. But one desire began to obsess me: one last time, I wanted to see this man who had so changed my life.

In the autumn of 1978 Woody wrote that he had moved into "our" new home in a village outside Charlottesville. "Well, you have become a *pomeshchitsa* [lady of the manor]. I would have preferred to wait until you come to buy, but for a variety of reasons it was now or never. The place is small but comfortable; when you come we'll find something bigger. . . . "

A *pomeshchitsa* in a communal apartment—socialist surrealism! Of course, Woody meant to cheer me up, and give me hope. Easy enough for him, I thought venomously, to make jokes living in a private home.

The situation in the kommunalka worsened. Our neighbors were as tired as we of living under such conditions, but the 1980 Olympic Games, which involved construction of a massive Olympic Village, forced thousands of Muscovites, among them the Voronovs, to wait several additional years for private apartments. They had put their name on the housing list soon after the birth of their daughter, now twelve years old. The absence of privacy in their one room generated ever greater tension and irritation. They took it out on me.

As my fortieth birthday approached in September 1978, I slipped into a deep depression. Forty is a critical birthday for many people, a time to reflect on the first half of life, but I had nothing to sum up. My husband was unimaginably far away; we had not seen each other for four years. I had lost my mother, who condemned me as a traitor to the motherland. Anastasiya Nikolayevna filled the gap in my life to some extent, but then Sergei Yakovlevich died, and some of the spark went out of her.

When I awoke on September 4, I could not move. My limbs were like putty. Nature called, but I could not rise from my bed. At the slightest attempt to move, pain shot from head to toe. Unaware that the pain indicated I was not, after all, paralyzed, I panicked. My first thought was of Lena, asleep on the sofa across the room. Would she be saddled with an invalid?

Lena, ill and unhappy, in 1978, age nineteen.

After a few minutes I tried again to move but the lightning stab of pain defeated me. Finally I called out softly to Lena and asked her to help me. Groggily, she slid me off the bed, propped me upright, and somehow got me to the toilet.

"At least I've got a good excuse to duck the birthday party," I said when we were back in our room.

"Mama, don't say that. You'll feel better soon . . . everybody is looking forward to it."

I stayed in bed all day. Several friends who could not come in the evening dropped by with flowers and gifts and, when they saw my condition, sympathy. Around 8:00 P.M., a dozen or so people assembled in our apartment. Lena got me on my feet, dressed me in my favorite black velvet pants—a present from Woody—and a knitted red blouse-shirt, draped a large, brightly colored shawl over my shoulder, and led me into the other room to greet the guests.

They thought it was a joke.

"*Vo dayosh, Mamasha!*" Just look at you, Mama! they yelled in delight. "Now quit fooling around. Let's have something to drink!"

Doing my best to smile, I crouched on the edge of a chair and barely moved for the next three hours. The guests drank, ate Lena's tasty *zakuski,* talked, enjoyed themselves, tried to cheer me up.

A couple of physician friends later claimed the semi-paralysis was wholly in my mind. Another doctor said I had been struck by some organic dysfunction. It was never clear what had happened. The next day I awakened quite healthy. The physical pain had disappeared, leaving only the incurable ache in my soul.

I began to learn how to live one day at a time. The first priority was to find new students; again my friends spread the word. Gradually people appeared for English lessons, and the rather well-paid job of typing the *samizdat* journal *Culture and the Jews* came my way. Between lessons I sat at my typewriter and pounded away at the journal. Stiff prison sentences awaited people caught working in *samizdat,* and naturally I kept my actions secret. It was a cat-and-mouse situation. Sooner or later the Voronovs would report the sound of late night typing.

(After about a year, the KGB discovered the identity of the journal's editors, summoned them to the Lubyanka, and ordered them to cease their activities. There was no alternative but to comply. The fact that the publication dealt with culture rather than politics probably saved everyone connected with it from arrest.)

I rarely went out. I spent the evenings alone in my room, smoked, sipped tea, listened to the Kremlin chimes mark the passage of time, and mulled over a forgotten poet's words:

> And among a thousand-strong crowd
> you are alone,
> Even with solitude your companion
> you are alone.

Solitude gradually taught me to think—and my thoughts brought me out of my lethargy. Memories of my beloved babushka, Grannie Sanya, crowded into my mind. She was twenty years in her grave, but I felt her absence keenly. The happiest period of my childhood had centered on Grannie Sanya in the postwar period when our clan had regathered around her.

A small, thin woman with cornflower blue eyes, Grannie combed her graying blond hair straight back from her high Tatar forehead, braided and rolled it into a becoming bun. She made her own long dresses with white collars. Those oddly girlish dresses and her open, innocent gaze gave her the look of a high school girl in uniform. It was fitting that her appearance produced an impression of arrested youth, for catastrophe had struck Grannie just as she began to live. In the summer of 1916 the War Office in Petrograd notified her that Ivan Babyshkin, my grandfather, "Died for the czar-father and for Russia" while fighting on the Southwestern Front.

There were no pensions for war widows. Obliged to support herself and two small children, my mother and Aunt Anna, Grannie continued to work at the textile mill in Balashikha. In 1918 the new Bolshevik government conscripted her and millions of others into the "labor front"; Grannie went into the woods to fell trees under the supervision of the commissars. Alas, as she was fond of saying, a tree felled her and crushed her leg. Her daugh-

With Grannie Sanya in Balashikha, 1952. I am on the right; the other children are neighbors.

ters were placed in different orphanages, and Grannie spent more than a year in one hospital after another. Her leg healed crookedly and she was finally discharged as a hopeless case. Gathering up my mother and Aunt Anna, she went to live with her parents, my great grandfather Mitrofan and great grandmother Lena.

Never able to walk normally again, Grannie concealed her deformed leg under long dresses, used crutches to get around, and wore some sort of prosthesis whose squeaks reminded us of a suffering borne with uncomplaining dignity. No longer fit for factory work, she earned a meager living by sewing, taking in washing, and watching the children of working parents.

Like most Russians before the Revolution, Grannie Sanya was devoutly religious. She lived according to the Ten Commandments, loved God and all around her—children, grandchildren (my cousin Vitalik and me), friends, neighbors.

But the Revolution dealt a colossal blow to religion in Russia and drove most young people out of the churches, into the Communist Party. Two such young Party members, Mama and Aunt

Anna, forbade their mother to practice her faith openly or display icons in her home. Meekly bowing to the winds of change, Grannie hid the family icons and worshipped in secret. She never spoke of religion, but every now and then, as if praying silently, she would whisper, "Lord, forgive me!"

Despite her handicap and her poverty, Grannie was forever helping other people. When her own daughters went to work and the strain on the family budget eased a little, she would often sew and knit for friends without charging a kopeck. She cooked simple meals for the sick and spent hours at their bedsides, hobbling painfully all over Balashikha to visit elderly friends. She always had time to tell stories to Vitalik and me and our playmates. "Go to Grannie Sanya," people would say to someone in difficulty. "She is wise . . . she'll know what to do."

Grannie's home was poor but filled with the gift of love. Relatives and friends flocked to visit on Sundays. Grannie would set a big table with potatoes and mushrooms fried in oil, salted herring, and *shchi* made from the sauerkraut she prepared in a huge vat every summer. She was especially famous for her mushrooms pickled in garlic, bay leaves, and other spices; people said they were the best in all Russia. Uncle Misha—Vitalik's father—gathered mushrooms for her in the woods around Balashikha, teaching Vitalik and me to distinguish the edible from the dangerous.

After those Sunday dinners at Grannie's, Vitalik and I listened to the adults talk and joined in when they began to sing the old Russian folk songs. We and any other children present would stand on chairs and recite verses, winning spirited applause. On holidays we danced folk dances; there was always some uncle or cousin who could do the knee-ruining Ukrainian *hopak*, and I loved to watch the adults dance the *barynya*.

The Red Army summoned Aunt Anna's husband, my Uncle Mikhail, to the colors during World War II. When he came home on a short furlough after basic training, Grannie Sanya secretly sewed a prayer to the Mother of God into the hem of his greatcoat. Uncle Mikhail fought on several fronts, helped liberate both Bulgaria and Hungary, was seriously wounded several times . . . but did return with one of the last groups of front-line soldiers in 1946. In the midst of the rejoicing in our home, Grannie took her little scissors, cut a few threads in the hem of the threadbare military greatcoat, and produced the tattered, water-stained prayer for everyone to see.

"See how the Mother of God saved you, Mikhail!" she sighed quietly.

Astonished, the adults in the family—Communists all—stared open-mouthed and uttered not a word of contradiction.

In the hot, dry summer of 1946, a few months before Uncle Misha returned, the crops failed, dealing war-torn Russia another terrible blow. That was the summer when Grannie Sanya secretly took Vitalik and me—I was going on eight, he a year younger—to the Church of St. Nicholas outside Balashikha. On a cloudless July day our little procession made its way down the dusty country road. Vitalik and I skipped along, dashing now and then into birch groves to pick a flower or hunt for wild strawberries. Grannie lurched behind us on her crutch, bent on the sacred mission of escorting her grandchildren to the church five kilometers away. Vitalik and I began to complain, but she resisted our entreaties to turn back, convinced that the day would witness a great event.

We passed through one cluster of hovels after another, each more miserable than the last. The few people we came upon sat listlessly under the trees, eyes registering nothing but defeat. Tiny garden plots overgrown with weeds obscured sagging, decrepit fences. No chickens scratched in the dirt. It was a summer of abject, universal poverty in the Russian countryside.

Tired and thirsty, we turned a last corner and there, at the end of the road atop a small hill, loomed the Church of St. Nicholas. White limestone walls gleamed under the brilliant sun, an Orthodox cross thrust heavenward on the topmost of the five onion-domed cupolas. The splendor of that rural church seemed all the greater after the misery we had passed. For some mysterious reason, the Communists, who destroyed thousands of churches, mosques, and synagogues all over Russia, allowed the Church of St. Nicholas outside Balashikha to survive.

People filed unhurriedly into the church, mostly women

dressed in simple cotton dresses or skirts and blouses, kerchiefs on reverently bowed heads. Silently they crossed themselves, paid a few kopecks for small candles which they lit and placed before the icons, stepped back, crossed themselves again, and offered unspoken prayers. As in most Russian churches, the cupola ceilings were decorated with paintings of scenes from the Gospels. Far more important, however, were the icons: a large one of St. Nicholas dominated the iconostasis. St. Nicholas is the patron saint of travelers in Russia, and Grannie Sanya had brought Vitalik and me to his icon as we prepared to embark on the roads of our lives.

After the service the parishioners dispersed slowly, some to their homes, others to visit graves in the nearby cemetery. A small group of adults with babies in their arms or young children at their sides gathered around the baptismal font in the narthex. The priest was an old man in a black cassock; a huge gold cross was suspended from a gold chain around his neck. With an open prayer book in his hands, he walked slowly around the font reading in a language I could not understand. Once in a while I made out words like *"Bog"* (God) or *"Gospodi"* (Lord), but that was all. Only later did I realize that he was speaking not in Russian but in Church Slavonic, the liturgical language of the Russian Orthodox Church. Then the priest stopped, put the prayer book aside, offered yet another prayer, and beckoned the people to step forward.

The babies were first. The priest baptized each one in turn, the cold holy water producing distinctly unholy screams. Then he nodded to us, perhaps half a dozen seven- and eight-year olds dressed in coarse light brown linen baptismal robes. We followed him as he circled the font three times reading from the prayer book. After the third time, we lined up, and approaching each one in turn, the priest said a prayer and poured a small dipper of holy water on our heads. The newly baptized customarily don crosses, but Grannie had hidden ours away. She had, however, given us the cross of baptism, fulfilling her duty to God and her grandchildren . . .

Grannie Sanya died ten years later, when I was eighteen, soon after Khrushchev delivered the "secret speech" that toppled Stalin from his pedestal. The speech marked the beginning of my political maturity, Grannie's death the end of an innocent, happy childhood. Several hundred people attended the funeral. If, as in *Dr. Zhivago*'s opening scene, a passer-by had enquired, "Who are they burying there?", everyone in that crowd would have answered, "A truly good person."

With Grannie's passing, our clan seemed to fall apart. A small woman on crutches had held us together. Once she was gone, we were lost. People fell to quarreling for no reason and family reunions ceased. At one point Uncle Misha, Aunt Anna's husband, disappeared for a year and a half. He later told me that Grannie had exerted such a powerful magnetic force that without her we spun away crazily in different directions.

Today, now that I too am a believer, I know that Grannie's strength lay in her faith. She was our guardian angel. It was only natural that we were bewildered and confused when she died. It took me many years to grope my way back to the truths she had instilled in me when I was a child.

In the autumn of 1978, when all seemed lost, I cried out to Grannie Sanya in pain, feeling her near. Waking after yet another restless night, I decided to go to church. Something was lacking in my life . . . the core that had helped my grandmother survive. After a bite to eat, I set off eastward along Chernyshevsky Street, no fixed destination in mind, past Clear Pond Boulevard to Karl Marx Street—down to Yelokhovsky Cathedral. I lingered near the main entrance for a while, watching as people approached, stopped, and crossed themselves before going inside. I was ashamed to make the sign of the cross: my arm would not obey—and God forbid that anyone should see me! After a while I simply edged in and stood in the immense nave.

It was a weekday. A few dozen communicants, mostly old and middle-aged women, stood around the altar where a priest was conducting the liturgy; silently, I came up to them. Not understanding a word, I concentrated on the haunting, majestic, palpably *spiritual* sound of the unaccompanied choir, the only music in Russian Orthodox churches. The worshippers listened attentively to the priest, crossed themselves, and made the responses in unison, joined the choir for brief passages. How strange, I thought, that these modestly educated (so I assumed) women follow everything precisely. I turned to an old woman standing next to me and asked in a low voice, "What is the service all about? What is the priest saying?"

At that moment he was reading the homily. Splendidly attired, hands folded across his pot belly, eyes half-closed, he spoke softly, as though to himself. The woman's stage-whispered response rocked me back on my heels.

"If you don't understand, there's nothing for you here. Don't interfere!"

She started to growl something else but I was already on my way out . . .

With time the resentment faded, and I decided to try again at a different church. In the Russian Orthodox way, I stood through the liturgy, neither comprehending nor feeling anything beyond an appreciation of the choir, both ashamed and afraid to ask questions. After the service, worshippers lined up to kiss a cross the priest held in front of the altar. I looked at the faces, which seemed so peaceful and content when they turned to leave the church, and was seized by envy: What is going on here? Why can't I understand anything? But again I left with nothing . . .

Why had Grannie Sanya never told me anything about her faith? Who was God, how did she find Him?

In the summer of 1979 my friends and fellow refuseniks Liliya and her mother Bronya, Irene, and several other lucky ones received exit visas and left for the United States or Israel. We who remained were happy for them; but the parting hurt us deeply.

Lena celebrated her twentieth birthday on May 28, 1979, with a party attended by her own young friends and some people from my new circle. Not surprisingly given the circumstances, her health had not improved, but the bloom of youth was on her, and she had become an attractive young woman. Her longing for independence grew stronger with each passing year. She wanted to get out from under my wing, but neither the housing situation nor our finances permitted her to do so. Our relationship was full of contradictions.

Rabbi Engel still called two or three times a year and with those calls and his community's other activities would not let the Soviet government forget our plight. The rabbi's voice was always calm, confident, full of goodwill, but it was difficult for me to respond. I did not understand his determination or his refusal to capitulate when even Woody and I were slowly relinquishing hope. Woody participated in the conference calls—how I loved that voice, although it now sounded less intimate, even when he repeated the same words: "Irina, I love you . . . I'm waiting for you . . . I will continue to wait . . . "

In October 1979, Woody wrote:

Life goes on here; I grow older and all too accustomed to living alone. As your relationships with some old friends have changed, so have mine. . . . Our situation is so unique, so abnormal, that it would be foolish to expect anyone to understand it.

I am almost ashamed how dull and comfortable my life is. The house is cozy, and I have become a plant-lover. Early in September I planted a clump of *beriozy* [birches] and a hedge. I have ordered three pear and three crabapple trees, more birches.

Woody was living his own life, and I was searching in the darkness for mine. In the spring of 1979, a woman acquaintance had offered me the job of typing multiple copies of prayers for the Sergius-Trinity Monastery at Zagorsk for distribution to believers. It was good to have the work, but at the typewriter something would not function. My fingers refused to execute the instructions my brain tried to send. I did not understand the words, could not grasp their meaning. Finally I began to bang on the keys mechanically, made and corrected numerous mistakes, became angry with myself. There was no satisfaction in such toil.

When my acquaintance came to get the first batch of prayers, I apologized for the less-than-perfect typing. We talked for a while, the conversation jumped from one subject into another, and I told her the story of my life. She suggested I go to the monastery with her and make confession.

We took an early morning elektrichka to the town of Zagorsk northeast of Moscow, a journey of about two hours. As we traveled my companion explained that confession involved telling the priest honestly and openly of one's sins. I thought ruefully that time would not suffice to recount mine . . . and how could I possibly speak of such things to an unknown person, even if he were a priest? Sensing my doubts, my companion reassured me, insisting I would feel better afterward.

Zagorsk: the town loved by millions upon millions of Russians, and not only believers. I think that Russians by nature possess an organic connection with religion, including their conscious and subconscious struggle against it. I had been to Zagorsk several times on excursions to see the ancient, exquisite churches and view the icons. Now I was coming to recount my life story.

My companion and I stood through the long service, then went to the basement of a nearby chapel where a half-blind elderly priest with gray hair flowing down to his shoulders heard confessions. He seemed very feeble. Dressed in a black cassock frazzled at the edges, he received penitents sitting in an armchair. Each individual approached in turn, kneeled, kissed the cross and the Bible, then confessed, often shedding bitter tears. The priest's peaceful, benevolent expression never changed. The confession concluded, he covered the penitent's head with his stole and offered a prayer of absolution. Then the penitent presented cupped hands to the priest, who made the sign of the cross and said, "Go in peace. God has forgiven your sins." People left with radiant faces, burdens lightened.

At last it was my turn, and I approached fearfully. For the most part my confession has fled memory, but I do recall that, when I came to the story of my marriage to Woody, to our separation and sorrows, the priest said, "You, child, should have come here with your husband before your marriage to confess, to ask the blessing of the Church, to be married in the Church. If you had done that, all would be well. Now there is nothing I can do."

"But, *Batyushka* [Father], I'm lost . . . help me . . . "

He had already beckoned to the next person.

Not long after, I went to see Mary Pringle, the wife of the American consul. We spent a lot of time together in 1978–79, and talked at length about religion. A devout Catholic, she attempted to cope with my questions: Why does God permit war, murder, suffering, evil, violence, the KGB? She did not have answers, and her husband, Bob, would admonish me, "Don't torment her . . . how could she possibly explain all that?"

Wanting to ease my pain, Mary tried valiantly. Knowing how much the trip to Zagorsk had disappointed me, she proposed something new.

"Let's pray together—every morning at ten, you in your apartment and I here. I will pray for you, and you for me. Make sure you *concentrate*. Don't let anything distract you."

"But I don't know how!" I protested. "I don't know a single prayer and don't know God—and He does not want to know *me.*"

"Let's just try," Mary said soothingly, anxious to avoid another fruitless discussion. She gave me a book of daily prayers in English, and we began the following day.

It was like meditation. No sort of spirituality welled up within me, but at least for a while I did feel better, perhaps from Mary's presence in my life.

In that difficult period during the late 1970s, Mary Pringle helped preserve my strength and sanity. Polio had struck in her childhood, leaving her crippled for life. Barely five feet tall, Mary had strong, well-developed shoulders and arms from years of getting around with canes. On meeting her, one inevitably noticed the physical infirmity first, but almost immediately one would be drawn to her lovely, warm, dignified face. She had overcome disability to create a happy, healthy family which she supervised with enormous love and patience. Fiercely independent, she got along with very little help. Like Grannie Sanya, she never gave in to self-pity, even in the trying initial period in Moscow when she had not yet made friends, knew only a word or two of Russian, and had no idea how to cope with the inefficiency and discomfort of life in the Soviet capital.

Several times I accompanied Mary to the Polish Catholic

church on Little Lubyanka. I liked the service, the organ music, the calm, reverent atmosphere. Deeply impressed by Mary's faith, I decided to join that church after she left Moscow with Bob and the children in 1979.

The gray-haired Polish priest listened to my story, a faint smile crossing his kind face. I told him about Mary Pringle. He handed me the Lord's Prayer in Latin.

"Memorize it and come back," he instructed me amiably.

For hours I paced a circle in my room, reading and rereading the prayer, trying to memorize the words in the correct order without regard for meaning. My efforts failed; some force inside me constantly pushed the prayer out of my mind. Returning to the priest, I begged him simply to talk to me first rather than insist I learn the Paternoster. But that was not his method. He urged me to try again—and I left in defeat, knowing that fate did not want me in the Polish Catholic Church. Perhaps God did not want me there.

In the spring of 1980, six or eight months after Mary and Bob left Moscow, Olga—who had introduced me to Woody that fateful August day in 1972—unexpectedly came back into my life. We had not seen each other in the nearly six years since Woody left Moscow, and only rarely had she called to ask how things were going. By this time we knew little of each other's lives, which had taken such divergent paths. On the surface Olga looked as she always had—straight chestnut hair hanging to her shoulders, bangs covering her forehead. The glasses were a little thicker now, but she was still the same energetic, nervous Olga—and pregnant with her third child. Since we had last met face-to-face she had married, borne two children . . . and become a believer. She had come to my apartment to invite me to Easter services.

As easily as if we had never parted, Olga and I talked for hours about the past few years, and then suddenly she began to speak of her sense of guilt in relation to me: *that* was why she had not come to see me for such a long time. I reassured her as best I could. No one was at fault; it was simply fate. I felt much better after her visit, however. We were as close as ever. We could speak about anything and everything, secure in each other's understanding.

Walking along Potapov Lane, we recalled our superstitious "pilgrimages" to various churches on the eve of exams to light candles before the icon of St. Nicholas the Miracleworker. Unable to articulate our feelings but needing to offer some sign of gratitude for our success, we did the same *after* examinations. Tonight, however, marked the main holiday of Olga's spiritual life, the Resurrection of Christ. As for me, I simply accompanied her.

The Church of the Archangel Gabriel and St. Theodore Stratilates of the Antiochian Orthodox Church was built by one of Peter the Great's favorites early in the eighteenth century and restored eighty years later by Catherine the Great. At 10:00 P.M. on Easter Eve, internal passports in our pockets just in case, we set out for it. As we turned the corner into Telegraph Lane, we encountered a cordon of young civilian auxiliary police doing their Komsomol duty by preventing people from attending Easter services. The authorities were always especially vigilant at churches attended by members of the foreign community, like this one. Blocking the way, the men politely ordered us to turn around, saying, "You can't enter the church. There isn't enough room for the babushkas."

Equally polite, Olga responded, "Young men, move aside and let us through." She thrust her pregnant belly forward, leaving no room for discussion.

A few meters further on there was a second line, this one composed of uniformed police. A sergeant asked us playfully, "Why are you young and pretty women going to church?"

"What do you mean, 'young'?" I said. "I'll soon be a grandmother. I have a twenty-one-year-old daughter . . . would you like to see my documents?"

The police ranks parted good-naturedly. Just in front of the church, however, we ran into the third and most serious ring: men in civilian clothes, obviously KGB. They stood in a solid phalanx, sternly scrutinized everyone who approached, and permitted only older women and foreigners to pass. It would have been useless to argue with them and jokes were out of place. In my most solemn voice, I said to the two men who stepped forward to block us, "I want to speak to the precinct police captain."

The man was standing on the fringes of the guard; it was he who had come to the apartment the time the Voronovs had locked Lena and me out. The security people naturally did not want any disturbance in front of foreigners, whose automobiles were parked all along the curb. They summoned the captain. As the familiar pot-bellied, red-faced little man approached, I took off my kerchief and said with a smile, "I hope you haven't forgotten me—I'm Irina McClellan, and this is my close friend. We want to attend the service."

The captain looked at us for a brief instant, then nodded to the ring of plainclothesmen. A path suddenly opened up for us. Safely inside, Olga and I struggled to suppress our laughter.

"For once in your life that name helped," she observed drily.

Although the church was already crowded, we managed to get close to the altar and stood waiting for the service to begin. Almost everyone held a lit candle. From the choir loft came the stately sound of the Troparion. The church, with its recently cleaned murals, polished icons, enormous brass chandelier, and solid malachite floor-to-ceiling columns, produced an impression of massive, powerful solemnity. An unseen conductor seemed to unite the congregation in the Easter service. Slowly, inexorably, I began to share the experience.

Ten minutes or so before the procession around the church was to begin, Olga swayed and started to fall. The stuffiness in the crowded church, the musty odors of burning incense and unrefined beeswax candles proved too much for her advanced pregnancy. I took hold of her securely and tried to clear a path to fresh air; her extreme pallor and blue lips frightened me. As we jostled them people looked at her and immediately gave way with a breathless *"Gospodi, prosti!"*

Finally we reached the street. As we slowly retraced our steps toward my apartment, a sadness overcame me. Once again my efforts had failed.

17

A Reconciliation

SUSPENSE AND ANXIETY ruled my life, and I faced the future with dread. I was filled with anger: at the system which had treated me so cruelly; at my mother, who had renounced me; at Woody, whom I loved as before but who was not (so I thought) doing enough to reunite us. Anger at Lena, who wanted to be on her own. By the summer of 1981, three years after my abortive demonstrations, I was on the verge of collapse. Mired in an obliterating apathy, I could only sit for hours smoking mindlessly and posing unanswerable questions: What's the sense of it all? Who needs me?

Woody's mood seemed almost as bleak. He had written on January 12 to express only faint hope for better luck with the new administration in Washington:

I do not know anyone in the new Reagan Administration but a few old friends remain in Washington, and I shall try to reenlist their support; now that the do-nothing-to-upset-Brezhnev Carter crowd is gone maybe there will be some movement. The new people are not my cup of tea politically, but they won't be so damned naive dealing with Moscow. . . .

Months went by with no change in the situation. In June, Woody told me of his futile attempts to reach high governmental officials.

When he was a presidential candidate, George Bush—whose son was then my student—wrote me several good letters about his efforts to help us, but now that he is Vice-President I can't get through to him. Those people are of course incredibly busy. . . . The one bit of good news

is that Reagan will name Arthur Hartman to be our new ambassador in
Moscow. He is outstanding . . . and what a refreshing change after
[Malcolm] Toon!

Ambassador Toon had arrived in Moscow in January 1977
with the reputation of being tough with the Soviets, but as far as
we refuseniks were concerned, he played into the KGB's hands by
ordering American diplomats to give him twenty-four-hour notice
of any unofficial meetings with Soviets. He wanted to reduce such
contacts drastically, and he succeeded. Invitations dried up. Bob
and Mary Pringle were among the few embassy people who had
dared to maintain social relations with Soviet citizens. By Soviet
design, the Americans were already largely walled off from the real
world of the Soviet Union. Toon's order compounded the isolation and reinforced the KGB's attempt to break contacts between
the refuseniks and foreigners.

Ambassador Toon ignored all my requests for a meeting. At
first I thought he feared I would create another disturbance like
the one that embarrassed Cyrus Vance, but then a more sinister
explanation emerged. One Saturday afternoon at the synagogue
in the fall of 1978 my friend Rima Yakir warned, "Listen, people
at the American Embassy are saying you work for the KGB, and
that's why you are denied permission to leave. You've got to do
something, defend yourself!"

The news saddened but did not surprise me.

"Rima, how can I do that . . . hang a placard around my neck
proclaiming innocence? I have nothing to defend myself against."

The KGB itself originated this story. Woody had written
three years earlier that a Soviet émigré who had worked at
IMEMO was spreading it, evidently with little success, around
Washington. Enraged, Woody wanted to pick a public fight with
this "informant," who had emigrated with astonishing ease despite his high Komsomol rank, but I urged him not to do so. It
seemed to me that our best defense was to ignore the rumor. One
cannot easily prove a negative, especially across oceans and continents and ideologies, and I was confident that my innocence

would quickly be recognized. The charge was so preposterous.

Fortunately, my friends among Moscow's Jewish refuseniks, the people best able to spot KGB types, never believed the rumors and continued to associate with me. A few Americans remained my friends, others shunned me. Not until the arrival of Arthur Hartman as ambassador and Warren Zimmerman as deputy chief of mission in October 1981 did I again become persona grata at the American Embassy.

Once again we refuseniks and divided spouses could believe that our plight concerned the Americans, and the two dozen of us who hoped to join husbands or wives found in Ambassador Hartman and Minister Zimmerman two strong champions. For the very first time, the United States government recognized the issue of divided spouses in American-Soviet relations.

In the late summer of 1982 Warren Zimmerman and his wife Teenie invited me to dinner in their embassy apartment along with Alex and Rosa Ioffe and several other refuseniks. My friend David Satter, an American who reported from Moscow for the *Financial Times* of London, was also on the guest list. The only time I had tried to visit the embassy since my 1978 demonstration, the KGB had intercepted me.

David crammed five of us into his little burgundy-colored Soviet Zhiguli and drove to Tchaikovsky Street. The sight of half a dozen Soviet uniformed policemen in the archway and three Volgas full of men in civilian clothes parked nearby did not reassure me. A wave of fear rose deep from my stomach as I remembered how policemen had hurled me to the ground and twisted my arms after unshackling me from the fence.

Warren Zimmerman was waiting at the curb. Opening the rear door and offering me his arm, he said in a firm voice, "Don't be afraid. They won't bother you while you're with me."

We walked briskly past the guards, who merely looked at us with that special police curiosity and saluted.

That evening reopened my route to the American Embassy. I received many invitations now, not only to the Zimmermans' apartment but also to Spaso House, the American ambassador's

residence. Arthur and Donna Hartman regularly entertained
refuseniks, divided spouses, and dissidents, often introducing
them to visiting congressmen and senators and other American
officials concerned about human rights in the USSR. I wrote to
Woody about the Hartmans' and Zimmermans' support, and in
September 1982 he went to Washington to see Arthur Hartman,
then on home leave.

Ambassador Hartman [Woody wrote a few days after their meeting]
greeted me cordially and took me to a private room, where we talked for
more than an hour. I was struck by the obvious sincerity of his concern
for you and all the divided spouses and refuseniks; he sees helping you as
one of his most important tasks in Moscow. And not only that: he
assured me that the President himself will not rest until these long-
standing cases are resolved.

Sensing my depression in the melancholy summer of 1981,
before the change of command at the American Embassy, Rosa
Ioffe invited me in July to join her and Alex and their children on
their summer vacation. I had inherited the Ioffes, as it were, from
my friend Irene, who had emigrated to the United States in 1979,
and when Rabbi Engel "adopted" both our families the bond of
friendship grew even stronger. With a number of other refusenik
families from Moscow and Leningrad, they were going to Ust-
Narva on the Baltic, a small village near the boundary between
Russia proper and Estonia. With half-timbered, well-constructed
cottages of North German design, tidy gardens, manicured paths
through carefully preserved forests, reasonably well-stocked local
stores, and polite Estonians who spoke heavily accented Russian,
Ust-Narva was almost foreign.

"But what would I do there?" I objected. "Everyone will be
busy with children and husbands—and I'll be alone."

"Never mind," Alex interrupted, putting aside his mathemati-
cal formulas. "Bring along some books and put together a children's theater—in English! *That* will keep you busy."

Rosa and Alex screened off a corner for me on the porch of
their rented cottage overlooking a lilac garden. Every morning I

awakened to a sweet, heady smell that soon merged with the irresistible aroma of Rosa's famous pancakes, a luxurious stack of which waited on the wood stove. Every morning was a fiesta as the two Ioffe children and their playmates devoured the pancakes with three kinds of homemade jam, fresh raspberries, thick Estonian sour cream, then raced for second helpings. We adults found the pace infectious.

After a few days of rest I got busy. Using various fairy tales and traditional stories for sources, I wrote several scenarios, held try-outs, and assigned roles. Rehearsals began: every day after lunch we gathered at someone's cottage to learn and walk through the roles. When Mark Terlitsky brought his guitar and his daughter Olya her violin, we transformed the production into a musical and rehearsal became even more fun. Parents prepared costumes and built sets; soon the entire community was involved.

From early in the morning everyone waited impatiently for rehearsal time. In the evenings, after the young actors and actresses had gone to bed, the adults gathered in groups at various dachas to have a drink and discuss the latest news from Moscow, Leningrad, and the world beyond.

Finally it was time to announce the premiere. The children tacked up notices throughout the village: ALL VACATIONERS IN UST-NARVA INVITED TO THE CHILDREN'S THEATER 5 P.M. SATURDAY, JULY 25, 1981. BANQUET IN THE WOODS FOLLOWING THE PERFORMANCE. We prayed it would not rain.

The day before the premiere I was awakened by an uneasy, insistent summons to Moscow. I bustled about nervously, trying to dispel my sense of foreboding. Two days earlier Lena had said on the telephone that everything was fine at home, so why was I so restless? Moscow would still be there . . . what *was* it that propelled me home? I tried to reason with myself: tomorrow was the premiere and the picnic, everyone looking forward to a good time. No, my heart said, go to Moscow—*today.* I began to pack my things.

I went upstairs to Rosa. Having nothing to explain, I simply said, "Rosa, I've got to go to Moscow. Boris is driving down today and I'll go with him."

Her eyes wide with surprise, Rosa was at a loss. After a few moments she stammered, "But . . . but what's the matter? Is something. . . ?"

"Please understand," I broke in, "everyone will be angry with me but that can't be helped."

I dressed hurriedly and trotted over to Boris's cottage to ask for a lift, then came back and sat on the porch to wait for him. After a while Rosa said quietly, "Don't worry, I'll take care of things here. Everything's ready . . . Mark can handle the premiere."

For most of the long drive I remained silent, checking off the hours and kilometers in my mind. At first Boris tried to amuse me, but when I did not respond he turned on the radio and concentrated on his driving. I grew more and more impatient, as though afraid to miss something in Moscow . . .

A warm, stuffy day greeted us as we reached the outskirts of the city; perspiration glistened on the faces of people on the streets. Cars, buses, trolleybuses, trucks, squealing brakes, an occasional horn, taxi drivers shouting at errant pedestrians, all the big-city noises—such a contrast with peaceful, quiet, Ust-Narva on the northern sea. But whatever it was that had brought me careening back was on the verge of erupting into the open, and I experienced a certain satisfaction.

I dashed up the three flights of stairs to my apartment and hurriedly unlocked the door. Startled, Lena looked up from the chair where she sat reading.

"What's happened? I wasn't expecting you . . ."

She began to apologize for the messy apartment but, only half-conscious of her words, I was already dialing my mother's number. She picked up the receiver on the first ring.

"Mama . . . it's me. Your daughter . . ."

I had no idea what to say next, but Mama answered immediately.

"Irochka! I'm *so* glad you called . . . I'll come over right away."

Without another word she replaced the receiver. Lena stared at me with a puzzled look, but I myself did not know what was going on. There had been times during the three years of our estrangement when, tormented by guilt, I had picked up the telephone to call my mother, only to have so such anger well up that I could not dial. Sometimes I begged Lena to call, but she resolutely refused.

Hurriedly, Lena and I cleaned and dusted, put away clothes and books and newspapers, prepared some food. The doorbell rang much sooner than we expected and there stood my mother—not decisive and authoritative as before but confused, aged, more overweight than ever. Eyes moist, we embraced in a tight little family knot. The separation had at last brought us closer. Mama hung on; the tension of those years fell away. She needed me.

We went into my room. Mama sat down heavily on the sofa, sighed deeply, and said, "Irochka, Lenochka—tomorrow I'm going into the hospital for an operation . . . " A flood of frightened tears gushed forth.

So *that's* it! Contradictory emotions swept over me: concern for my mother, happiness that we were reconciled.

"Mamochka," I said soothingly, "I'm here now—tell me what's wrong."

Years after menopause, she had begun to bleed. The doctors insisted on an immediate operation. In the Soviet Union a diagnosis of cancer is almost never revealed to the patient; the physicians ask relatives for permission to operate. But seriously ill people usually know what afflicts them, and so it was with my mother. She knew.

She could not stop crying as I sat next to her on the sofa, hugging her and stroking her hair.

"Mama, we're together now and everything will be all right. I'll go to the doctors with you."

We had some tea and something to eat, talked as animatedly as if the three years had passed in a twinkling. But suddenly Mama rose to her feet, face taut. She insisted that Lena accompany her to the bank.

"I want to put a thousand rubles in your account—for your wedding."

"But, Babushka," Lena protested, "I'm not even thinking of getting married! I don't need any money."

"Never mind," Mama said, already heading for the door and beckoning Lena to follow. "If anything happens, I want to be sure you have something from your grandmother."

The next day we took Mama to a KGB hospital a short bus ride from the October Field metro station on the northwest side of the city. It was a huge, U-shaped, solidly Stalinist edifice surrounded by its own park with crushed-rock paths, flower beds, shrubs, and little groves of birch and spruce where ambulatory patients could enjoy nature during good weather. The contrast between that KGB hospital and the shabby ones where Lena went twice a year for her ulcer was striking. The large, sunny wards had only three or four beds each, there were ample supplies of everything, including fresh bed linen daily and plenty of good food, and the solicitous staff maintained cordial relations with patients.

The surgeon, an attractive, intelligent woman in her late forties, took me aside to explain the situation. My mother had second-degree cancer of the uterus; her condition was extremely serious.

"The success of the operation depends to some extent on the patient's morale," the surgeon said earnestly. "If you can calm her down, her prospects will be brighter."

Mama waited on a bench in the little park. Trying to conceal my own anxiety, I walked a tightrope, reporting and not reporting at the same time, making jokes.

"Well, the important thing is that you're with me," she said finally. "You always did know how to perk up my spirits!"

The hysterectomy was basically successful. The cancer had not metastasized. But my mother's recovery was abnormally slow, in part because she was so overweight: the stitches kept snapping through the thick, weak-celled layers of fat, and infection set in. She became agitated and capricious, convinced that the doctors were not paying her sufficient attention.

I visited her almost every day. Although the food was far better than in ordinary hospitals, Mama did not like it and asked me to bring caviar, vitamins, and special home-cooked dishes in order to replace—such was her understanding—the blood she had lost. Mama behaved like many sick people, subconsciously making family members pamper them as punishment for their good health. I did not mind. I was happy to serve her, to know she needed me.

The KGB surgeons removed Mama's tumor, but they could not heal the incision. After two months of unsuccessful treatment they gave up and sent her to an ordinary municipal hospital. She was occupying a bed needed for KGB personnel on active duty, and they could not tolerate that.

The municipal hospital, an ugly, badly designed box of a building, had never been remodeled and probably not repainted since it was built half a century earlier. In that respect it was identical to the ones where Lena was treated for her ulcer. Branching off long, badly lit corridors, each ward was filled with beds from which sick women, draped in colorless tentlike hospital smocks, stared listlessly at newcomers.

There was nothing we could do. My mother needed further treatment and this was the only place she could get it. I came every other day to walk her around the stark inner courtyard. She was undergoing chemotherapy and insisted she needed fresh air to speed the expulsion of the poisons from her body.

The turn of events embittered Mama. They had taken away her privileges. She cursed the KGB, which for thirty-six years she had served "with faith and truth," as she put it, and which had now thrown her out into the street. She could talk of nothing else when we strolled around the courtyard and she was sure no one could overhear. So full of anger was she that I felt sorry for her.

I was both sympathetic and perplexed: why do human beings act this way? Not until they had hurt and offended her personally did my mother appreciate the KGB's cruelty. Why had not *my* story, her own daughter's suffering, produced understanding? I did not speak of this to her. She was in enough pain, and this was no time to clear the air. My parents needed my support and help, and we were bound to each other by ties of blood, not ideology, and by our common fear of illness and death.

Tired after four months in the hospital, more preoccupied than ever with her health, my mother rejoiced when she was able to go home again. I visited her and my stepfather often, bringing food and whatever else they needed, thus sparing my stepfather, who had aged visibly, from those maddening queues in the stores. I did their laundry, washed windows, and sat with them for hours, trying to compensate for my absence in their lives during the three years of our estrangement.

My mother treated me much more carefully, and did her best not to raise sensitive topics. Ideology disappeared from the daily menu. She did ask about Woody: "He's still waiting for you?" I brought her a letter in which he mentioned her illness.

Poor Elizaveta Ivanovna! I am so sorry this has happened to her but delighted she is recovering. It is hard on you, of course, but at least you two are together again. I can well understand what you are going through. . . .

With a satisfied expression, she said, "I always knew he was a fine man!"

We talked long hours about the family, and especially Grannie Sanya. Mama seemed wistful at such moments. When she spoke of our now scattered clan, I detected a certain sadness.

"Mama," I said, "our babushka evidently had something we lack . . . something better to live by. . . . " I paused for a few moments, then added, "Maybe faith in God?"

Mama remained silent—a *thoughtful* silence.

18

An Unusual Guest

THE RECONCILIATION with my mother and her recovery from cancer brightened the late summer of 1981. A second joy, one I had almost ceased to believe possible, materialized equally unexpectedly in the middle of August, a couple of weeks after Mama's operation: the Voronovs left the kommunalka for a new apartment.

Preoccupied with visits to the hospital and the frustrating search for special food, I had not noticed the changes in the Voronovs' behavior as—faces radiating happiness—they ignored me . . . and my Jewish friends. They brought home empty boxes and the sound of heavy objects being shifted around came from their room, into which they took the telephone for long, supersecret conversations. I was flabbergasted when I came home one afternoon and found their door wide open for the movers—my dream come true!

The relief was almost too much to bear. In those seven years since Woody left Moscow I had almost forgotten how to handle good fortune. Creeping into my room, I softly closed the door, sat down in my favorite armchair, covered my face with my hands, and burst into tears of sheer unrestrained joy. A silent wail came out of the depths of my soul: "Oh Lord, you have after all bestowed your mercy on me!"

The next morning I went to the Bauman District Housing Office to see the director, a primly dressed woman in her sixties. I told my story and assured her that within the year OVIR would grant permission for me to join my husband in America. By waiting until my departure, she would have an attractive three-room

apartment to allocate as she saw fit. Retrieving the document on
the room from her files, she wrote DO NOT RENT on it, signed with
a flourish, smiled, and wished me luck.

With the help of a friend I forced the lock and left the Voronovs' door—and our two—open wide, turned on all the lights,
began to rearrange the furniture, shuffled vases and knickknacks,
and walked around in a loopy daze, anticipating the housewarming. A rush of strength replaced the hatred of the Voronovs that
had eaten at me for so long. Another miracle! Free at last in my
own little fortress . . .

My friend Marie-Hélène, an interpreter at the French Embassy and David Satter's fiancée, declared that we would have the
housewarming on my birthday, September 4. For the first time in
years I actually looked forward to a party. Many people came to
help. Two artists painted the Voronovs' room—lilac on two walls,
gray on the others—to destroy the aura of the former occupants.
A friend drove into the forest to collect some birch logs from
which we fashioned stools and four sturdy table legs. Still another
friend, an actor, liberated a table top from a theater warehouse.
From my "American" suitcase—full of presents intended for
Woody—I retrieved a handstitched Ukrainian tablecloth bought
in Kiev and put it on the table in the new room, hung matching
curtains, fixed shelves and put souvenirs from the same suitcase on
them, and hung my collection of lacquered black metal trays of
various shapes with handpainted flowers on the walls. Marie-Hélène gave me big white candles she had brought from France; we
put them on the table and suddenly found ourselves in a real
Russian *izba*, a peasant cottage. In the Moscow tradition, we had
created something out of nothing.

Like an unexpected birthday-housewarming present, a third
near-miracle came when David Satter appeared at my door late
one afternoon. David and I often talked about the situation in the
country; he sympathized deeply with the plight of those of us who
wished to leave. In June 1981 he asked his friend of many years,
Strobe Talbott of *Time*, to carry a letter from me to President

Reagan; Strobe agreed to do so. Grateful though I was to him and David, I did not expect much, and indeed the summer passed and nothing happened.

We chatted about the upcoming party for a few moments, then David motioned me to be silent, turned up the volume on the radio, and gravely handed me a letter.

THE WHITE HOUSE
Washington

Dear Mrs. McClellan:

Your letter of June 22 [1981] is an eloquent and poignant reminder of your many efforts in these past years to obtain permission from the Soviet authorities to emigrate to the United States to live with your husband.

Your situation is a particularly tragic one. Your numerous attempts to try to gain exit permission from the Soviet Union have touched the heart of all of us who believe in freedom and fundamental human rights. Your courage in the face of continued harassment from the Soviet authorities inspires our admiration and deepens our concern, which we share with your many supporters and well-wishers in the United States.

With Kevin Klose of *The Washington Post* (left), Strobe Talbott of *Time* (center), and David Satter of the *Financial Times* (right), autumn 1981.

In past years high U.S. Government officials have raised your case with their Soviet counterparts on numerous occasions. We will continue to express our concern and indignation about your case to Soviet officials at every appropriate occasion. The lack of Soviet responsiveness to our representations on your behalf has not lessened our concern or our determination to try to help. Your name was placed on the United States Government Representation List of Divided Families once it became apparent the Soviets would not readily grant you permission to emigrate. Your name will remain on the list until the Soviets do permit you to be reunited with your husband in the United States. In this way, as well as in others, we have continued and will continue to remind the Soviets of our long-standing concern that your tragic circumstances must be resolved to allow you to be reunited with your husband.

In addition to expressing . . . our concern to the Soviets, we want to keep abreast of your situation in every possible way. Please contact the American Embassy in Moscow any time you feel we can be of assistance. We have asked your husband to do the same with the Department of State in Washington. It is our hope that through continued, determined efforts you may soon be reunited with your husband.

Sincerely,

[signed] Ronald Reagan

Unable to believe my eyes, I gaped at David, who again put his finger to his lips. I read the letter once more. Still not fully comprehending, I scrawled on a piece of paper, *Is it real?* David smiled and nodded his head vigorously, then said, "Why don't we go for a walk? It's a shame to stay inside on such a nice day!"

On the street David said, "Unfortunately I have to take the letter back to the embassy. The White House fears it might cause you trouble if the Soviets find out about it."

"Does this mean the President will push my case?"

"Surely a lot more than Carter did," David answered.

Woody was as surprised as I was by the President's interest in our case. He wrote a few weeks later, "I have been in touch with the White House . . . they asked me not to publicize . . . [the letter] and so of course I will not. I don't know what this means but it cannot hurt; at least Reagan himself knows about you. . . . "

In general we refuseniks and dissidents welcomed the new administration, which promised to take the Brezhnev regime to task for its cynical disregard of human rights. Six years after the signing of the Helsinki Accords our situation was worse than ever. Moscow had let thousands of poor Jews from the Caucasus and Central Asia—some of whom had to be persuaded to file the papers—emigrate to Israel; the Carter people, including Ambassador Toon, trumpeted this as evidence of the success of their human rights policy vis-à-vis Moscow. But Brezhnev—or rather KGB chief Andropov, who really ran the country from the late 1970s—had cracked down hard on the refuseniks, divided spouses, and dissidents. By 1981 the number of those who had waited at least five years to emigrate had reached several thousand. If Ronald Reagan meant what he said about holding the Kremlin to account for this barbaric policy, we were solidly for him.

Encouraged by the latest developments, on September 4 I prepared *zakuski* and welcomed my guests—Russians, Jewish refuseniks, foreigners, my students. About thirty people came bearing presents, flowers, bottles. My birthday was merely incidental. Everyone was caught up in the celebration of a rare victory: a three-room apartment in central Moscow! Toast after toast to new life, new hope, freedom . . . Rosa Ioffe hugged me and said, "You'll see—soon they'll let you go to your husband!" Mark Terlitsky had brought his guitar and after a while a group of guests began singing to his accompaniment. When they took a break, I put on a record and the dancing began. The festivities were in full swing when around eleven-thirty the telephone rang and a thin little voice said plaintively, "Mama, I'm at the Kirov metro station. Happy birthday. Don't worry, everything's all right . . . can somebody come to help me with my suitcase?"

Lena had gone to the mountains for a couple of weeks' vacation, and suddenly here she was back in Moscow after just a week. My spirits plummeted as I imagined all sorts of horrors. One of the men went to the Kirov station. I tried to keep a happy face, but everyone sensed my concern. Then in she walked, tanned after a week in the sun and seemingly healthier, all smiles; but there was about her something a little guilty, a bit tense.

"Lena, what has happened? It's best to come straight out with it."

"*Nothing,* Mama, nothing special. We can talk when your guests leave."

When at last we were alone she gave me a birthday present— some rose-colored sandals she had found in a local store in the Caucasus—kissed me, wished me health and happiness. I could not relax.

"Lena, for heaven's sake—*out* with it!"

"I've decided to live in the mountains. I found a job running a little library. I've got to go back in a week or I'll lose it."

Silently, I berated myself for celebrating the summer's victories too soon. What good were a private apartment and President Reagan's sympathy and normal relations with my mother if I were to lose my daughter?

Lena intended to live at a resort in the Caucasus to which people from the cities came for a week or two to ski during the day, carouse and show off in the evenings. The local men—Georgians, Ossetes, Abkhazy—firmly believed that all "white" women came to the mountains principally for sex, and acted accordingly.

Lena's special diet was hard enough to follow in Moscow, where food supplies were better than anywhere else. Skiing would place a severe strain on her delicate constitution. The weather was not the best. Just when we had the apartment all to ourselves . . . A protective mother can conjure up all sorts of objections! Lena would have none of it. The next day I called a physician friend and asked her to talk to Lena. Several other friends also tried to dissuade her, but she remained adamant.

"It's time for me to live my own life," she insisted. "I'm twenty-two, I want to ski . . . become an instructor."

A week later she left. As I watched the train glide out of the station, once again a terrible sense of loss overcame me.

Lena wrote only rarely. We called each other now and then,

but I knew little of her life in the mountains, and my heart was uneasy.

For years I had dreamed of having pets, but at every stage of my life someone opposed it. First it was my mother, who believed that cats carry infection and dogs filth. Then came Lena's father with similar views. And it was unthinkable to keep pets in the kommunalka. All families had to agree in writing if anyone wanted them, and the Voronovs would never have consented.

But now I was absolutely alone. Fortress, time, energy—all belonged to me. I went to the "bird market" near Taganka Square, a fenced-off section on an open lot where Muscovites have gathered for generations to buy and sell animals and birds. The exotic place is like a zoo, the gallery of humans no less interesting than the fauna. Birds are the main attraction—big ones, little ones, talking parrots from overseas that cost five thousand rubles and more, other birds trained to "say" a few words, brilliantly colored tropical fish in aquariums, reptiles, cats and dogs, kittens and puppies. The sellers of cats are frequently strange, shifty-eyed people who often simply find or steal cats on the street, clean them up, and bring them to the bird market to make a ruble or two.

I walked among the cages and boxes and little stalls and aquariums, longing to buy every kitten and puppy, and finally selected a fluffy, month-old, rust-white Persian kitten with huge sandy eyes on a mischievous mug. I brought it home and the comedy began: it got into everything, wanted to play constantly, and innocently scratched me so badly that I became ashamed of my hands and forearms. But I loved the little creature, named it Kotya, and let it sleep at the foot of my bed. The apartment became a happier, less lonely place. We were always together. When I came home from a lesson or shopping the kitten greeted me with a great show of affection, and it would meow softly as though replying when I related my problems.

A few days later a friend gave me a chocolate-colored female poodle with a baby-crocodile snout, expressive dark eyes, thin tail—which I left intact—and silky-smooth fur. It would be company for the kitten. A month old when I brought her home, she smelled like espresso coffee; I named her Manya. Very quickly the cat and dog—my new "family"—grew accustomed to each other, licked each other, played constantly, brought me endless diversion.

As soon as Manya was old enough, we went on long daily walks. Attention focused on the dog, I ceased looking over my shoulder for KGB "tails." New responsibilities and little joys made my life a bit more normal, taking some of the pain out of Lena's departure.

In December 1981 I received the regular biannual rejection of my application for an exit visa, as usual without explanation. No more, no less devastating than the two dozen refusals that preceded it, this one again merely confirmed my status in Limbo.

A couple of weeks later, my doorbell rang at midmorning. I was not expecting anyone, and friends invariably called before coming, but I was not alarmed. Life had been relatively calm and peaceful. A young uniformed policeman stood outside the doorway. Handing me a piece of paper, he said, "The Housing Office has assigned me the free room in your apartment. Here's the order. I want to see the room."

"But—there's been a mistake!" I stammered, glancing at the paper. "This apartment isn't suitable for communal living."

Ignoring my objection, he stepped in and immediately went into the room, the first one on the right. I thought it odd he knew exactly where to go. He looked around for a minute or two, poked his head into the kitchen, bath, and toilet, then said in smug, satisfied tones, "I like it. I'll be back in a couple of days with my things."

Disaster threatened. How could I live with a policeman? Had the KGB decided to establish its headquarters here? I imagined agents in and out of uniform wandering through the small apartment, keeping me under twenty-four-hour surveillance. But after a while I remembered a municipal regulation that stipulates an apartment with a kitchen smaller than five square meters has to be private, for one family. My kitchen was barely four square meters.

I went to see an inspector at the District Housing Office; to my relief he turned out to be a very decent person. I explained the situation, then listened carefully to his advice.

"Install a couple of new locks, get copies of all official papers relating to the apartment, don't open the door to strangers . . . and just wait. This will turn out all right."

Some friends came to put the new locks on the door, and I got a strong piece of wood to prop under the doorknob. Mark Terlitsky, an architect, inspected the apartment and declared that my room and the adjoining one, where the Voronovs had lived, were originally connected by a door. The wall between them was not a load-bearing one; it provided only a slight barrier to sound. Unrelated families could not be forced to share such a wall.

The occupants of the apartment above mine let me look at their rooms. The floorplans were identical. Their two rooms were connected by a door, exactly as Mark said mine had once been. This was the last bit of proof I needed that someone had illegally walled up that door.

Mark contacted a friend with a reputation for outwitting the bureaucracy. Clutching a box of expensive French cosmetics Marie-Hélène had given me, I accompanied Mark and Valeri, the conqueror of bureaucrats, to the division of the District Housing Office where architectural plans and blueprints were stored. While Mark and I sat in the waiting room, Valeri—the cosmetics now in his coat pocket—went to an inner office where, as he had established, a young woman worked alone.

Valeri persuaded her to show him the drawings and blueprints for all the apartments in my wing of No. 7 Chernyshevsky Street. There it was: someone had tried unsuccessfully to erase the tiny red lines that indicated a door between the two rooms. Valeri approached the young clerk, unhurriedly put the French cosmetics on her desk, and told her in a low voice that someone had made a mistake. The floorplans for all the apartments were identical except for that one minor change, where someone had tried to disguise the sealing of a door. Would she permit him to restore those two little lines?

Apprehensive, the woman started to protest, but Valeri spoke persuasively—and one would never find such cosmetics in Moscow. She gave in. Not only was Valeri able to draw in the door; she also allowed him to take the drawings for the entire wing and have them photocopied.

I obtained a copy of the 1926 regulation concerning kitchen size, and a friend gave me the particulars of a modern ordinance that forbids the perpetuation of communal living except where unavoidable. When one set of occupants of a kommunalka moves out, their living space must ordinarily be assigned to those who remain. The ordinance had been in effect, or at least on the books, for several years, but Moscow City Council did not publicize it. When it suited the authorities to keep an apartment communal, they did so.

There was still another housing regulation on my side. This one concerned permissible noise levels: no room that shared a wall with an elevator shaft could be used as a bedroom. The room in question adjoined the shaft.

The director of the District Housing Office was not so agreeable this time. She glanced at my documents for a couple of seconds, then asked sarcastically, "What is this, have you come to pump some law into me?"

The slang and the vulgar tone were unworthy of a bureaucrat, much less a woman of her dignified years.

"Excuse me, *Madame*," I replied. "I don't understand your language. What do you mean by 'pump'? I'm defending my rights."

She glared at me for a moment, then looked out the window and said with a bitter, resigned sigh, "And what am *I* supposed to do when the KGB gives me instructions? They came in here and said, 'McClellan claims she's leaving. She's not going anywhere! Don't listen to her—*we* need that room.'"

She had probably never had to deal with the KGB directly. Only lack of experience and advanced years could have given her the foolish courage to blurt out everything. Be that as it may, she grudgingly promised to investigate and give me a final decision within a couple of months.

The young policeman returned, but by now my new locks were in place. A strange dialogue ensued.

"Let me in!" He rattled the door.

"Young man, I told you there's been a mistake. Go back to the Housing Office and they'll reassign you."

"I like *this* room." More shaking and pounding.

"Go away."

"Let me in!"

"Never! They'll give you a *better* room . . . "

The next day the Interior Ministry captain, the one on whose head our banner had hung in 1978, telephoned and ranted at the top of his voice for a few minutes. Finally I interrupted him.

"Comrade Captain! Is this your own *son* you're fighting for? Since when are you allocating living quarters?"

I hung up, knowing this was not the end of the matter.

This took place between August 1981 and April 1982, near the end of Leonid Brezhnev's regime. Brezhnev had been afflicted with Alzheimer's disease and other illnesses for years. Anticipating his death, Yuri Andropov launched a reform campaign from his position as head of the KGB. Gaining momentum as Brezhnev stubbornly clung to life, the Andropov campaign began right in central Moscow, in my own Bauman District that was "represented" in the Supreme Soviet by none other than Leonid Brezhnev. Andropov cracked down severely on corruption and—indicating the sensitivity of the problem in the crowded central city—one of his prime targets was the housing bureaucracy. Several housing inspectors and other officials went to prison for accepting bribes, circumventing laws, playing favorites. No one knew where Andropov's investigators would appear next.

I had presented the director of the District Housing Office with a dilemma. The law was clearly on my side. If she violated it,

I could bring a case against her personally, and in the reform
climate of 1982 she might have gone to prison. But the KGB itself
had instructed her to break the law.

In mid-April 1982 I received an official document assigning
the third room to me. There would be no neighbor. I would not
even have to pay extra rent. The authorities had decided that, in
view of the substandard kitchen size, the third room would be
designated a "dry kitchen," in effect a dining nook, for which
there would be no rent increase. I framed this letter and put it in a
place of honor, the "red corner" as the Communists restyled the
icon corner in Orthodox Russian homes. Victory of victories . . .

A new round of celebrations began. On my birthday we had
rejoiced unofficially, according to the irregular regulations of
Limbo. Now we celebrated officially, strictly in harmony with the
majestic impartiality of Moscow City Council ordinances.

Marie-Hélène came to one of the parties with a friend, a tall,
handsome young man of perhaps thirty whom she introduced as
Father Nikolai. Dressed as he was in normal clothes, only his full
beard hinted at the man's calling. He smiled rather bashfully as he
shook my hand. I had never met a clergyman socially and felt
confused. How does one treat a guest who happens to be a priest?
In a foolish effort to conceal my embarrassment, I laughed and
said, "It's nice to meet you, Batyushka. Welcome to our sinful
world!"

The priest sat in an armchair the entire evening, quietly observing the merriment, speaking cordially enough but only when
spoken to. Discomfited by his presence, I thought to myself, Let
everything go on in its natural way. No reason to act any differently because a priest is present.

Marie-Hélène and Father Nikolai were the last to leave. As he
was saying goodbye, the priest handed me a card.

"Here's my address. I work in a small village church on the
border between Russia and the Ukraine. It's a beautiful place—
come to see me."

Taken aback, I replied, "But, Batyushka, who needs such a
sinner in your holy places?"

Satisfied with my own joke, I laughed nervously.

"No, no, Irochka," he insisted, "you must come. I can see that you're very tired, and our village is so peaceful. You can enjoy a summer vacation in the country . . . or ski next winter."

"Well, I . . . I thank you."

"And here's the telephone number of my parents. They live here in Moscow. If you should ever need anything . . . " He left the new offer up in the air, open-ended.

Father Nikolai and Marie-Hélène left, and I stood in the little hall trying to interpret this strange sign—a priest in my home.

19
Revelation

IN THE SUMMER of 1982 my friend Maria lost both her parents. Although her mother had long complained of various ailments, she looked vigorously healthy at fifty-six, and—preoccupied with their own petty cares—family and friends paid little attention to her muted grumbling. When she finally went to a doctor it was too late: cancer consumed her eight weeks after it was diagnosed. Six months later, Maria's father died suddenly in his sleep. The medical examiner wrote "coronary infarct" on the death certificate, but everyone who knew him understood that he died of grief.

A tightly knit, loving family was no more. The envy of everyone, they had seemed to have more fun together than most families. Every summer Maria and her sister took their husbands and children and pets to the parents' large, comfortable dacha outside Moscow. Maria's mother grew flowers and vegetables; her father, having taken up art in his retirement, painted landscapes. The children would tag along when he went into the woods with his sketchbook and watercolors. When he tired of painting he showed them how to find mushrooms, took them swimming in the little river, produced treats from his rucksack. After summer vacations the extended family gathered at the parents' apartment for dinner every Sunday without fail.

Now all that had come to a sudden end. Maria was shattered. Her appetite disappeared, she slept only fitfully, and she suffered from a recurrent nightmare in which her parents wandered through the countryside homeless and destitute, begging for alms. She would awaken in a cold sweat, moaning and gasping for breath.

Shortly before Christmas of 1982, an elderly, pious cleaning woman at Maria's laboratory told her she should go to church and light candles for her parents.

"They were never baptized, *golubushka* [my little pigeon]; they didn't know God, you see, and they're in torment! You have to do something."

Raised in an atheist home, Maria had not been baptized, and therefore, according to Russian Orthodox belief, her own candles would serve no purpose. When she told me about the old woman's suggestion, I volunteered my help.

"I was baptized—I can go immediately."

I returned to the Church of the Archangel Gabriel. Behind the counter a nunlike babushka dressed all in black, hair and forehead covered by a large white kerchief, sold devotional candles. Her manner reserved but kind, she listened patiently and with obvious sympathy as I related the story of Maria and her parents—in short, my mission. She gave me two medium-sized candles and showed me the special place for them before the crucifix. When I had lit them and placed them in the holders, she said softly, "Now go to the Icon of the Mother of God and pray for your friend's parents."

"I don't know any prayers," I replied apologetically.

"All right, then. Just *think* about the parents and stand for the whole service. Afterward there will be a special memorial service in front of the crucifix."

I did as she directed and went to the left of the altar where the large Icon of the Mother of God stood. There were many others, but I was glad the babushka had sent me to this one. The mysteriously enchanting icon attracted me powerfully. Eyes half-closed, only dimly aware of the tiny flames that danced before it, I looked at the angelic face of the Mother of God and mentally related the story of my friend and her parents, beginning, Mother of God, help my friend, she is wasting away in her despair . . . she has a son for whom she is responsible . . . I repeated this over and over.

I drifted into a strange, semi-conscious state. Time slowed, slowed more, then stopped, and finally—utterly irrelevant—disappeared. My mind was unshackled by a wave of liberating peace that impelled me toward . . . something . . .

The sudden bustle of the congregation at the close of the service restored me to consciousness. People softly nudged each other toward the priest, who stood in front of the altar holding a large cross, crossed themselves, kissed the cross, knelt and repeated the sign of the cross, then quietly left the church. A few people who remained near the burning candles in front of the icons began to sing a hymn, signaling the beginning of the memorial service.

Afterward, as I went out into the street, a sense of peace again swept through me. I walked slowly, almost weightless, through the narrow streets toward home, reluctant to go inside for fear of losing the sensation.

A week of normal routine and cares flew by—visiting my mother, lessons, shopping for food, caring for the pets—but at its end a nagging anxiety made me impatient for Sunday morning. I walked rapidly to the church and stood in the exact same spot, which was empty, almost as though reserved for me. Again I silently addressed the Icon of the Mother of God, first about Maria and her parents, and then, gradually, about myself—about Woody, Mama, Lena. Holy Mother of God, I have made a mess of my life . . . I cannot get my bearings . . . I do not know how I should live . . .

Weeks passed, one after another. Afraid of their reaction, I said nothing to anyone of my experiences, which I could not explain anyway. Maria knew only that I had fulfilled my promise. Every Sunday I hurried back to the church, a sense of joyful relief growing stronger with each visit. I had found a refuge where all people, no matter their station in life, were equal, children of one mother. I felt more secure than I had in years.

Maria slowly recovered. Her grief remained, but the nightmares became less frequent and finally ended altogether. We spent a great deal of time together and one day she asked, "What *is* it with you? You act so mysteriously calm. I've never seen you quite like this."

I confessed. "Since the day I went to light candles for your parents . . . I've been going to church. Every Sunday."

No discernible emotion registering on her face, she looked at me silently. Grateful that she did not press me, I did not go into details.

My icon was called "Rejoice O Bride Unwedded." The marvelous name fascinated me. I had come to feel close to her and now prayed from the depths of my being, feeling my hand make—for the first time in my life—the sign of the cross easily and naturally, almost of its own volition:

Mother of God, let all be as the Lord God wishes. I do not know what I need, let it be as He wishes. Give health to Lena, my mother, my husband, my friends. Help us sinners overcome our tribulations. I ask nothing else. I, a sinner, am in Thy power. . . .

Gradually I came to understand the service. One day when the choir and congregation began to sing the "Magnificat," I dropped to my knees, overcome by happiness and peace. As I rose to my feet after the hymn and vaguely watched people light candles and place them at the altar and in front of the various icons, I gazed at "my" icon, illuminated by an otherworldly inner light: her sorrowful expression gone, the Mother of God "Rejoice O Bride Unwedded" smiled directly into my eyes . . .

Unnerved, I glanced around me. Was I hallucinating? I shot a quick look at the small windows high on the wall, thinking the rays of the sun had created an illusion. The sky was overcast. Had anyone else seen it? Preoccupied with their own worship, the others in the congregation were not, at least not at that moment, looking at my icon. Timidly, my eyes again sought it—the smile remained. Spellbound, I gulped, then closed my eyes to offer a silent prayer of thanksgiving.

When I sought the icon again, it was as it had always been. The smile had disappeared, the eyes full of inexpressible sorrow as usual.

From that day I have felt the protection of the Mother of God.

One Sunday Olga appeared at the Church of the Archangel Gabriel. Because it was difficult for her children to stand through the entire two-hour service, her husband brought them only when it was half over. I looked on as Olga led them forward and positioned each child in front of the altar. After a while our eyes met, instantly full of unspoken deep meaning on both sides.

After the service we greeted one another in the church courtyard. Olga had been coming to the church for several years, and as we stood there, various friends and acquaintances of hers came up. She introduced me, and in the ensuing weeks my own little Sunday circle widened. Olga and her close friend Evangeliya, or "Gela," who sang in the choir, sometimes came to my apartment for tea after the service, while Olga's children went home with their father.

My life had become fuller and richer, more meaningful. I breathed easier, the feeling of desolation disappeared. Then a new worry appeared: I felt in need of a guide, a mentor, someone to talk to about my past life, someone to see to it that I did not "succumb to life's charms," as the Church's language put it. I mentioned this to Olga and Gela over tea one Sunday afternoon.

"You, friend, need to make confession, and for that you need a confessor," Olga said in her decisive manner. "Gela, you know everybody in Moscow—help her find a good reliable priest. Given what's happened to her, she needs to be careful."

By that time I had learned that the modern Church existed on two levels: the official one of church services and public worship under close KGB supervision, and the second, underground one outside the churches. The underground Church held special importance for new believers, many of whom were young people who worked in government and Party offices and needed to hide their faith and their attendance at services. A considerable number of young priests served the underground Church. Many held official positions and conducted services openly, but they also worked secretly to help new believers find their spiritual way, to acquire that faith and hold on to it. Each of these priests had a large unofficial "flock" and was extremely busy.

We began the search for a confessor, but the results were not good. One priest flatly refused, acknowledging that he found my personal situation vis-à-vis the authorities too risky. A second one was so busy that I could not even make contact by telephone. I became discouraged. Then one morning I jumped out of bed and without fully realizing what I was doing, dashed into the hall to the telephone and grabbed my address book. He had been in my apartment, but I had forgotten his surname. I leafed feverishly through the pages and at last found a Moscow telephone number.

A woman answered.

"Please," I said, ragged voice almost out of control, "let me speak to Father Nikolai!"

There was a moment of silence, then, perhaps alarmed by my tone, the woman said quietly, "Just a minute. I'll get him."

Waiting for the priest to come on the line, I looked at the clock. It was 7:00 A.M., an altogether inappropriate time to be calling someone I did not know. A strong baritone voice said, "Yes, who's calling?"

"Father Nikolai," I stammered in confusion, "this is Irina McClellan. You've probably forgotten me—Marie-Hélène brought you to my apartment once. I need help."

"What's this? I certainly haven't forgotten you." There was a brief pause, then he continued, "I came only a few hours ago, just for the day—barely had a chance to say hello to my mother. But I'll find time for you. Shall I come this evening around six?"

"Please, Father—*do come!*" Shuddering with relief, I mumbled thanks and gave him my address.

Father Nikolai was a tall and muscular man, with large, intense brown eyes, full, reddish beard, and slightly unkempt shock of hair. When he crossed the threshold into my apartment that evening, he brought with him the end to my search. I had found my spiritual father.

He declined *zakuski,* saying he had promised to have dinner with his mother, but accepted tea. As I related my story, it dawned on me that nothing surprised or shocked him, and that it was unnecessary to recount every detail. At the time it seemed as though he already knew everything. Later I understood that he had simply grasped the logic of my life. One step had followed another along a route less mysterious than I—in my false pride—had realized. There was a natural symmetry about the way I had found and lost happiness, about the cycles of joy and despair, about my attempts to find something to replace of the happiness I claimed to have renounced. I told him of coming to the Church accidentally—he smiled at that—and of being unable to find anyone to guide me.

Concluding my story, which I had told as easily and with as little embarrassment as if talking to myself, I apologized for rambling at such length and offered to make more tea. Shaking his head, Father Nikolai said slowly, "No, thank you. Let's be quiet for a moment."

He stared out the window at the late evening twilight and remained silent for several minutes.

"I will be your spiritual father," he said at last. "I'll be back in Moscow in two months and we can prepare you for general con-

Father Nikolai blessing some of his parishioners with holy water, spring 1982.

fession. You have to remember everything—this is a very serious step. After confession you will have a new life." He paused again, then asked, "Do you have a Bible and a prayer book?"

"No, I don't—and I'm absolutely ignorant. But I have found God, and I don't want to lose Him."

Withdrawing a Bible and a prayer book from his briefcase, he handed them to me, saying, "This is my gift to you. Read every day, at least a little. And write down any questions you have."

He stood up, made the sign of the cross over me, placed his hand gently on my head, and said softly, "God bless you."

Then he left.

It was another miracle. Overwhelmed, I dashed to Maria's home late that evening and told her about the priest's visit. She heard me out, then suddenly announced that, at the age of forty, she wished to be baptized.

I prepared myself seriously. Painful though it was to recall my sins, nevertheless I felt such complete security in the love of God, and such total trust in Father Nikolai, that I eagerly looked forward to confession.

When the priest returned at the beginning of June, Maria and I greeted him in my apartment and she told him her wishes.

"I'll have to baptize you in someone's apartment," he said. "If we do it in a church it would be registered."

Clergymen must inform the state of the names of everyone who receives baptism. Maria's acceptance of the sacrament would have branded her "ideologically unreliable," a label that usually carries the unwritten codicil "unemployable."

"You can do it here," I offered, saying yet another prayer of gratitude for my privacy. I rejoiced that my dearest friend would come to God in my apartment.

As an adult new believer, Maria too would have to make general confession. Father Nikolai had brought us a thirty-page type-written "Guide to General Confession" prepared secretly by believers. He told us what we would have to do: recall all our sins, recount them in confession, repent, and begin a new life with

God, observing Christ's Commandments. Beyond all that we had
to pray daily for God's forgiveness.

While the rest of Moscow went about its legitimate business
on that warm, languid June day in 1983, Father Nikolai conducted the sacraments in my apartment. What we did was illegal.
Maria and I made general confession, and she and the infant son
of some friends were baptized. One can indeed worship and praise
God—but legally only under the supervision of the authorities.
We had neither asked permission nor registered our intentions.

While the others waited, Father Nikolai took me into Lena's
room. Dressed in his beige and purple linen Sunday cassock, he
opened the small suitcase that contained his "traveling church": a
large gold-plated cross, a Bible, candles, a vial of holy oil, a tassel,
several other things. He carefully arranged them on the table, said
a prayer, then looked at me.

"Well, tell me what you remember."

At first it was difficult to speak at all; there was much in my life
of which I was ashamed. Some memories brought tears, a few
produced heartfelt sobs. Father Nikolai heard me patiently, silently. When my silence indicated that I had finished, Father
Nikolai said a prayer, covered my head with his stole, and said,
"The sins of God's slave Irina are forgiven."

I experienced an ineffable sense of relief, of a weight lifted,
the lightness of a soul released from the clutter of meaningless
corporeal and emotional impedimenta.

After hearing Maria's confession, Father Nikolai prepared to
baptize her and the child in my bathtub. Maria changed into a
seamless linen baptismal gown. The nervous, excited parents had
brought along two male friends who were to act as godfathers;
I was to be godmother to both Maria and little Fyodor. We
all stood holding lighted candles. I hardly recognized Maria's
flushed, radiant face. She stood in the tub while Father Nikolai
blessed the water, then anointed her with a small dipperful; he
repeated the process with the infant, whose father's outstretched
arms held him in a semi-reclining position over the tub. During

the sacraments I recited the Lord's Prayer. Fyodor smiled sweetly throughout.

Then Father Nikolai said another prayer and blessed my home, tracing crosses in holy oil on all the walls and above the doors and windows. When he had finished he looked at me and said in that deep, majestic voice, "Your enemies will not disturb you here. You are defended."

20

A Journey to the Monastery

THE COMMUNISTS have made savage efforts to stamp out religion and culture in Russia. Stalin usually receives most of the blame, but Nikita Khrushchev closed more than fifteen thousand churches that still functioned after Stalin's depredations and conducted a sustained anti-religious campaign in the media and the schools. Some churches, including historic and architectural treasures, were simply razed to the ground, while others were turned into propaganda centers, dance halls, or warehouses. Stalin and Khrushchev both imprisoned or exiled thousands of clergymen, hundreds of the best Russian writers, artists, and poets. Despite decades of persecution, however, the Church and Russian culture survived—precariously.

From the souls of those who perished in the Gulag came shoots that sprouted in the millions of people who began to seek religion in the sixties and seventies, in the souls of us new believers. These people attended services in the official Church, studied religion underground despite the lack of Bibles and prayer books and despite the official atheism that had been drilled into them all their lives, and were baptized. Many of the new believers came from the intelligentsia, people who had drunk thirstily at the officially approved well of science but who now, with the assistance of energetic, dynamic young priests, sought God and new values with equal fervor. Their searching made the underground Church even stronger.

It was Grannie Sanya who left the tiny seed in my own soul. It grew only slowly and painfully in the desert of my life for many years, unnourished by "living" water. To my eternal joy, I at last became part of the Church, which gave my life meaning and direction.

Father Nikolai taught me humility and forgiveness. Humility allowed me to find happiness in the simple things I had always taken for granted—health, life, people. Forgiveness took away the malice that had filled my heart, made me less intolerant, more able to think of others. Through the underground Church, new friends appeared; doing things for them helped me overcome my own problems, get outside them. A new calm, a solid internal integrity, spiritual peace became my habitual condition. Old friends soon noticed the change, and my apartment became the site of frequent unofficial gatherings devoted to religion. We did all this in secret, never discussed anything on the telephone. If the KGB was aware of our activities generally, it evidently decided that merely talking about God was harmless.

More and more people in my circle began not only to talk about God but to seek Him. Father Nikolai was a great help to those who worked for the state and were therefore not free to be received into the official Church. He baptized them either in their own apartments or, if they lived in communal apartments, in mine. Soon I became godmother to seven people, adults and children.

The underground Church gave me manuscripts to type. This work I did gladly, banging hard on the keys to make five copies. The material provided spiritual sustenance, and typing it gave me the satisfaction of fulfilling a Christian duty; as soon as one manuscript was completed, I began another. The books opened up to me the map of the catacombs of the Russian Orthodox Church, where thousands of priests and nuns murdered by the Communists rest in unmarked graves. They reopened the question of the tragic fate of the last legitimate Patriarch, Tikhon, who died in suspicious circumstances in 1925 and was almost certainly mur-

dered by the secret police, and of the saintly metropolitan of
Petrograd, Veniamin Kazansky, whose execution Lenin sanc-
tioned in 1922. I learned of the last days of Lev Tolstoy, who on
the eve of his death went to Optina Pustyn, the great Hermitage
of the *startsy*, or saintly elders, to confess, only to find that pride
would not allow him to open the door to the cell of the *starets*
Varsanofy.

The story of Father Serafim Rose fascinated me. A well-edu-
cated American who converted to Russian Orthodoxy and became a monk, he helped found a monastery in California. One of
his godchildren, a Russian émigré, translated his works and smuggled them into the Soviet Union especially for the use of new
believers. I typed those manuscripts repeatedly, along with works
about the monks of Mount Athos in Greece and classics of Russian Orthodox literature.

An American friend came to see me at the end of a day when I
had typed for eight hours. Noticing my swollen fingers and el-
bows, he said in all innocence, "Look here, why torment yourself?
I'll send you a copying machine."

I could not help but laugh at such naivete.

"That road leads straight to the Gulag," I told him.

"But they are so *common!*" he insisted. "Almost like typewrit-
ers. No one makes carbon copies any more."

"That's *your* country," I replied. "This is ours. We go to
church secretly, are baptized secretly, marry secretly—and type
Church literature secretly. We trust in the Lord . . . and pray."

Each morning I said a prayer to the Mother of God before
beginning work and felt myself secure.

Profoundly caught up in my new life, I paid little attention to
the rapid-fire changes in our country. In truth the essence of
things did not change, only the leaders. This was the Era of Great
Funerals. They died one after another, these men, so quickly that
one corpse was barely cold when the Communist Party announced the arrival of another.

First to die was Leonid Brezhnev, in November 1982. Yuri

Andropov, KGB chief from 1967 to 1982, succeeded him and greatly intensified the anti-corruption campaign already in place. This was the KGB-led drive that actually began in my own Bauman District of Moscow and—ironically enough—transformed a kommunalka into my private apartment, despite KGB wishes.

From December 1982 to April 1983 the streets of Moscow were virtually under martial law. Without the slightest pretext, hordes of regular police, KGB agents, and civilian auxiliaries swooped down on people in stores, theaters, public baths, public transportation, or simply on the street, and demanded internal passports. One evening a pale and frightened Maria appeared at my door.

"Are you all right?" she gasped. "Nothing's happened?"

Perplexed, I assured her that everything was quite normal.

"When I got off the trolleybus," she said as she took off her coat and sat down, "a policeman came up and said, 'Your documents, citizeness!' I said to him, 'What's going on? Don't I have the right to go anywhere I like after work?' He came back with, 'Show me your passport, then we'll talk.' "

It is a waste of energy to challenge the police in our country. Right and might are always on their side. The policeman examined her passport carefully, found it in order, and permitted her to go on her way. But a couple of hundred meters from my building another officer suddenly appeared and demanded that Maria identify herself.

"What *is* this?" she asked him. "Do I look like a criminal? They just *checked* my passport!"

She pointed to the bus stop, where the first policeman was busy perusing someone else's papers.

"Let's not get into a discussion," the second policeman snapped. "Passport, citizeness!"

A short, feisty young man, he looked at Maria's document, then asked, "Where are you going?"

"For a walk."

"Where to?"

"What kind of question is *that?*"

"Now, don't take offense . . . we're just here to keep order."

The man returned her passport and she hurried on to my apartment, convinced that the check-up was connected with me. Decent people found it almost impossible to realize that this humiliating verification of documents had become the norm in our country.

The campaign eased up in the spring of 1983. The Andropov people arrested many corrupt officials—including several at OVIR and the Ministry of the Interior—and sent them to prison or in a few instances even executed them, but in the end nothing changed. A new set of masters replaced the old. I occasionally read in Western newspapers and magazines brought by friends that Andropov was a "liberal" who liked jazz, drank scotch, spoke English, read widely in good literature, and genuinely wanted reforms. Even Roy Medvedev, the "dissident" Leninist historian, believed this. People who accepted this story evidently forgot who had run the KGB during that savage period 1967–82, and the entire country in the last years of the Brezhnev era.

One of Brezhnev's old cronies, Konstantin Chernenko, became General Secretary of the Party when Andropov died in February 1984. Almost devoid of a personality, Chernenko was—as we Soviet people said privately—Brezhnev's faithful arms bearer; for years he bore his master's briefcase and cigarette lighter. Aged, decrepit, suffering from asthma, Chernenko was incapable of running the country. Someone—at the time it was not clear who—stood behind him and made decisions.

Virtually unnoticed by the Soviet people, Chernenko died in March 1985. Someone would replace him, but no one believed any significant changes would take place. The Communist Party seemed unable to renew itself. Jokes took the place of political analysis, which was forbidden us anyway:

One day Ivanov does not show up for work. The next day his boss asks, "Ivanov, where were you yesterday?"

"On Red Square," Ivanov replies laconically, "at the Kremlin wall. Buried Brezhnev."

Assuming Ivanov was one of the token workers invited to the funeral, the impressed superior falls silent.

Some months pass, and again Ivanov fails to report for work. The following day his boss enquires respectfully, "Well, Ivanov, among the invited guests on Red Square again?"

"No—I bought a season ticket."

Popular cynicism sharpened when Andropov died. It was common knowledge that Brezhnev had worn a pacemaker for years, and that for months only a kidney-dialysis machine kept Andropov alive. Radio Armenia (the mythical voice of popular humor) asks: Why did Brezhnev travel abroad, while Andropov did not? Answer: Brezhnev worked on batteries, but Andropov was hooked up to wires.

May 1984 approached—and the tenth anniversary of my marriage. Alex and Rosa Ioffe and Lena and Erik Dubyansky came to my apartment on May 4 with a beautiful wall clock as an anniversary present, champagne, and flowers. Erik borrowed a small stepladder from someone and solemnly hung the clock on the wall, Rosa set out a little banquet, and we waited for the telephone to ring.

In America, Woody went to the Capitol Hill office of Senator John Warner of Virginia for a three-way conference call—Washington, Moscow, and West Lafayette, Indiana—arranged by Rabbi Engel. Senator Warner and Rabbi Engel spoke to me briefly, assured me of their continuing support, and then Woody came on the line with a surprise. He read me a letter that he had received that day:

THE WHITE HOUSE

Washington
May 4, 1984

Dear Professor McClellan:

Today, on the tenth anniversary of your marriage, I would like to offer you my personal wishes that your wife will soon be allowed to join you.

I know that you married Irina during an academic stay in the Soviet Union ten years ago. Despite official policy to the contrary, your wife was not allowed to leave the Soviet Union with you. It has been almost ten years that the Soviet authorities have refused to issue her an exit visa. And during this time, you have not been permitted into the Soviet Union to see her.

Surely, it is among the most basic human rights that a husband and wife should not be forcibly kept apart. It is of great concern to me when a family is involuntarily separated as yours has been.

I know that yours is one of the longest-running cases of its type, and I realize how painful this must be for both of you. You can be sure that Nancy and I are keeping you and Irina in our prayers on this special day.

Sincerely,

[signed] Ronald Reagan

As grateful as I was to President Reagan, it was difficult for me to appreciate the significance of this letter. Mr. Reagan had written to us before and nothing had changed. Woody and I remained apart.

The conference call marked the official, public celebration. In Moscow, we now began our private observance. Alex poured champagne, there were toasts to Woody and me and the American President—and my heart felt torn in a thousand pieces.

Friends in the Soviet Union and the United States encouraged us to be optimistic. Ten was such a nice round number—the KGB was sure to relent after a decade of tormenting us. Woody and I knew better.

Nevertheless we were determined to make a major effort in 1984. Woody fought his way through the maze necessary to invite his wife and stepdaughter to live with him in the United States. The Soviet forms he had to submit involved these steps: he had to have his signature on the forms notarized; the notary public's seal and signature authenticated by the County Clerk of Albemarle County, Virginia; the County Clerk's seal and signature verified by the Secretary of the Commonwealth of Virginia; the latter's bona fides authenticated by the Secretary of State of the United States; and finally, the Soviet Embassy had to vouch for the Secretary of State. Then Woody could send the forms to me . . . so that I could enter the still more complex maze inside the Soviet bureaucracy.

My husband had to go through this time-consuming process every six months. By the time I received the forms, they were so bedecked with seals and ribbons—the blue and gold Virginia state decorations were the most colorfully impressive—that they ought to have liberated whole masses of divided spouses and refuseniks, but for a decade now they had failed to reunite our family.

In Moscow, I went through the complicated process of filing papers to invite my husband to visit me and to prepare my own documentation—and Lena's—for departure from the Soviet Union, just in case. I could only complete certain applications in certain offices on certain days. For at least the twentieth time, I had to get detailed medical certificates—touching reassurance of the Soviet state's sincere concern for our health and that of the foreigners among whom we wished to live. I needed my mother's permission, even though I was nearly forty-six. I had to state once again exactly when and where my father died and was buried, and once again I had to say that I did not have the precise information—which necessitated filling out more documents to indicate that I could not fill in all the blanks in the original documents. Lena had to have her father's permission to emigrate. And so on.

All this accomplished and everything quite in order, or so it appeared, I went to OVIR, where a fortyish blond in military uniform, a pleasant-looking woman whose angry expression and tone of voice clashed with her appearance, confronted me. She studied my documents carefully, as though they were written in Chinese. Rage mounting, she reacted as if I were petitioning to live with *her* husband.

She began to call me every day and summon me to her office: this comma is misplaced, there should not be a period there, you have left off a question mark, this should be capitalized, that written in lower-case letters. After several such encounters I could no longer contain myself.

"Why are you mocking me?" I demanded. "OVIR has X-rayed me down to the guts in these ten years and knows everything by heart!"

She opened her mouth as if to unsheath a suitable reply but I would not let her.

"Do you really want to tell me I can't go to my husband without these damned commas and periods? Is *that* your game?"

I stood up to leave, unable to bear the humiliation any longer. The pleasant-looking officer with the savage temperament had obviously been waiting for that moment. She beat me to the door, yanked it open, and shouted, "Guard! Come at once! Citizeness McClellan is acting like a hooligan—preventing me from doing my work!"

This looks like a provocation, I thought, stomach churning. A chubby, uniformed KGB captain appeared, all smiles and goodwill; if he felt any hostility toward me he certainly did not show it. He sat down on an empty chair, ready to be a dispassionate witness to my "hooliganism." I produced a piece of paper and a pencil from my bag, placed them on the table in front of the woman officer, and said coldly, "Please make a list of everything you're dissatisfied with in my application. I have neither the wish nor the time to come in every day to discuss fine points of punctuation."

Two months later I received—over the telephone as always, never anything in writing—the usual refusals. Lena and I could not join Woody in the United States, nor could he visit us in Moscow.

Thus, in their own way, OVIR-KGB celebrated our tenth wedding anniversary.

After the double-barreled refusals of 1984, I decided that it was simply not my fate to be with my husband. The words of the old priest at Zagorsk haunted me: Because Woody and I had not been married in the Church, it was too late for the Church to do anything. That terrible judgment in mind, I tried to make the sense of what had happened, to understand God's design for my life. I thought: God has called me to the Russian Orthodox Church, which has given me tasks—typing manuscripts, copying books, helping people—that constitute the real meaning of my life. And I am destined to remain in Russia.

The only thing I could not understand was how the Soviet government and especially the KGB would look on my conclusion, and that, naturally, worried me. But I relied on God's will and the protection of the Mother of God.

In the fall of 1984, just when I had at last learned to live alone and enjoy it, Lena finally returned from the mountains, pale, unhappy, and angry with me because my prediction had proved accurate. She was desperately ill, unable to digest food. Through friends, we managed to get an appointment with a leading specialist, who after his examination reported that Lena would have to undergo a resection of her stomach. Only such an operation could cure her perforated ulcer, and even then something would have to be done about her outlook on life.

Once again I felt myself drowning in a tide of guilty despair: I was responsible for everything. And how could I possibly create positive conditions for Lena in this country of ours?

There was no thought of sorting out our relations, and there was indeed nothing to be said. We had to get Lena ready for the operation. She approached it heroically, bravely endured the tubes and probes, endless analyses and injections. Exhausted from a decade of stomach pain, she looked forward to the operation almost with joy, grasping desperately at the possibility of regaining her health.

I was skeptical about Soviet medicine, and nearly sick with apprehension. I could not sleep, prayed constantly for my daughter and for forgiveness of my sins that had—I was convinced—brought her such suffering.

The resection was a success; but now Lena had only half a stomach. For a year she had to watch her diet with extreme care in order to nurse the remaining half back to good health, and she had to work on her outlook on life.

While Lena was in the hospital, Manya the poodle presented me with a litter of five pups. The apartment became a kennel; the astonished cat did not know what to make of the increase in population. Manya was an extremely protective mother to her chocolate-colored offspring, and I was constantly coming and going, trying to provide Lena with all the things ordinary Soviet hospitals lack—decent food, juice, sanitary napkins, toilet paper. I spent hours in lines at stores, then in the hospital, then hurried home to clean up after my menagerie. It was hectic, but it was life, movement, new hope . . .

Another gray autumn descended on Moscow. Lena was back home now, the pups had been given away, and life slowly returned to what I had come to regard as normal. After the refusals of 1984, however, it seemed no longer possible to think with hope of my marriage, and I sought a way out of the predicament. That could only mean divorce.

Tired of bearing the cross of my ill-fated marriage, I would submit to God's will. If He did not want me to be with Woody, so be it. When Father Nikolai, in whom I confided these thoughts, asked how a divorce would help matters, I replied that I would be free of moral and legal chains, of my false status. I complained constantly, but Father Nikolai quoted from Luke: From everyone to whom much has been given, much more shall be required; and to whom they have entrusted much, they will ask the more. To me that made no sense. They had taken everything from me and still demanded more.

"You divorce your husband . . . and suddenly they'll offer you an exit visa," my priest cautioned. "You would never forgive yourself."

"What visa are you talking about?" I demanded heatedly. "I've already waited a lifetime. You're a monk, you don't know what it's like. I can't go on living alone."

We fought for several months. Without his blessing I would not begin the proceedings—but what if he *did* give it? Why indeed divorce after all these years? Even though there seemed to be no good answer, the question would not go away.

In January 1985 Father Nikolai brought the matter to a head.

"All right, *golubushka*, I'm tired of arguing. We're going to a monastery . . . let the *starets* decide."

All that I knew about the saintly elders came from Dostoyevsky's *Brothers Karamazov:*

The *starets* is someone who takes your soul, your will, into his own soul, his own will. Having selected a starets, you renounce your own will and turn it over to him in total obedience, with total self-abnegation. One who so consecrates himself voluntarily undertakes this novitiate, this terrible school of life, in the hope of overcoming the self after the lengthy ordeal, of so mastering the self that, in the end, through a lifetime of obedience, one can attain perfect freedom, that is, freedom from that very self, can escape the lot of those who have lived their whole life without finding their true selves in themselves.

I read and reread this passage with mounting apprehension. Still merely raw material, quite a new child of God, what if I could not cope with whatever advice the *starets* might give? And if I disobeyed, the consequences would be terrible.

The day we were to leave Moscow I called Father Nikolai.

"I'm just not prepared to go," I pleaded, feeling myself a sinful coward. It did not matter that the tickets for the night train had been bought, or that in a few hours it would be time to go to the station.

Father Nikolai, very upset, insisted that I come to see him at his mother's apartment, at least to return the ticket. I agreed because I had promised to take a present from a priest, a friend of mine, to someone at the Pskov-Pechery Monastery. Now Father Nikolai could deliver it.

At first he scolded me.

"You're a capricious and foolish lady. I don't want anything further to do with you."

"Aha! So this is how easily priests reject their spiritual offspring!" I gloated.

I was about to leave, but at that moment his mother came into the room and invited me to stay for dinner. At the table, Father Nikolai acted as though nothing had happened. As we were finishing the meal, Pavel, who was also going to the monastery, came to the apartment. Handing him a small suitcase, Father Nikolai said with a grin, "Here, take this untamed lady and pack her up. We'll take her to Pechery by force."

Confused, Pavel stared at Father Nikolai, who took a little package from a shelf, opened it, and threw a handful of beads at my feet.

"Look at her! We cast pearls, and even *that* doesn't help!" he said.

The performance melted my self-righteous posture. I burst out laughing and relented. We took a taxi to my apartment. Lena—who was not going—made sandwiches for the journey while I changed into warmer clothes.

Father Nikolai had chosen the time purposefully; during mid-week in late January there were fewer pilgrims now that the holidays had ended. On the train, seven of us gathered in one compartment. Though from different social circles, we were united in our regard for Father Nikolai. That night we had a party. There were a couple of bottles and Lena's sandwiches, and everyone was in a good mood. As the train rolled through the dark Russian night I looked at my dear priest, a strange, compelling mixture of intelligence, forceful personality, and little-boy mischief, a man who loved to joke and have innocent fun while struggling to solve serious problems. He never lectured. Already the possessor of a formidable reputation, all kinds of people flocked to him with their problems . . . and dreams of a more meaningful, fulfilling life.

There are few active monasteries left in the Soviet Union. Dating from the fifteenth century, the Pskov-Pechery Monastery in Pskov province northwest of Moscow is among the oldest, famous not only because of its rich heritage but also because of its monks' courageous defiance of Nikita Khrushchev. The monastery is the refuge of two of the last few *startsy* in Russia. Father Adrian is a renowned healer, Father Ioann a clairvoyant. Pilgrims from all over the Soviet Union throng to see them. A year earlier a deacon, a friend of mine who had once been his cell attendant, had forwarded a letter to Father Ioann, who promised to pray for me.

It was 30 degrees C. below zero when we alighted at the little railway station just after 6:00 A.M. We walked briskly along a narrow path through the snow-covered fields the two or three kilometers to the monastery and crossed a wooden bridge over a creek. There before us, in a deep ravine, lay the building. Nine lookout towers studded its thick stone walls, visible reminders of its role in the defense of northwest Russia against the knightly orders of medieval Lithuania and East Prussia. The tops of the cylindrical towers are ribbed cones on a beveled circular base. This Pskov-style architecture—also evident in the churches—is unique to northwest Russia. There is a little less oriental fantasy here, and lines tend to be straighter, concepts more ascetic.

Entering the large monastery complex through the main gates, on the right is a three-story dormitory for the monks and across from it the refectory. Seemingly growing out of the far fortress wall is the whitewashed limestone Church of the Annunciation, our destination. The massive center cupola is flanked by two smaller ones on either side. All five are painted dark blue, spotted with starlike designs fashioned from gold leaf, and adorned with the Orthodox Cross.

Approaching the church, we fell into a silence broken only by the faint crunch of yesterday's snow under our boots. Inside, enveloped by the cloistral calm, each of us lost in private thought, we moved into that river of worship that never ceases to flow in Russia's monasteries.

Russian Orthodox services last about two hours, but those in monasteries are much longer, move at a slower pace, and are more detailed. Besides the resident monks and visiting clergy, services at the Pskov-Pechery Monastery are usually attended on a regular basis by groups of pilgrims and the village babushkas. The elderly women in the Church of the Assumption that January morning treated us kindly. Aware of how difficult it was for people unaccustomed to monastery services to stand for such a long time, they brought small benches so that we could rest. Now and then they motioned for us to kneel when the service so required.

Following the service, Father Ioann prepared to hear confessions. Our priest, Father Nikolai, was the first to go to the altar. The *starets* was his spiritual father. After his own confession, he told Father Ioann about the group of people he had brought from Moscow: a married couple, both alcoholics; the disease threatened the husband's promising career. A baptized Jew utterly confused by religion, he was a so-called parapsychologist who claimed healing powers and had come to ask Father Ioann's blessing on his gift. He was not to receive it. A young man who assisted in services at Father Nikolai's church; his wife had run away with her lover, and in his grief he had decided to become a monk. There were a couple of others, and of course myself.

The men in our group went to the altar for confession; women were not permitted there. Father Nikolai came to me and said softly, "Your case is quite clear. I'll explain later."

He motioned me to remain behind while the other women in our group, other women pilgrims, and several of the local babushkas, went to the grilled confessional. Bewildered, I wondered why I was being treated differently from the others. Sinking down on a bench, I failed to hold back the tears. Father Nikolai attempted to comfort me.

"If Father Ioann has such great insight," I whimpered, "he would know how much I need to speak to him. A year ago he promised to pray for me. Now I've come all the way here and he doesn't even want to talk to me . . ."

Through bitter tears I suddenly saw Father Ioann standing before me.

"Where is Irinushka? Ah, it's you! Come to me, child."

Trembling, I stood and took a step toward the small, white-robed *starets,* a man of indeterminate age whose long, absolutely snow-white hair contrasted with ageless, fathomless, radiant eyes that—behind round metal-framed spectacles—projected saintly wisdom. When in response to his gesture I extended my hands, he took me by the wrists and held me lightly but firmly, and gazed deeply into my eyes. A sense of strength and purity flowed from his touch and spread through my whole being.

"Don't weep, my child," the *starets* said softly. "I cannot open the frontiers for you. I know how difficult your life has been these past many years. Nevertheless, this is what I advise: wait one more year. But remain celibate—do not have any relations with men. Come back in a year, cleansed of sin. Your husband is still waiting and you should not offend him. If after a year nothing has changed, you and I will write him a letter explaining everything, and *then* you will get your divorce."

Never ceasing to look into my eyes, Father Ioann was silent for a long moment, then continued, "You're thinking: These monks do not know anything about real life, yet they tell me to live alone, as they do. No, child, even though I am a monk I understand how difficult it is to be alone . . . But go now, go with God. I shall pray for you."

It was said of Father Ioann that his clairvoyance came straight from God.

We had come to the *starets*—each of us for the first time— with trepidation, even fear. We left enlightened and happy; and this was true even for those who heard advice or admonitions at variance with what they wished and expected. Such was the internal strength, the authority of Father Ioann.

21

Hope Fades

AS PLANS for a divorce slowly took shape in my mind, I calculated that my pension would be sixty-five rubles a month, not enough to survive. It would be necessary to find some sort of regular job to supplement the meager state stipend. When I broached the subject to my friends, their reaction was uniformly pessimistic. On every job application I would have to indicate my husband's name, occupation, and place of residence. The data about Woody would automatically close every door.

One well-intentioned but naive friend suggested I write to the Party Central Committee for assistance. The Party would demand that I renounce my past and confess my "mistakes," perhaps publicly—and that was unthinkable.

An acquaintance named Ludmila told me that the English-language edition of the journal *Soviet Science* desperately needed someone who not only knew English but could type in that language as well as Russian. She had learned of the opening from a man who had long worked for the journal and was a friend of the chief editor. Most of the people who translate the original Russian articles are either native speakers of English, German, or French (the journal also appears in those languages) or else highly skilled Soviets. They work at home, and the pay is excellent.

The first interview was by telephone. The chief editor introduced himself, then questioned me about my background. I told him about my education and previous jobs; he seemed satisfied.

"Now let me have your surname and date and place of birth," he said.

I made an effort to swallow "McClellan," but he immediately recognized its Scottish origin.

"We would like to talk to your husband," he said. "We are in great need of native speakers. Where is he?"

"At home," I answered laconically.

"Well—can I speak to him?"

"His home is in the United States."

A long, uncomfortable pause spoke for itself. When the chief editor finally got hold of himself and tried to put a good face on a bad situation, I knew it was all over.

"I have a list of candidates," he said brusquely. "When it's your turn, I'll call again."

He never did.

Olga's friend Gela suggested I look for work at the Danilov Monastery in Moscow. The state had recently returned it to the control of the Patriarchate, and some of the priests told her they needed translators and typists. I liked the idea at once; Gela arranged for me to meet the monk in charge of hiring.

When I arrived, the work of restoration was well under way, but part of the complex was still being used—as the whole monastery had been for many years—as a detention center for juvenile delinquents. It was strange to enter the main building and find uniformed policemen and women and closed-circuit television cameras that monitored the grounds and the interiors of some of the buildings. An officer summoned the monk whom I was to see by telephone, and as I waited a depressing thought took hold of my consciousness: Monastery and prison, such an unlikely combination. But everything is possible under Soviet power . . .

Finally the monk came, a black-garbed man with long hair and beard and a benign expression that inspired trust. He was Gela's friend—I could speak frankly. We walked outside the monastery. On the street, I briefly related my story and told him of my desire to work for the Church. He listened patiently, then we walked along in silence for a couple of blocks.

"I'm afraid," he said at last in a sad voice, "that it would be

useless even to try. The KGB is in charge here, and with your
history there is no point in making an application."

There seemed no way out of the trap. All doors were closed.
Even if I divorced Woody the situation would not improve. But
there *had* to be a solution, some way for me to live out my days.

I called Ludmila and asked for an introduction to her friend at
Soviet Science. Perhaps he would know about free-lance translat-
ing. She arranged the meeting for the day of Konstantin Chernenko's funeral, which we were watching on television when
Grisha appeared. A tall, imposing man, Grisha's youthful face
belied his totally gray hair—he was around sixty. When he introduced himself in English, I recognized an upper-class "Oxbridge"
voice.

"Where does your accent come from?" I asked.

Almost proudly, he replied that he had lived in England with
his parents until he was ten.

We were distracted by the events on Red Square. As she
served coffee, Ludmila related the latest joke:

Radio Armenia asks: What is the favorite sport of our leaders?
Answer: Racing funeral corteges around Red Square.

I told Grisha about my situation and asked his advice. From
his acquaintance with the chief editor at *Soviet Science,* did he
think there was any hope at all for me? With a heavy sigh, he
replied simply, "No." But it was clear that he sympathized with
my plight and sincerely wanted to help: he suggested that I work
for him personally. In constant need of typists, he even offered to
provide a machine with Latin characters. In time I might even be
able to translate from Russian into English myself and increase
my earnings considerably.

"Don't despair," he said as he went out the door. "There's
always lots of work."

And so I began to type for him; later I would also translate. He
used a dictaphone. This was my first experience with the device,
and at first my new "business" proceeded slowly and haltingly.
Grisha answered my questions and corrected my work with great
patience.

We spoke almost exclusively in English. He brought me English and American books, invited me to art exhibitions and plays, brightened my life, an interesting, highly intelligent older friend.

Then one day at the end of summer he proposed marriage.

"Why live alone? We work together, spend a lot of time together. Let's live together. I can take care of you."

I looked at him in astonishment. He knew my situation, knew about my meeting with the *starets* . . . so why the proposal? It flashed through my mind that this was a test, a temptation. The positive reaction of my friends—and Lena—to my work with Grisha, to our friendship, had obviously created a certain aura of encouragement.

"It's too early," I responded quietly. "Let's shelve the question for the time being."

He continued to court me in his gentlemanly way, always brought flowers when he came to see me, invariably set an attractive, elegant table when I visited him.

Father Nikolai had met Grisha in my apartment. Grisha had translated the text of many illustrated books on art, including several on icons, and the two men found much to talk about. I told Father Nikolai about the marriage proposal. Although he liked and respected Grisha, the priest scolded me for admitting a man into my life.

"Nothing will come of this," he predicted. "He has no chance."

"What do you mean? In three months I'll go back to Father Ioann and he'll give me permission to divorce. I'm *tired!* My situation is hopeless . . . I can't go on this way."

"I know, Irochka, I know," Father Nikolai said soothingly, "but nothing will come of this."

In late September of 1985 I received a telephone call from a KGB agent who had come to Moscow from the Tbilisi office. Some affair was under investigation in Soviet Georgia, and my telephone number appeared in the accused person's address book. He ordered me to meet him at Lefortovo Prison.

Lefortovo—the very name strikes fear into Russian hearts. It is supposed to be the KGB's worst prison, the innermost circle of hell. Solzhenitsyn described his imprisonment there in *The Oak and the Calf.* Yuri Orlov, Anatoli Shcharansky, and God knows how many others also sat in Lefortovo's cells.

Only once had I met the man under investigation. It was through a mutual friend, and I had forgotten the wholly inconsequential encounter. Knowing nothing about the matter, I refused to go to Lefortovo.

At first the Georgian investigator did not press the issue, but he called every day and politely "invited" me to the prison to "have a chat." Just as politely, I refused. This went on for several days, then he abandoned his civility.

"See here, I'm tired of this. Either come tomorrow at two P.M. or I'll send some people to bring you in by force."

"But you don't have the . . . "

"I don't think I'll have any problem arranging this," he interrupted. "Be here at two."

He hung up before I could reply, but anyway there was nothing I could say. Indeed I did not want to be manhandled by the KGB.

After a sleepless night I made some coffee and willed myself to be calm. Over and over I said a prayer: "Lord Jesus Christ, Son of God, have mercy on me, a sinner." I dressed carefully, kissed Lena goodbye, and took a taxi to the prison.

A modern glass entrance has been added to Lefortovo, a prison built by Peter the Great's Swiss adviser, Francis Lefort. As soon as you pass through it, you find yourself behind walls two meters thick. A young uniformed KGB enlisted man who sat behind bulletproof glass carefully examined my identification, then asked the name of the investigator whom I was to see. I told him, he wrote it down, then pointed toward a room opposite marked VISITORS. Visitors!

I had been sitting in the characterless room only a few minutes when the investigator appeared and introduced himself. His uniform bore the insignia of a KGB major. I tried to remain composed, but my heart was pounding: what would happen now?

The investigator led me up to an interior door operated by a dozen numbered pushbuttons. He pushed a few in sequence and the door opened, then closed automatically behind us. How many people had heard that same door shut behind them on the first leg of their journey into the Gulag Archipelago? Lord Jesus Christ, Son of God, have mercy on me, a sinner! And how many had repeated the same prayer? There was no conceivable reason to imprison me, I reminded myself, but this was the KGB, which needs neither reasons nor laws when it has instructions.

Down a long corridor, then another door with a bank of pushbuttons, then up a flight of stairs to the second floor, where several young men in dirty coveralls were painting the walls. I wondered whether they were prisoners or free men. Brushes suspended in midair, they stared at us curiously.

The investigator and I continued down a long, narrow, high-ceilinged corridor with dirty windows every few meters, so high as to admit nothing but a little light. Those facing the outside were barred even though it would have taxed a pole vaulter to reach them; the interior ones were not. At the end of the corridor my guide opened an ordinary door, stood aside, and motioned me to enter.

We had come to an austere office with dingy, ash gray walls not graced—I noticed with surprise—by portraits of Lenin and Dzerzhinsky. The only furniture was a scuffed wooden table, once painted olive drab, with nothing on it but a telephone and a gun-metal gray chair behind it, and three straight-backed chairs. A single forty-watt bulb hung on a short cord from the ceiling.

The interrogation began. I refused to answer the man's questions and silently repeated my prayer. Armed with God's protection, I lost all sense of the KGB man's presence in that small room. Some time passed before I realized that he was shouting at me at the top of his voice.

"A Soviet citizen who refuses to help the Motherland! We raised you, educated you, and now you betray the Motherland with your American husband and his friends!"

Now aware of him but no longer afraid, I remained silent. He tried to trick me, blackmail me.

"We know *everything!* The accused has told us all about your relations with him."

There had been no relations, so at last I had a ready answer.

"All the better, then. There's nothing to talk about."

Changing his tone, the man wheedled, "But you *live* here, this is your *Motherland* . . . and you don't want to help?"

When I did not respond, he shouted, "You'll sit here until you talk!"

Well, I thought, there's nothing to be done. If it is necessary to sit here, so be it . . .

We remained almost immobile for perhaps an hour, in total silence. I stared at the small, dirty window high up on the wall without any idea of how the day would end and wordlessly repeated the prayer.

The harsh ring of the telephone shattered the silence so unexpectedly I almost fell off my chair. At first I could not figure out what the noise was or where it came from. The investigator appeared every bit as startled. In response to whatever was being said on the other end, he grunted from time to time. Then he replaced the receiver, took a form from his briefcase and placed it on the table. Pen poised over the paper, he asked, "Name? Date and place of birth? Profession?"

To the last question I responded simply, "Housewife."

"What do you mean?" the investigator asked, both surprised and angry.

"Exactly what I said."

"But you have a higher education!"

"That has no bearing on this interrogation," I replied.

Incensed, he wrote across the form, "Citizeness McClellan refuses to give a deposition," and ordered me to sign. Irritated, I refused.

"This is not correct," I insisted. "I told you what I know, not what would satisfy you."

He produced a new interrogation form and recorded my answers exactly as I gave them. I signed.

Our footsteps echoed as the officer led me back down the

same corridor . . . to what destination I did not know. Then he motioned me through the electronically controlled doors to the glassed-in entrance, and I found myself on the street.

It was *babye leto,* the Russian equivalent of Indian summer, when the leaves turn and the days are warm, the nights refreshingly cool. I was so drained I could not enjoy it. As I wandered along the street, that terrible feeling of defenselessness seized me. After calling Lena to say I was free, I went into a shop to buy my favorite chocolate-covered nuts. There was not even a queue. Then I pointed myself in the direction of home, nibbled the nuts one by one, and let my thoughts swim where they would.

I needed fresh air, and above all space . . .

When I finally reached home, my temperature was several degrees above normal. I was in bed for two days.

Grisha was finally beginning to understand how complicated my life was, how much stress I was under. For the second time he proposed marriage. When I did not respond one way or the other, he began to make plans: he would move into my apartment, and we would find a small place of her own for Lena. Tired of my hopeless situation, of living with me, Lena was all in favor. My friends also approved.

There was no need to hurry; everything was in Father Ioann's hands. Whatever he said, I would do.

In November 1985, General Secretary Mikhail Gorbachev, who had assumed his post within hours of Chernenko's death in March, would meet President Reagan in Geneva. The Soviet media had adopted a new tone with regard to the United States and its President. Suddenly the Americans in general and Reagan in particular were not such ogres, such implacable foes, after all— even though there had been no personnel changes in Washington.

The Gorbachev-Reagan encounter would be the fifth "summit" since my marriage to Woody. There was no reason to expect any more from it than from the preceding four. Early in November someone from the American Embassy invited me to join other divided spouses—there were about two dozen—in a meeting with Rozanne Ridgway, Deputy Undersecretary of State for European Affairs, who would be in Moscow in the middle of the month with Secretary of State George Shultz to make final preparations for the Gorbachev-Reagan meeting. For several years our little group of Soviet citizens married to Americans but denied the right to leave the USSR had held occasional informal meetings, written letters to various Soviet and American officials, spoken to American diplomats and visitors at the embassy and Spaso House on July 4, Thanksgiving, and other holidays on which the Americans held open house. By far most the senior member of the group, having been separated from my husband for more than eleven years, I went to the meetings and signed the letters but without any hope of success.

The analogous group in the United States, the Coalition of Divided Spouses, was led by two American women married to Soviet husbands. Woody joined the group and wrote to me:

Our case stands as a terrible warning to people planning to marry Soviet citizens; sometimes I get the feeling that both the State Department and the Kremlin use it to discourage such marriages . . . "Just look at the McClellans!" Over the years more than one person has admitted that they were afraid to associate with me out of fear of being tainted. . . . But this new group's leaders are tough and determined, and those are the qualities the situation demands.

We gathered at the embassy around 6:00 P.M. on Monday, November 11, 1985. A junior diplomat waited for me on the street. The Soviet policemen on duty merely looked at my identification and one of them, pronouncing my name as though he knew me, asked, "What's this? Still coming here, Irina Igorevna?"

Detained at the Foreign Ministry, Rozanne Ridgway appeared two hours late. A businesslike, charming middle-aged woman, she apologized and invited us to smoke if we wished. She lit a cigarette and asked someone to bring coffee. But only good news could put us at ease, and Ms. Ridgway had none. The Shultz delegation had again raised the issue of divided spouses; the Soviets were immovable. Foreign Minister Edvard Shevardnadze and his aides listened but did not respond. There was no reason to hope for a change in the Soviet position.

My mind drifted away and I thought, This must be what it's like just before you die. You know the last, frayed threads are breaking, but it doesn't hurt, doesn't even matter . . .

Lena and Grisha were waiting for me when I got home around 10:00 P.M. They looked at me anxiously.

"Finished," I said, sinking into a chair. I did not elaborate.

Lena brought me some tea and turned the television on, then she and Grisha sat at the table, talking quietly.

A terrible, all-consuming emptiness. The posthumous existence I had led since that August day long ago when Woody had flown away was now at an end—what could possibly come after?

To my relief, Grisha said nothing about his plans for the future. I surprised myself one day by blurting out, "If I marry you it will be on the condition that if my husband ever comes to the Soviet Union, I *must* see him."

"Of *course* you must," Grisha replied quietly. "I myself would love to meet this man who has played such a role in your life."

On Sunday, November 10, on the eve of the Geneva meeting between the leaders, the *New York Times* published a story about Woody and me on the front page. The newspaper reached Moscow a couple of days later. Someone at the embassy gave me a Xerox copy of correspondent Phil Taubman's article, which began with these words:

The photographs of each other that Irina and Woodford McClellan keep are faded and outdated, worn mementos of a marriage that was defeated by a government.

In tears by the time I reached the end of that sentence, what followed in that long, sympathetic piece was no easier to read.

Phil mentioned the birch trees Woody had planted, and quoted my husband's reflections:

I think of Irina when I see these trees. . . . The way she has handled this [separation] makes me realize the marriage was the best thing I [ever] did.

Phil had interviewed Woody in Virginia in August before taking up his new assignment in Moscow, where he had spoken to me in October. I quickly became fond of him and his journalist wife, Felicity Barringer, not least because they did not treat me merely as a news source. Phil concluded his article:

Mr. McClellan said he would continue to press for his wife's release. "I'll never give up," he said. "I wouldn't give [the Soviets] a cheap victory."

Mrs. McClellan seemed less certain.

"I don't know how to end this," she said.

22

Liberation

ON NOVEMBER 15, 1985, my friend Chara
marked her first birthday since her husband's sudden, unexpected
death two months earlier from a brain tumor. She was in a state of
near-collapse and we all felt responsible for her. No matter how
sad, a birthday cannot pass unnoticed; we gathered in her apartment simply to show our love and concern. Chara was famous for
her cakes, and we insisted that she bake one, hoping the chore
would at least briefly distract her.

After the subdued party, I went to Grisha's apartment around
eleven thirty. We talked for a long time about Chara, her late
husband, life and death, then went to bed. In the middle of the
night there was some sort of loud noise, maybe a siren—no, the
telephone. Calls at that time are never pleasant—bad news,
wrong number, or someone hoping (and invariably succeeding) to
upset you with an anonymous call.

I looked at the clock: 2:00 A.M. Grisha picked up the phone. It
was Lena, and she had to speak to me. I shuddered apprehensively
and took the receiver.

"What's happened?"

"Vadim just called. He says they will give us exit visas. Mama,
come home and call him . . . he's waiting."

Stunned, unable to move, after a few seconds I began to trem-
ble uncontrollably. Thoughts raced frantically through my mind
and I could not separate one from another. As supposedly happens at times of great crisis, my entire life seemed to flash before
my eyes. Grisha stood next to me, totally unaware of Lena's message. Only after some minutes could I tell him what had happened.

When I recall that shock now, I imagine the sensation someone long ago doomed to life in prison must experience when
suddenly, out of the blue, a reprieve comes, and freedom beckons.
He has dreamed about freedom every night for years, but when it
arrives, it comes not as a joy but as a shock. It stuns, bewilders,
confuses. It is impossible to conceive of a free tomorrow; one is
powerless to comprehend the message. For the prisoner, freedom
is something absolutely new and unfamiliar. When it suddenly
summons him he has no idea how to live with it and—terrified of
the unknown—loses his last shred of confidence and strength. His
friends in confinement, with whom he has spoken a common
language and shared his experiences, will not be with him now.
Among free people, he will be an alien.

In those first moments, I did not think of Woody, of the
sudden possibility of a meeting with him. Nor of Grisha, Lena,
Mama, friends. One primitive emotion dominated all the others:
fear. Fear of decisions that loomed ahead and of my inability to
make them, fear of my lack of emotional and physical strength to
begin a new life . . . and fear of continuing a precarious existence
in my homeland.

I collapsed in a chair. Perplexed, Grisha draped a blanket
around my shoulders, silently sat down across from me, placed a
bottle of cognac on the table, and suggested a drink. He poured
half a small glass; I took a sip, another, then gulped it all. No
reaction, not then, not ten minutes later. I asked for more. The
trembling did not cease.

After a while I became chilly again, as though I had been
bathing not in alcohol but icewater. I drank half the bottle but
could not relax. My mind did however slow down enough for me
to realize that I did not want to go home to Chernyshevsky Street.
If anything had to be done, let someone else do it for me. I felt
very lonely.

At four o'clock in the morning it was frightfully cold in the
deserted Moscow streets. As Grisha tried to hail a taxi I thought,
We won't find one—and that will put off the moment when I
have to call Woody.

Lena opened the door, lost, looking to me for answers. I had none. In response to my halting request, the operator gave me America in less than a minute.

"What's happened?" I asked, voice sinking.

Woody sounded so excited I thought he was out of his mind. He shouted into the telephone,

"Call the American ambassador immediately! They have to get the documents ready!"

I reminded him that it was 5:00 A.M. in Moscow, an inconvenient time to telephone Arthur Hartman. Woody gave me all sorts of instructions about what to do and how to do it. He sounded like the Woody of old, as though the years and the pain of separation had suddenly evaporated.

I replaced the receiver and sobbed helplessly. Lena put her arm around my shoulder, held me close and softly spoke.

"Mama, don't cry. I'll go with you."

Decision made. After more than a decade of vacillating, in the crucial moment my daughter was on my side, as she had been at the American Embassy in April 1978. We would go, and it did not matter what would happen there. The important thing was that the nightmare would end.

Experience and instinct told me not to celebrate prematurely. There would be time to rejoice when the Soviet authorities made my release official; so far all I had to go on was Woody's report. Michael Armacost, a high State Department official, had called him in the late afternoon on November 15 to say that Washington had just learned of the impending reunification of eight families, including ours, on the eve of the Gorbachev-Reagan meeting in Geneva. Ironically, the previous day Woody and a dozen other members of the Coalition of Divided Spouses had met Mr. Armacost in Washington. That meeting had generated only slightly more optimism than the one we Soviet spouses had had with Rozanne Ridgway. After it, Woody had quoted Kafka when some journalist asked him about the future: "There is infinite hope . . . but not for us."

For seventeen of the longest days of my life, the Soviet authorities refused to confirm the decision. Everyone became edgy, including the officials of the American Embassy. Finally, Ambassador Hartman directed a representative of the embassy staff to accompany me to OVIR.

Comrade Karakulko received us in Room 22, where exit visas are issued.

"Well, what do you want to know, Irina Igorevna?"

"No questions," I said. "The only one I had has been decided at the highest level. But why do you continue to play this game. Aren't eleven and a half years enough? What documents must I bring in order to get the exit visas?"

Karakulko enumerated all the papers which Lena and I had to produce, then had us sign the OVIR daybook.

The news spread quickly. People sobbed into the telephone as they tried to express congratulations. For believers and nonbelievers alike, and certainly for me, it was God's providence. Three months away from the fatal step of divorcing Woody, God saved me and my family, gave us the opportunity to be together in a free country, make a new start. Had anyone asked me about either the past or the future, I could only have answered that the ways of God are unfathomable.

Lena and I hurried to collect our documents, leaving the form from her father until last. That permission would be the most difficult to obtain because Volodya would fear the effect on his career of having a daughter in a capitalist country. Lena went to see him alone first. Her father and his daughter by his second marriage were alone in their apartment; his wife was in the hospital. Lena asked him to sign the paper for OVIR one last time, promising never to bother him again about the matter. He refused instantly, fed up, he told her, with her mother's schemes. Furthermore, it was time for Lena herself to start living a normal Soviet life. He acted—as Lena told me—like a lecturer and propagandist rather than a father.

She came home in tears, without the signature.

At nine o'clock the next evening, a time when good Soviet

Rabbi Gedalyah Engel listening to me on a speaker telephone in West Lafayette after learning that Lena and I would be released.
Greg Jensen, Journal and Courier, *Lafayette, Indiana*

people are in front of their television sets, I rang Volodya's doorbell; Lena stood nervously by my side. Resolute as the Bolsheviks at the gates of the Winter Palace in 1917, I had carefully thought out all details of the encounter, and Lena and I had thoroughly rehearsed our roles. Without asking who was knocking, Volodya opened the door. He stood stock-still, benumbed. Pulling Lena by the hand, I pushed past him into the apartment and said, "Forgive the intrusion, but circumstances demand it."

Without waiting for permission I took off my coat, hung it on a peg in the entryway, and asked if we could go into the sitting room. He made a gesture of helpless assent.

I sat down and crossed my legs. Drops of melting snow ran down my boots onto the beautiful oak parquet floors and distracted Volodya's attention; that was part of my plan. He stared silently at the puddle, then asked coldly, "Why have you come?"

"I've given you more than twenty-five years to establish normal relations with Lena," I answered quietly, "and never interfered. It would have made me very happy if you had succeeded. But when she comes home in tears after seeing you, I've got to do something. It's not my fault that the state demands you give permission for her to leave the country. I have to submit my documents for the last time. I promise you we will *never* ask you for anything again."

He started to repeat the sermon he had given Lena the previous day, but I interrupted him.

"All right, if you want to discuss the problems of our daughter's life and education, let's meet another time."

He realized I would not leave without resolving the OVIR matter. Two days later, he kept his word: he met Lena at the office of a notary public and affixed his signature to the form.

Like so many people, Volodya had been convinced that I would never be permitted to leave the Soviet Union. He did not listen to the Voice of America, was not acquainted with refuseniks or dissidents; thus he did not know our real situation. The rest of the time until we left, almost six weeks, Lena and I lived in fear of the one chance in a million that he would learn of our impending departure. I could only trust in God.

Then came Karakulko's December 30 bombshell: Lena could not go with me. After writing to Gorbachev I called Woody, who instantly agreed with my decision not to leave the Soviet Union alone.

The Western press, especially the American, reacted quickly with a flurry of stories. My friend David Satter was living in Paris and wrote occasionally for *The Wall Street Journal.* Thanks to him, our family's plight figured prominently in the lead editorial, "Parading Peace," on January 3, 1986. The editorial led off with a quote from Gorbachev's address to the American people, followed with a complaint from a citizen who had missed part of a parade on television because of the Reagan-Gorbachev exchange, and then quoted me:

I will not leave without her. I have not waited all these years to unite only one part of my family. Irina McClellan, on being told in Moscow that her permission to join her husband in the U.S. doesn't include an exit visa for her daughter by a previous marriage.

Mrs. McClellan's words were not broadcast from Moscow to the American people on New Year's Day. No, this valuable air time was set aside for the two spokesmen for the "Year of Peace"—Ronald Reagan and Mikhail Gorbachev. . . .

We couldn't help but notice . . . that Mr. Reagan's speech had a brief paragraph using a word absent in Mr. Gorbachev's speech—"freedom." . . .

This may have had to do with the lack of connection between what Mr. Gorbachev was saying about humanity New Year's Day and what press reports this week have been saying about his release to the West of separated Soviet spouses. The stories suggest that even when the Soviets try to do the right thing, they just can't. The Soviets wanted international applause for finally agreeing to the spousal releases, but . . . these folks won't be getting out without being made to suffer, deeply, for their decisions.

On January 9, Karakulko called again. Lena's exit visa had been approved.

At OVIR, an officer handed us a set of rules for the behavior of Soviet citizens going abroad—tourists, people on state business, and all the rest, one pattern for all. Among the warnings: "Do not permit foreigners to carry your suitcases," and "Do not have any contact with foreigners." Before giving us our passports, the man asked whether the instructions were clear.

"Not entirely," I responded. "My husband is a foreigner—am I to carry five suitcases myself? Can't I ask him to help? And what about 'contact'?"

This enraged the bureaucrat, and of course I enjoyed the situation. Today *I* had the last laugh. He made us wait a little longer in the hall, but when he gave us our brand-new foreign travel passports he smiled sweetly and said, "You can come back to the Motherland in a year. You'll be welcome."

Lena and I said "Thank you!" in unison, flew out of the room, and ran all the way home, afraid that suddenly they would change their minds and take the passports away. For the remaining two weeks, we slept with them under our pillows.

We planned to leave on January 28, 1986. Much remained to be done: sell or give away most of what little we owned, arrange to ship my collection of Gzhel porcelain, buy souvenirs, say goodbye to Mama, friends, relatives, acquaintances, students. And I had to make a trip to the monastery to see Father Ioann.

The days went by swiftly. Full of complex, sometimes contradictory emotions, friends came singly and in groups to sit for a while, talk, rejoice, grieve a little. I understood what they were going through. Enormously happy for me, knowing how I had suffered for my right to be with my husband, to begin a new life in freedom—at the same time, trapped in Limbo, that semi-society without end or rest, they could not help feeling sorry for themselves.

Grisha came around in the evenings. He too was happy for Lena and me, but the situation was extremely difficult for him. You could see the sense of loss on his face. My friends were sad for him, but above all they were overjoyed at my release.

Maria came in tears and asked plaintively, "What will I do without you?"

There could be no answer. I too was losing my dearest friend, a woman closer to me than a sister. Despite her grief, she came almost every day to help me prepare for my departure.

Exactly a year after my first visit I returned to the Pskov-Pechory Monastery with Father Nikolai, eagerly anticipating my second meeting with the *starets*, Father Ioann. My purpose was entirely different from the one I had planned: it was to ask his blessing on my journey to a new life in America. After the service, Father Ioann came over to me with a gentle command: "Go to the altar and pray. I'll come later."

My prayers were for the friends I would leave behind, for my aging mother, for Anastasiya Nikolayevna, for the souls of my father, my stepfather, and Sergei Yakovlevich, for strength to cope with whatever the future would bring.

I looked up when I heard a footstep. The church was absolutely empty—except for the *starets* and me.

"What's this crying, child? Now you see what miracles God performs! And you wanted to divorce . . . "

I dropped to my knees.

"Father Ioann, hear my confession. I did not follow your conditions . . . a man in my life these last few months. I'm a sinner . . . I quarreled with Father Nikolai about it . . . angry with him for knowing of my sin. . . . "

My tears flowed freely now. It was difficult to speak, and I was ashamed before Father Ioann. He heard me out silently, a kind, peaceful, concentrated look on his face as he whispered a prayer. Then he covered my head with his stole and said in a firm voice, "Lord Jesus Christ, Son of God, forgive the sins of God's slave Irina."

He paused a long moment before continuing, "Stand, Irinushka, and pray to our Lord, pray and you will be forgiven."

Before us was a magnificently painted, gold-framed icon of the Mother of God. The *starets* read a special service for my journey. Then, fixing his eyes on mine as if seeking the innermost depths of my soul, he said, "You are charged with a mission from the Russian Orthodox Church, an important mission. Now go with God. Marry your husband in the Church."

The word "mission" shocked me.

"But what can I do, Father? Please explain. I don't know anything. I just believe in God with all my soul . . . how am I to know what to do?"

"Don't worry, child. The Lord will show you the way."

Majestically, he made the sign of the cross, then escorted me from the church.

Outside, I whispered the words of the ancient prayer: O God, grant me the serenity to accept the things I cannot change, courage to change the things I can, and wisdom to know the difference.

A triumphant smile on his face, Father Nikolai waited for me on the church steps. It was his victory, too.

The last three days were the most difficult. The apartment was almost empty, but friends and acquaintances streamed in and out constantly. Everyone brought flowers, small souvenirs, huge victorious smiles, happiness. There was a party each night. One was for my closest friends, among them Father Nikolai. Having recovered from his initial depression, Grisha helped prepare the food. Now and then someone would suddenly become sad and the tears would fall . . . but mostly tears of relief, triumph. Who would have guessed, three months ago, that Irina McClellan would be packing her bags for America? One had to believe in miracles; and all of those dozens of people who came to say farewell *wanted* to believe.

Our last night in Moscow Lena and I spent with Mama, whose holiday table was as festive as ever. But sadness was in the air. The unspoken thought that this might be our last dinner together haunted us.

My mother, Aunt Shura, Father Nikolai, and a few close friends came to Chernyshevsky Street on the morning we departed. The priest gave each of us a candle and said a prayer for the journey. He read a prayer, sang a psalm in his glorious baritone voice, and I looked at my mother. To the best of my knowledge this was the first religious ceremony she had experienced since very early childhood. She stood there crying throughout the service that invoked God's blessing on her daughter's journey to faraway America, but Father Nikolai conducted it with such dignity, and the atmosphere was so festive, that it was difficult to separate grief from happiness. When it was time to go, Father Nikolai sang *"Dolgie leta"*—"Long Life to You."

We said goodbye at home. I would not take those nearest and dearest with me to the airport . . . it would have been impossible to hold back the tears.

I was about to leave everything summed up in the concept of homeland: my native city, which I loved deeply and in which I had spent all forty-seven years of my life; my street; my mother; the many friends who had helped me survive through the long, difficult years; the land—so sad and yet so alluring, those white birches and firs and mossy-banked creeks, the gentle hills and fields of central Russia. I was about to bid farewell to all that I loved, and after eleven and a half years of struggling to leave, the thought that I might never see it again brought inexpressible pain.

An unknown new life awaited me in America. Although it seemed that, through American friends acquired during the years in Limbo, I knew something about that country, I realized that such knowledge was merely a mirage. Everything would be unknown, unfamiliar. The flight across the ocean would be like being born a second time. I was hardly eager for adventure; the age for that had passed. It would be difficult suddenly to become a Robinson Crusoe seized by the spirit of the unknown.

But I thought about this only on the road to Sheremetyevo Airport. There, Soviet customs did not give me any leisure time for reflection. The struggle began again, or rather continued, at the airport, in some ways still more terrible, more tense. Like wild animals after prey, the customs officers pounced on the five big yellow suitcases Lena and I had bought. After eleven and a half years we had very little to put in them, nothing that would interest Soviet customs: clothes that would no doubt be unsuitable for America, souvenirs, two bottles of vodka, in truth the most expensive and packaged in festive boxes—a present for my husband. And two cages with the animals: in a large, impressive one bought from Lufthansa sat my terrified, freedom-loving Manya; in a smaller blue one languished my reddish Persian cat, so frightened he could hardly breathe.

The customs people opened all the suitcases at once and tossed our carefully packed things aside. They dug zealously, as if seeking a corpus delicti, but the search was really unnecessary because the corpus was simply on my face in the Soviet concept of crime: I was going to America. Case closed. Nevertheless they meticulously searched our things and the bags themselves, then X-rayed everything. The process moved slowly. No reason to hurry—theirs was a long working day.

Behind the low wooden partition that separated the customs inspection area from the public corridor stood American friends from the embassy who had brought us to the airport, along with some American correspondents there to report our almost histori-cal departure from the USSR. Several of my Russian friends were there too; they had come to give moral support and help me repack if necessary. Anticipating complications, the embassy peo-ple had arranged beforehand to have Lufthansa hold the plane. Lena and I were a "special case," they told the airline staff, and the plane must not leave without us.

And indeed departure time came and went. The other passen-gers had long been strapped into their seats, but my "leavetaking" from the Soviet Union continued . . .

They found nothing of interest in the suitcases. Then one of the customs inspectors held up the two bottles of "Golden Ring" vodka and announced triumphantly, "I won't pass this—250 grams above the legal limit."

"You can *drink* the 250 grams," I snapped, "or pour it out somewhere. The rest I'm taking with me."

It was a typical Soviet impasse, drama at the level of 250 grams of vodka. The inspectors ran around in circles; what was to be done? Behind the barrier, friends and correspondents looked on, helpless. Then one little agent dashed off for instructions from his chief. I tried to shut the suitcases. They would not close. The inspectors had made a mess of our careful packing and now nei-ther Lena nor I had the strength to force the lids down. Our friends were not permitted to help.

The customs people watched with satisfied smirks as we strug-gled. But then the wind shifted, as it so often does in the Soviet Union. The little agent who had gone off for instructions re-turned: we could take the vodka. Now all the inspectors rushed to help close the suitcases. The pet carriers were already on board . . .

They would not let us go back to our friends; we had held up the flight long enough! And so we could only wave, blow kisses . . . and then the tears came. I realized that this, at last, was it.

The engines were already running when a stewardess led us to a small compartment at the very rear of the plane. We sat down. Several moments later I realized that, as though in fear of falling out of that airplane back onto Soviet soil, I had reflexively gripped the armrests so tightly my knuckles were white.

But the plane taxied down the runway and took off normally. Able at last to lean back in our seats, Lena and I looked at each other. Thank God, they could not touch us now . . .

I was flying to a freedom I knew only in theory and a husband whom, after eleven and a half years, I did not know at all.

The future, the rest of my life, lay ahead. The present was only the one day necessary to fly from one continent to another, from one system to another, diametrically opposite one. God had blessed me by granting my wish, but beyond that—all was unknown.

And then a voice came over the intercom:

"Irina McClellan and her daughter are to come to the forward cabin."

We did as directed, obeyed the FASTEN SEAT BELTS sign, and the plane began to descend. To spare us waiting in line, the crew let us debark first at Baltimore-Washington International Airport. We went through United States customs in a twinkling. Then they directed us to the elevator.

The abrupt elevator stop made my stomach sink. The door opened, and I took one step forward into the embrace of my husband. He hugged Lena and me tightly and I could not understand a word, it seemed he was speaking a foreign language, not English, not Russian. Then the three of us cried out in unison, *"Pobedili! Pobedili!"*—We won! We won!

Afterword

FOR THE FIRST TIME twice: that is how I felt when I met Woody at the Baltimore-Washington International Airport. We had, after all, been together in Moscow only eight months, then apart for eleven and a half years.

The Vadim of Moscow no longer existed. Not only had he aged during the long separation; he was now an American Vadim, or rather, Woody, a man I had never known. Our roles were reversed. He was the host in his country, his culture; I was the wide-eyed visitor, but still an independent and strong-willed woman.

We faced a monumental struggle to find again the qualities we had known in each other. The chemistry that had swept over us at our first encounter now languished beneath an overlay of tormented years and emotional exhaustion, beneath a past we had not shared, lives we almost did not know.

Woody often did not understand how to take her, this strange woman, his wife, for so long only a voice on the telephone and words on paper. He too had expected, or at least hoped for, someone else. As the days of regaining each other unfolded, he would often say, "Stop fighting. The battle's over. We won." But after so many years of tension, it was not easy to relax.

Quite soon it became clear that victory over the separation meant the beginning of another task—to restore what was once so dear and important. As I struggled for my "new" husband and new life, at times I did not know which was more difficult, defeating the KGB or starting all over again at forty-seven.

Three hectic days at the Four Seasons Hotel in Washington were filled with constant meetings with the press and television people, telephone calls from friends all over the United States, a couple of bewildering drives around the city. Sleepless nights: because of jet lag, which I experienced for the first time, and because of the awkwardness that struck when Woody and I were finally alone. How to share the privacy? Were we really husband and wife? After eleven and a half years we had forgotten how to act. Lovers? We could not create that overnight. The situation was too serious, too much of a test, to make any false moves, to pretend. At a given moment I said, "Vadim, our whole life lies ahead . . . no need to hurry. Let's try to sleep." Grateful to me for taking the responsibility, he hugged me gently.

After those confusing January days—I hardly remember the kaleidoscope of faces and conversations—Woody took me to Florida for a desperately needed second honeymoon. The situation had become unbearable; we had to have rest and privacy.

I loved Florida in February in all its lush greenery, strong sun in a clear sky, cool refreshing nights, the warm, peaceful Gulf of Mexico. I marveled at the beautiful homes on large, meticulously groomed lots, little palaces with flowers everywhere and botanical rarities—or so I assumed—in every corner.

The seemingly innumerable funeral homes with all sorts of bizarrely inviting names—"Heavenly Peace," "Quiet Gardens," "Green Comfort"—attracted my attention. In a country where they do everything to make people comfortable and ensure long life, why so many such places? Was it respect for death, or merely competition for its business? As Woody drove along in our rented car, lost in his own thoughts, my mind wandered back to the Soviet Union, where it's hard to find a funeral home even when you need one badly. Maybe it's because atheists don't believe in eternity; afraid of death, they don't want reminders of it on every corner.

In Florida, we had a room in a small, cozy motel on a remote little peninsula—the first place where we could really be alone. Large plate-glass windows faced the Gulf, and the room was done up in soft earth tones from light beige to deep brown. I had never seen such a large bed; "king-size" seemed appropriate. There was a kitchenette where we could make coffee and toast, a small table with two chairs next to the window, a gigantic television set. Everything was so new and so fresh it seemed no one had occupied the room before us. I liked that.

One day Woody stopped the car, went into a florist shop, and came back with a bouquet of flowers as fragile as our relationship. I opened the tiny envelope and found a card on which he had written in Russian: "I love you. Vadim." Somehow the small gesture began to break the ice, but our fear of talking very seriously to each other still hung heavily in the soft Florida air.

On the fourth day we both awakened with headaches and queasy stomachs. "Oh Lord, you save us again!" I thought happily. Now we had no strength to talk; we simply slept most of the next two or three days and nursed each other. Woody's friends George and Branka Brozak flew down from New York to meet me and be with us for a while. Spending time on the beach, sightseeing, and going out to dinner with them provided a welcome distraction.

Like all honeymoons, ours came to an end. We returned to Washington, picked up Lena and the dog and cat and luggage—Woody's friends Sam Berner and Lynn Crane had taken them in so that we could get away—and drove to the village of Ivy near Charlottesville. It was a cold and gloomy day, one that matched my spirits as the reality of my new life in a strange world pressed down like the winter clouds.

"This is your home," Woody said proudly but a little nervously as he opened the door. I glanced around quickly: a *bachelor's* house. One bedroom and a loft which he used as a study, cathedral ceilings with two large skylights—the loft seemed to be flying into the sky. Bookshelves crammed with books everywhere but kitchen and bathrooms; a woolen handmade Polish wall hanging in the living room; windows everywhere; dozens of large and small plants. It was a cheerful little place, yet my heart sank: it was not mine, everything was strange, and it was too open, with no place to hide. Manya the poodle and Kotya the Persian cat wandered around looking for familiar sights and smells; like me, they couldn't find any.

Woody was torn between his usual life—university, neighbors, friends, everyday chores, books, newspapers—and me. For the first week and a half I simply sat in an armchair, virtually unable to move, and looked through the huge glass sliding doors into the Virginia woods and the pond in front of the house. It rained non-stop. Alienated from everything, I had no strength for anything, least of all to begin a new life, to discover my husband. I thought about Moscow, where everything was familiar, even the misery.

America stunned and blinded me with its brilliant and rich variety. In years of dreaming, I had not given a thought to strangeness. Was I not, after all, a teacher of English? And did I not have many American friends to tell me about this country? It is, however, one thing to read and hear, another to encounter reality: gaudily dressed, dauntingly self-confident women; hordes of carefree children of all hues; everyone speaking English, which even dogs seem to understand; comfortable private homes; brightly colored, flashy automobiles; on all sides everything new, new, new.

In the stores—such a headache!—clothes, boxes, gadgets, packages, bottles, jars, cans, *things* cried out, "Buy ME!" The first time we went to a shopping mall, Lena stared uncomprehendingly at the lavish displays. Sheer confusion clouded her face. Disbelief in her voice, she asked Woody, "Why so many things?" He laughed and could only reply, "Capitalism!"

Lena helped a great deal. We gave her the bedroom and used the loft for ourselves. She awakened in the morning interested in everything from new food for breakfast to shopping to learning how to drive. With Woody she could speak Russian and feel comfortable in her native language. The two quickly restored the father-daughter relations they had established in Moscow.

I had not realized how fond the American media are of human-interest stories. It seemed that Woody and I were such a story, a happy ending. Crowds of television and newspaper people attacked, all refusing to understand the uniqueness of our situation. One story had indeed just ended happily, but at the moment it did a new one began: the rebuilding of our marriage, complicated by my difficulties as an immigrant in a new country, a strange culture, a foreign language. The absence of my friends and the impossibility of maintaining anonymity compounded these problems still further.

The press people would ask, "Irina, what about cooking? What do you cook for your husband?" Irritated, I thought, Does it matter? How do you use this stove with all the knobs and buttons . . . how to translate recipes I've forgotten anyway? Trying to be polite, I would answer truthfully, given the food shortages in Moscow, "I don't care much about cooking."

This did not satisfy them. They asked time and time again, looking hopefully through the windows at our garden, "Irina, what about gardening?" Having lived all my life on Moscow's asphalt, I knew nothing about gardening. Two years later, however, I would take it up with great pleasure, spending hours planting hundreds of flowers and bulbs, weeding, digging, mulching.

Yes, they all wanted a happy ending, but we didn't have one to the story we were now living through. Everything was in the beginning. I would not tell them about the pain and the difficulty, about the sleepless nights struggling over the past we had lived separately.

The situation with the media reached an impasse. For all those years journalists had helped with their reports, but they were more or less sophisticated correspondents in Moscow. Now we had to pay for *their* help by giving one interview after another to people most of whom had never been outside the United States. There was however no other way to show our gratitude to the press, and through those interviews we were at least able to speak out on behalf of the divided spouses who remain behind in the Soviet Union.

After three weeks or so Lena appealed to me, "Mama, come on, bestir yourself, *do* something." But when Woody and I went shopping, my inability to take in the abundance and variety and color made me miserable. The shelves turned into a blur. A ringing in my ears would not stop, my head spun, I felt faint. People moved their carts slowly, with dignity, a list in one hand and a pen in the other. They would take something from a shelf, put it in the cart, make a check on the list. All very impressive, I thought hopelessly, dragging myself after Woody. How do they know where to find these things?

Charlottesville is a small world, and many people recognized us. They spoke to Woody and me, saying cheerfully, "Welcome to America!" Their sincerity was obvious, but the constant attention depressed me. The next time shopping had to be done I stayed at home.

When I tried to conquer the kitchen, it puzzled me with its appliances, its cabinets and refrigerator full of boxes and packages and fresh food I couldn't understand. I had never seen breakfast cereal or biscuit dough in cans, never encountered artichokes or broccoli or zucchini. I needed a special dictionary for the food and an instruction manual for the stove—everything I touched seemed to burn or boil over.

Neighbors appeared with "Welcome to America!" smiles and small gifts: champagne, flowers, music cassettes, cookies, cards. The sheriff came by with roses and a hearty "Welcome to Albemarle County, m'am!" The attention touched Woody, but I was lost. I could not remember faces, names wouldn't stay in my head, the lilting southern accent was impossible to understand. No, I would never be able to adjust . . .

A defensive mechanism took over, and I concentrated on hot dogs, the dream of all Soviet citizens—smoked, aromatic, meticulously shaped Oscar Mayer hot dogs. In my frequent reveries, a scene from Moscow life floated across my mind: it is the middle of the day. A robust woman in white retail-trade smock and kerchief places a large wooden box of sausages in the middle of the sidewalk. Not packaged by sixes or tens, they are all linked, from first to last, in a chain. Around her a crowd of people gathers, famished for a taste of decent food. On the fringes of the crowd, where they can't see the box, others raise the universal Soviet cry, *"Chto dayut? Chto dayut?"* What are they passing out there? The ones who manage to reach the box tear off some links and pay. Perspiring, gleeful, they hungrily clutch their naked, unwrapped sausage chains—there's a paper shortage—and fight out of the crowd.

I am fixated on hot dogs. To Woody's astonishment, every morning I eat two, with Dijon mustard and dill pickles. Never eggs or cereal, only and always hot dogs. He cannot understand; it has been so long since he was in the Soviet Union. As soon as he leaves home, I dash to the refrigerator, yank out two more, boil and devour them. When he comes home for lunch, we both eat hot dogs. I let him think it is because there isn't time to prepare anything else.

In a day or two, the hot dogs are gone. Woody brings home more; they too quickly disappear. After a week or so Woody asks, "What the hell is happening? Have those crazy pets of yours figured out how to open the refrigerator?"

I had told him the story of the Hungarian chicken, a plump, two-kilo, frozen chicken I had miraculously found at one of those Moscow sidewalk stalls and left in the kitchen sink to thaw for dinner with friends. The pets were six or eight months old. When I returned late in the afternoon from giving lessons, only the thick plastic bag with the giblets remained; the dog and cat had even crushed and swallowed the bones. Manya and Kotya stared at me in a listless stupor, swollen bellies telling all: the cat had leaped into the sink and in his frenzy had dumped the carcass on the floor, where Manya claimed her share of the feast.

The pets barely moved that evening; the next morning their condition appeared unchanged. With a heavy heart I left for another lesson, certain I would need two small coffins by evening.

Again, God was kind. On my return two lively, hungry, loving creatures greeted me, as did a dozen mounds of shit. Relieved that the pets were alive, I cleaned up.

Not until maybe six months later, when I had finally had my fill of hot dogs and couldn't bear the sight of another one, did I reveal to Woody the mystery of their strange disappearance. Today I eat them only rarely.

At every turn my ignorance of American culture and language manifested itself. Not long after my arrival, the telephone rang and a man said something about dogwoods and a parade. I thanked him. Proud of Manya, I asked Charlie—Woody's son who was then home on vacation from Kenyon College—where to take her to be groomed. He stared at me in confusion, then broke into a broad grin, led me into the yard, and pointed to a dogwood tree just beginning to bud.

It turned out that *I* was to be the grand marshal of this parade, which takes place every April when the dogwoods blossom and Charlottesville looks like a bride all decked out in white and pink. I still did not fully understand; to me, "marshal" was a military rank.

Woody bought me a brightly colored dress with reds, pinks, and blues on a yellow background, and a chic off-white hat. They put me in some sort of elegant one-of-a-kind open car in the middle of a long line of floats, cars, and marching bands, and we drove slowly through the streets. I looked on in astonishment as grown men in fezzes roared crazily along the route in tiny gasoline-powered cars made for small boys . . . what in the world was *this?* Thousands of people turned out. They stood on the sidewalks and sat on the curbs with their children, holding cans of soft drinks and eating popcorn and ice cream. They shouted "Welcome to America!" and I waved for the forty minutes it took to complete the circuit. What a job!

The restrooms in some hotels and fancy stores and restaurants impressed me when I first encountered them: unobtrusive classical music in the background; subdued, elegant wallpaper in pastel shades; soft lighting; some sort of perfumed scent in the powder room—these rooms seemed to belong in great palaces, and it was easy to forget why you had come there in the first place. Well, these Americans respect you, I thought with a smile as I sat on an elegant little padded bench in front of a huge mirror and lit a cigarette.

But another side of that same story, the very abundance of everything, upset me. The reserve rolls of toilet paper scattered around discreetly recalled a painful Moscow scene: a long, unruly queue in a shop where they sell household sanitary items. *"Chto dayut?"* cry people in the rear. Before the answer came, the product itself appeared. Faces reddened in the stuffy atmosphere. Men—who usually don't carry those "just in case you find something" string bags that women always keep in their purses—pushed their way out of the crowd, satisfied in anticipation of forthcoming comfort, chests and shoulders bedecked with garlands of strung-together toilet paper rolls like wreaths bestowed on champion athletes or beauty queens.

Despite ups and downs in our relationship, Woody and I moved forward. In May 1986 we had our wedding in a Russian Orthodox church in Washington, thus fulfilling Father Ioann's behest. At the most difficult times I would remember his words: "You are charged with a mission from the Russian Orthodox Church, an important mission. Now go with God. Marry your husband in the Church."

Alongside the problems between Woody and me, I sensed myself caught between two different fears. One, from Moscow, gradually faded except in nightmares where I was still followed and haunted by eavesdropping: the KGB. I would scream, rise up in bed, and sob until I calmed in Woody's arms. During the day I shuddered at every ring of the telephone, and talking to someone made me uneasy; surely everything would be overheard and reported! Accustomed to speaking conspiratorially with my Moscow friends, I could not, in those first few months, break the habit. My paranoia knew no bounds. Putting down some book banned in the Soviet Union, I automatically hid it under the mattress when we left home. Woody tried to reassure me, saying, "This is America. No one's going to search us!"

But as the Moscow fear slowly evaporated, a new, American one came into being, one that sprang from my near-complete lack of understanding of American culture, life, and language. It also weighed on my poor husband, who remembered the competent, educated, worldly-wise woman he had known in Moscow. That was

Our wedding in St. Nicholas Russian Orthodox Church, Washington, D.C., May 24, 1986. Charles McClellan holds the crown over his father's head, an unseen Strobe Talbott the one over me, and Lena is on the right. *George Brozak*

the woman he wanted, the one he had waited for. What he got was a child in a woman's body: questions, questions, questions . . .

We both needed forbearance. My faith in God, and the Russian Orthodox Church, had taught me that. "If you'll be a patient teacher," I told Woody, "I'll learn more quickly, and life will be easier for you. Remember how patient I was in Moscow? Now it is your turn." As always, patience and time would be the great healers.

The breakthrough came in November 1986. We were driving to Washington, where I had a lecture engagement; it was a rainy, miserable day and the road seemed to go on forever. As we neared the city, Woody suddenly turned to me and said, "Why don't we move up here for good? We'll start all over together . . . we'll have privacy, the city."

It was so unexpected. Oh how I had longed for those words! But it was not for me to propose the move; Woody's job was in Charlottesville. Sensing my concern, he said, "Don't worry, I'll commute. I only have to teach a couple of days a week. Several of my colleagues live in Washington and don't have any problems."

That move saved us.

We settled down in Alexandria, Virginia, across the Potomac River from Washington, in May 1987. Here no one knew us; we could be ourselves. We did not have to put on smiles every time we left the house to pretend all was wonderful, with no sadness or pain. We regained the trust of those earlier years and appreciated each other's company more and more.

Through tears, resentment, happiness, endless talks that were now stormy, now peaceful, talks in which we now understood each other, now did not—through all this Woody and I painfully unearthed each other and all that had been dear to us in our relationship, rediscovering that chemistry which now emerged into the light after the painful scraping away of all those years, all that sorrow.

When Woody's son Charlie first learned that Lena and I were to be released, he wrote a poem and entitled it "To the End of the Nightmare." Despite his natural concern about his place in his father's new life, he soon accepted the relationship between Woody and me. He and Lena got along well from the start; raised as only children, they were delighted to have each other as sister and brother.

Charlie is now on Taiwan, where he teaches English and studies Chinese. Lena is a student—an astonishingly good one—at Purdue University. Last year she married Tom, an electrical engineer who earlier graduated from Purdue, and in October they produced a daughter, a little American citizen called Lara, the first sweet fruit of all our suffering, living evidence of our new American roots. Woody and I became grandparents for the first time.

Three years have now passed, years full of exciting events. Perhaps the most extraordinary was that my mother came to the

United States to visit for two months.

December 9, 1988, Dulles Airport. The plane was two hours late. Woody and I were nervous and excited; I had not seen Mama for nearly three years, and fourteen had gone by since Woody left Moscow. And then at last she appeared, lurching along after a cart piled high with her suitcase and several ridiculous little bags of different colors stuffed to the bursting point with presents for everyone, a bunch of red carnations from Moscow in her hand. The cart seemed to roll along of its own accord, so feebly did Mama move behind it. A white scarf, no doubt knitted twenty years ago, had almost escaped from the old greenish winter coat that hung loosely around her ample body; a brown fur hat was cocked to the side at a comical angle. She wore black felt boots zippered in front, the kind our people call "Goodbye Youth," the only ones she could find that would fit over her arthritic feet. Her pale, worn-out face had lost all expression.

Imagine a woman of seventy-four on her first journey, not just abroad but to America, the most dangerous enemy of Soviet power—as she had been taught all her life. Letters and photographs had eased her fears just a little; now she had come to see with her own eyes. Her face wore a look of total confusion, as though she had no idea where she was or what she was doing there.

I stepped out from behind the barrier and rushed up before despair overtook her completely. She clung to me and began crying quietly, helplessly. "Irochka," she said, "*dochenka* [little daughter], I thought I'd never make it to see you . . . " I tried to comfort her. Then Woody came up to take the bags and she began to sob again as she embraced him—tears of relief.

Recalling my own shock and the difficulties of the first two years of life in America, and thinking about my mother's age, I was concerned for her. But my fears were unfounded; she had after all come as a guest and would be in our home. There was no need to learn English or how to live in the United States. Woody and I speak only Russian when we are alone anyway, and when my mother came we anticipated her every wish, quickly solved every problem.

She liked the country immediately—the homes, the cars, the shops, the smiles; she was as tired as anyone of deprivation and rudeness. Watching African Americans on the street and in shops and restaurants, she exclaimed, "They tell us black people don't have any rights here. Just *look* how well these people are dressed, how normal they act!"

Before our eyes she became younger, straightened her posture, began to dress stylishly in clothes we bought. She liked Woody more than ever and told me constantly, *"Dochenka,* you've got an ideal husband."

Lena, baby Larochka (Lara), Tom, and Tom's parents and brother Steve all came for Christmas, and here we were around the table, four generations—my mother, Lena, Larochka, and I. Mama threw all her emotions into her great-granddaughter now, holding the baby for hours on her generous bosom, cooing in that special great-grandmotherly language.

Christmas was basically a social event; we called Charlie on Taiwan to make him part of it. The pile of brightly colored, beribboned presents in front of the fireplace in our living room awaited that afternoon. After exchanging gifts we sat down to a turkey dinner that Woody had been cooking all day, a kind of Christmas and Thanksgiving meal in one to show my mother something of American tradition. She loved everything.

Because they had had only a civil ceremony in Indiana, two days after Christmas Lena in a beautiful off-white wedding dress and Tom in formal wear were married in the Russian Orthodox Church of St. John the Baptist in Washington. Father Victor and Father Vladimir performed the ancient ceremony. Woody and Martin Davis took turns holding the crown over Lena, while Steve and Bob Pringle held the one over Tom. We had a modest wedding feast after the ceremony—it was a period of fasting for the Russian Orthodox—and then Father Victor baptized Lara. Woody and I served as godparents.

Standing off to the side, a little apart from everyone else, my mother held herself solemnly erect. Tears of joy filled her eyes and her lips moved slowly, as if in prayer for her children.